# Traditional Architectural Culture of China

Teaching series for undergraduate personnel training item,
Phase 2, State "985 Project", Tsinghua University

Written by Lou Qingxi
Translated by Su Guang

China Travel and Tourism Press

**图书在版编目（CIP）数据**

中国传统建筑文化：英文／楼庆西著；苏光译.—北京：
中国旅游出版社，2008.1
ISBN 978-7-5032-3346-3

Ⅰ.中...Ⅱ.①楼...②苏...Ⅲ.古建筑－建筑艺术－中
国－英文 Ⅳ.TU-092.2

中国版本图书馆 CIP 数据核字（2007）第 190188 号

# 中国传统建筑文化
## Traditional Architectural Culture of China

| | |
|---|---|
| 作　　者 | 楼庆西 |
| 翻　　译 | 苏　光 |
| 选题策划 | 赵小军　谭　燕 |
| 责任编辑 | 谭　燕 |
| 责任印刷 | 冯冬青 |
| 美术指导 | 海　洋 |
| 出版发行 | 中国旅游出版社 |
| 地　　址 | 北京建国门内大街甲 9 号　邮政编码：100005 |
| | http://www.cttp.net.cn　E-mail：cttp@cnta.gov.cn |
| | 发行部电话：010-85166507 85166517 |
| 经　　销 | 全国各地新华书店 |
| 设计制作 | 北京锦绣东方图文设计有限公司 |
| 印　　刷 | 北京翔利印刷有限公司 |
| 版　　次 | 2008 年 1 月第 1 版　2008 年 1 月第 1 次印刷 |
| 开　　本 | 787 毫米 × 1092 毫米　1/16 |
| 印　　张 | 21 |
| 印　　数 | 1-5000 册 |
| 字　　数 | 160 千 |
| 定　　价 | 180.00 元 |

ＩＳＢＮ　978-7-5032-3346-3

# Centents

# Chapter 1
# Structure of Chinese Traditional Architecture

In world history, China, Egypt, Greece and Rome have all created splendid ancient civilizations and their forefathers left behind numerous architectural relics: emperors' palaces and tombs, temples and churches, gardens and official residences, monumental tablets and triumphant arches. These architectures, recorded with the politics and history, art and culture, science and technology of the particular countries and regions, are regarded as the symbols and landmarks of that region and time, both materially and spiritually. Only by glancing over these architectural relics, we can easily find the evident differences in their images between China in the east and Greece and Rome in the west.

Fuling Mausoleum, Shenyang, Liaoning Province

Venice Square, Italy

Gate of Supreme Harmony Square, Forbidden City, Beijing

    Both China's ancient feudal emperors and Egyptian pharaohs invariably took pains in building their own tombs because they all believed in the immortality of human souls and sought to live eternally in the after-life world. The ancient Egyptian pharaohs built gigantic pyramids as their tombs by piling up big pieces of stone on the ground, while the Chinese emperors preferred to bury themselves into the underground palaces, and on top of them, groups of architectures similar to their imperial palaces were constructed on the ground. The famous Parthenon of the Athens Acropolis in ancient Greece was surrounded on all sides by colonnades of stone pillars enclosed in which was a standing statue of Athena of 12.8 meters high from base to top. In Jixian County of China's Tianjin City, there is a Buddhist temple called Dule Temple in which the main hall—the Goddess of Mercy Pavilion is a single story but double-eave structure built with timber which contains a 16 meter statue of the goddess. In the ancient city of Rome, there were many squares surrounded by the city hall, temples and shops, and in the squares, there stood the monumental pillars and obelisks, all of which were built with stone materials. What people saw

Giant Sphinx and Pyramids, Egypt

The Parthenon, Athens, Greece

Goddess of Mercy Pavilion, Dule Temple, Jixian County, Tianjin

and made contact with on the squares were stone pillars, stone terraces and stone steps, as well as all kinds of stone statues and stone carved decorations. The area inside and outside the Zhengyangmen Gate of the old Beijing was also a central area, where there were the gate-tower on top of the high platform, the official residences and shops on both sides of the streets as well as the archway standing on the street, all of which were built with timber.

From the comparisons of the buildings around the city squares, temples enshrined with gods and emperors' tombs, we may come to realize a fact that the reasons why there should be such a big difference in architectural images between the oriental China and the western civilized countries in ancient times, aside from the factors in geological environment, culture and custom, etc., the main reason is the difference in building materials and structural systems. Timber-frame structure was used in building houses in ancient China, while in the western countries, stone structure.

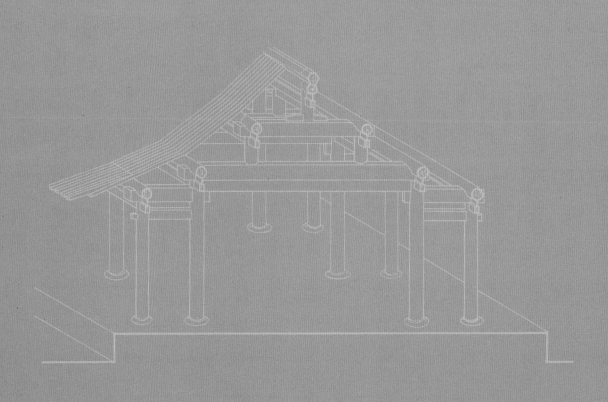

# Timber-frame Structure in Chinese Architecture

In Zhoukoudian of Beijing's Fangshan District, archaeologists discovered the mountain caves inhabited by the human beings in their early periods. Found in these caves were fossils of the Peking Men and the stone hammers and other stone tools they once used, which belonged to a time between 700 thousand to 200 thousand years from today. Such stone caves of the ancient human beings belonging to the Paleolithic Age have also been found in China's Yuanqu of Shanxi Province, Shaoguan of Guangdong Province and Changyang of Hubei Province, etc. These remains tell us that the ancients several hundred thousand years ago were not yet able to build houses for themselves, instead, they could only look for and choose suitable natural stone caves as their living quarters to keep themselves away from the attacks of the elements as well as wild animals.

Along with the human progress and development in productive activities, the ancients began to be able to build houses for themselves. According to ancient documents and the excavation of historical remains, there were mainly two kinds of houses: one is to build the house on a tree by using tree branches just like a bird nest built with twigs, thus called "nest house". Such houses were suitable for the southern region of China where the weather was damp with lots of rains. The other was to dig into underground to make a house in order to keep away from wind and rain, which looked like a cave, thus called "cave house". Such caves were suitable for the northern regions of China–the loess plateau region, where the weather was arid with few rains.

In Banpo Village of Xi'an's suburban area, Shaanxi Province, remains of a tribe of the primitive clan society were excavated in 1954, which was built 6,000 years ago in the Neolithic Age. On the remains the area of which amounted to 50,000 square meters, 40 to 50 densely arranged houses were discovered. These houses fall into two types; one is in square shape, dug into the ground 50 to 80 centimeters deep in square form with a slant slope leading to the cave from the ground. On the ground, there are thin pillars lined closely together on four sides. In the middle of the shallow cave, there are four thicker wooden pillars. It is these four and the surrounding smaller pillars that jointly prop up the roof which is also formed by tree trunks and branches. The other type is in round shape, mostly built on ground, instead of digging into underground. On all sides are also small wooden pillars closely lined up, serving as the walls, while in the center are two to

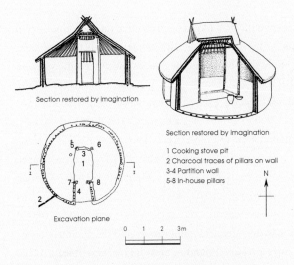

Section restored by imagination

Section restored by imagination

1 Cooking stove pit
2 Charcoal traces of pillars on wall
3-4 Partition wall
5-8 In-house pillars

N

Excavation plane

0  1  2  3m

Round residence, Banpo Village, Xi'an, Shaanxi Province

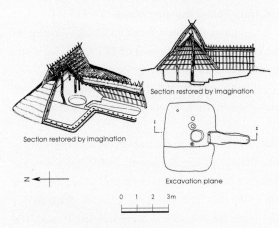

Section restored by imagination

Section restored by imagination

Z

Excavation plane

0  1  2  3m

Square residence, Banpo Village, Xi'an, Shaanxi Province

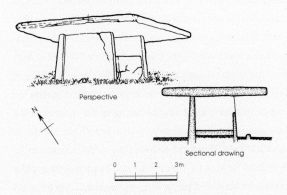

Perspective

N

Sectional drawing

0  1  2  3m

Big stone architecture, Haicheng, Liaoning Province

six big pillars which prop up the roof together with the surrounding smaller ones. These roofs, no matter whether for square or round houses, are all made into a ramp to help draining rain and snow. From the houses in Banpo Village remains and the other buildings, we get to know that the cave house of earlier human beings transformed gradually from deeper to shallow caves, and finally elevated to the ground, becoming houses entirely built on the ground.

In Shandong Province and the seaside area of Liaoning Province, stone sheds made of stone materials have also been discovered, among which the one in Haicheng of Liaoning is built entirely with large size stone slabs including the walls and the roof. It was made at the end of Neolithic Age, about 4,000 years from today. But such stone structures never developed in ancient China, perhaps because, as compared with stone materials, timber was both easier to collect and easier to process and fabricate. Therefore, the ancient Chinese chose timber as the building material, and through long time practice, gradually established a special system of timber-frame structure.

When we examine the remains of the early settlements at Banpo and other areas, we can see that they are usually situated on the terraces of both sides of rivers. The Banpo Village is on the terrace of the east shore of the Wen River, the residences of which are built on a higher land close to the river, the choice of the natural environment by the ancients for the sake of their own existence. It is because, both their living and production are dependent on water, however, the houses and other structures are afraid of the humidity, and even worse, the floods, therefore, the best place for houses is the higher terrace near water. If there were no natural terrace land near by, the ancients would have to build an artificial terrace which can also play the role of resisting humidity and floods. Thus, such artificial terrace becomes the base of the house, an inseparable part of ancient construction. Now, the whole image of China's ancient architecture composed of the roof, the body and the terrace base has come into being. It's a pity that we can no longer see the whole image of the early stage constructions, but their remains on the ground. However, we can still see, indirectly, their patterns from early Chinese characters because the characters are "pictographs" created after the actual images of objects. For examples, the ancient characters of 京(capital), 高(tall), 圂(lavatory),貯 (store) are all composed of three parts: Sloping roof, erect house body and terrace base, only the terrace is either solid, or hollow formed by timber-frame.

圂　　京　　亯　　貯　　高

Ancient inscriptions on oracle bones concerning architecture

Among the three parts, the house body is by far the major one, for it provides living space. The house bodies of Banpo Village are all made by the surrounding walls under the roof, no matter for the square or round houses. Inside the house body, propping up the roof are several pillars whose arrangement are not made to a set rule, which indicates that there are not yet a set rule to the roof structure. In Dadiwan of Tai'an, Gansu Province, remains of a house have been excavated, belonging to the late period of Neolithic Age, some 4,000 years ago. It is in rectangular shape, with walls on four sides made up of little pillars lined together just like that in Banpo, and in addition, there is a row of well-ordered pillars clinging to the inner side of the walls. All these pillars are corresponding to each other in all directions, and together with the two standing pillars in the middle, a net of them is formed which prop up the roof above in common efforts. This fact shows that during this time, the standing pillars and the roof have formed a relatively fixed structure, while the walls only perform the role of fencing, instead of propping up the roof. In Fengchu Village, Qishan County, Baoji City, Shaanxi Province, the remains of a courtyard style building have been discovered, belonging to the Western Zhou period (11th century to 771B.C.). From it we

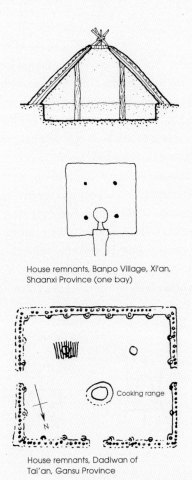

House remnants, Banpo Village, Xi'an, Shaanxi Province (one bay)

House remnants, Dadiwan of Tai'an, Gansu Province

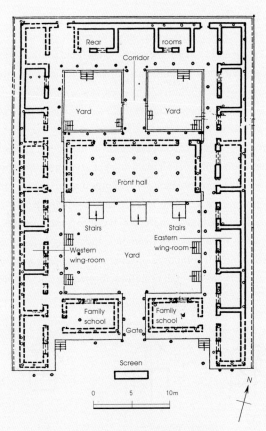

Architectural remnants, Fengchu Village of Qishan, Shaanxi Province

can see well-arranged pillar bases not only along the hall on the axis, but also the wing-rooms on the sides. Comparing to the house remains of Dadiwan, Gansu Province, this one is not only larger in scale, but the pillar bases are more regular and neat, corresponding to each other in all directions. This example testifies that the timber-frame structure in China's ancient architecture of this time has become a system with a set rule.

The remains of a large square-shaped house excavated at Banpo Village shows that in the middle of the house, there are four timber pillars propping up the roof, the area inside the four pillars we call it a "bay" which can be regarded as the basic unit of the house floor-space. In Banpo, the size of most of the half-cave houses is only a single bay. But in the courtyard style architecture in Fengchu Village, the size of houses is much larger than a bay. For example, the front hall, center of the courtyard, is six bays from left to right, three bays from front to rear, which is called, according to habit, six bays wide and three bays deep. For a single building, with more bays, the more space, naturally the bigger proportions. From this courtyard style house of the early stage, we come to know that in Chinese architecture, the bays are combined into a house, and the houses are combined into a courtyard style group of houses.

# Big Roof

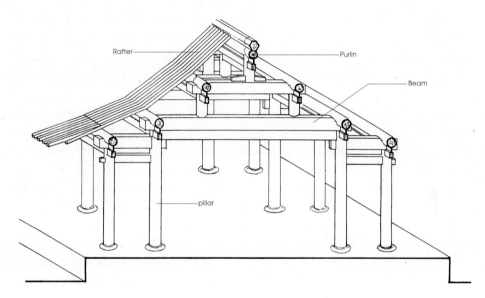

Rafter

Purlin

Beam

pillar

Sketch. Timber-frame structure of Chinese ancient architecture

Apart from the house body, the roof is also very important which protects the house from wind, rain and snow attacking from above. Since the roof is entirely a timber-frame structure except for the tiles on top, it is therefore big in size, and the more the bays, the bigger the roof. Therefore, big roof is the special feature of the image of Chinese ancient architecture. In many countries of the world, roofs made of timber are not uncommon, e.g. in European countries like France and Switzerland, etc. many houses in the city and countryside use timber-frame for the roof and the sizes are also big, the height of some roofs is even two to three times higher than the house body, but their images are totally different from the big roofs in China. Firstly, the eaves of a Chinese roof project out especially far from the walls on four sides, for only a big projection of eaves can protect the walls from the erosions of rain water. The walls of Chinese architectures, either built with clay in early stages, or bricks afterwards, together with the wooden doors and windows installed on them are all subject to rain water erosion. Secondly, the image of Chinese roofs has been transformed in molding.

Such transformation, first of all, manifests in the creation of the overall images. We may find, after giving it only casual look, the roofs, ranging from emperors' palaces, halls, temples to the pavilions in gardens; from theatres and conference halls in the cities to Buddhist and family temples in the countryside, are curved on top, with the four corners of the roof raised upward, so that the eaves on four sides are in curved lines, flat in the middle part, but raised at the ends. As for some farmers' houses, even the ridge in the middle of the roof is also made into a curve line with both ends raised up. The reasons to the birth of such images are manifolds, among which is the reason of timber skeleton, e.g. the four corners of the roof being far from the walls, bigger pieces of timber are needed for support, which make the four corners higher. There are also reasons for functioning. The front margin of the top cover of the ancient horse chariot is purposefully raised in order to provide the rider a better view forward from within. Therefore, to make a curved roof with raised eaves would enable more light into the house and better view outside from inside. Of course, the main reason for adopting such an image is to make the house more appealing to the eye. Curved roof and curved eave lines with four raised roof corners, the house is like a bird, flying toward the clouds with head raised high. And the big house roof would seem light in weight and graceful, instead of being clumsy. Thus, the ancient people refer such house roofs to be like divine birds, flying high in full swings.

The transformation also manifests in the decoration of the parts of roof. When looking at a roof, one only sees a layer of tiles on the surface, but not the timber skeleton inside the roof, and on the surface, beside the tiles, there is the house ridge where the two slopes meet and the inter-section where several ridges meet. The ancient artisans would make artistic transformations to those tiles, ridges and the intersections. The tiles, one line after another, run from the upper to lower reaches, and when they come to the eave edge, flowery decorations are added to them. The ridges are decorated either with flowery patterns formed by bricks and tiles, or images of various

Roof of temple architecture in the countryside of Hejiang, Sichuan Province

Raised eaves of roof of a temple in Fuzhou, Fujian Province

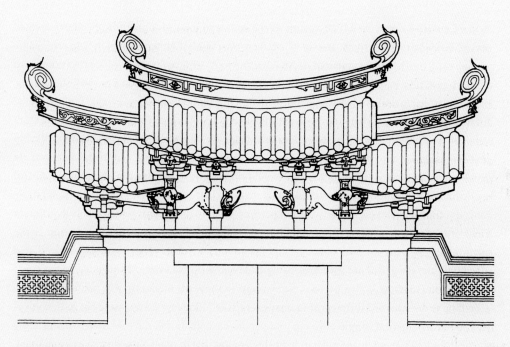

Curved house ridge, countryside residence, Zhejiang Province

Sketch. Ancient horse chariot

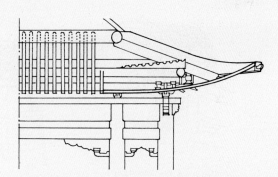

Elevation. Protruding eave of a roof

kinds of animals and plants. And the intersections on the roof can be transformed into the images of dragon, phoenix or pagoda, etc. Originally, these are integral parts of the roof structure, and after going through artistic transformation, they have become the objects of decorations. These decorations are not only beautiful in images, but also convey, through symbolization and analogy, certain cultural connotations, e.g. dragon represents the emperor and divinity, phoenix for affluence, tiger for divine power and strength, etc.

After such transformation and decoration from the overall image to component parts, a simple, large and clumsy roof has become lively, graceful and interesting. This is really a unique creation by the Chinese artisans. And furthermore, in the course of long-time practice, they have created several different types of roofs, among which there are mainly four types, namely: hip roof, gable and hip roof, overhanging gable roof and flush gable roof. Hip roof is a four-slope roof composed of five house ridges; gable and hip roof is an irregular four-slope roof composed of nine ridges; overhanging gable roof is a two-slope roof with the right and left ends projecting out of the walls; flush gable roof is a two-slope roof with the right and left roofs closely sticking to the walls. More variation types derive from these basic four, e.g. there are single and double eave roofs to the hip roof and gable and hip roof; gable and hip roof, overhanging gable roof and flush gable roof are divided into central and non-central ridge (round ridge roof) types. Besides, there are pyramidal roof with several ridges joining into one in the middle, half (pyramidal) and flat roofs. All these roofs use timber skeletons, the only difference lies in skeleton patterns which result in different kinds of roofs, being used on different buildings, big or small, and of different purposes. In the environment of ancient China where to rule the country by observing rites was practiced, and along with the images of architectures being endowed with the symbolic meaning of the ritual hierarchy, the roofs have also become the symbols to show the hierarchy. The roofs are graded, according to the sizes and differences in images, into the following: double-eave hip roof, double-eave gable and hip roof, single-eave hip roof, single-eave gable and hip roof, overhanging gable roof and flush gable roof, in the order of being high to low, big to small, important to less important.

On Dule Temple gate, Jixian, Tianjin

Wall ornamental piece on Lower Avatamsaka Temple, Datong, Shanxi

*Chiwen* (zoomorphic) picture of the Song painting

Incense-burning for high pavilion of the Song painting

Ornamental piece on Sweet-Dew Nunnery, Taining

Sketch. *Zhengwen* (zoomorphic ornaments) on roofs, Song and Liao periods

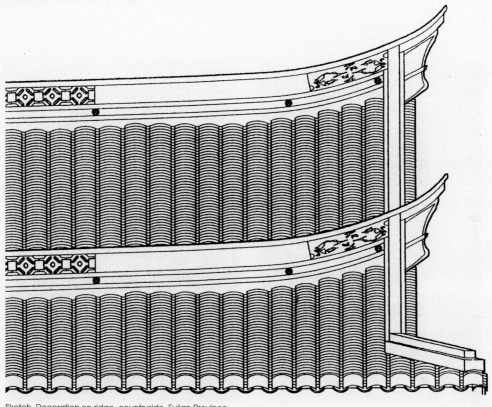

Sketch. Decoration on ridge, countryside, Fujian Province

Sketch. Decoration on ridge, countryside, Fujian Province

*Baoding* (precious roof-crown)

*Baoding* (precious roof-crown)

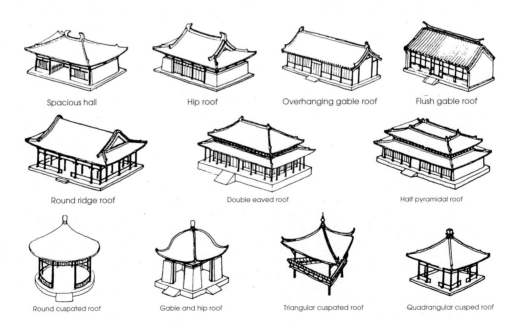

Spacious hall          Hip roof          Overhanging gable roof          Flush gable roof

Round ridge roof          Double eaved roof          Half pyramidal roof

Round cuspated roof          Gable and hip roof          Triangular cuspated roof          Quadrangular cusped roof

Ancient roof styles

In building some large halls or storied pavilions, several roof types are combined, e.g. Dacheng Storied Pavilion of Puning Temple in Chengde of Hebei Province, Yellow Crane Storied Tower of Hubei Province and Tengwang Storied Pavilion of Jiangxi Province. Those roofs are a combination of several types: gable and hip roof, pyramid roof and flush gable roof, etc. Such combinations make the architectural images seem complex, yet lively, far richer than a single type roof, thus, their artistic manifestation is much stronger.

It is the big roof which has not only made the architecture as a whole seem less heavy and clumsy, on the contrary, it has become the unique part full of charm and grace in Chinese architecture.

*Tengwang Pavilion*, Song painting

*Yellow Crane Tower*, Song painting

Corner tower roof, Forbidden City, Beijing

# Bracket Sets (*dougong*)

Between the house body and the roof, i.e. on top of the beam which is placed on the column, there is a set of members formed by small pieces of timber, evenly arranged on the beam. This set of members is called dovetail joints known as *dougong* in Chinese. It is a unique member in the timber-frame of Chinese ancient architecture. To understand Chinese architecture, one must have the knowledge of bracket sets.

What role does *dougong* play in timber-frame structure? Why is it called *dougong*? To project the eave of roof from the column and beam, a member to prop up the eave must be used. The ancient artisans used a bow-shaped timber piece to project the eave out from the column or beam, if one layer is not enough, add another layer. Such bow-shaped timber pieces, layer upon layer, can enable the eave projecting out of the house body, and they are called *gong*. To make the joint safe, a square timber block is placed in between. The block resembles the ancient measurement *dou*, thus, the member which combines the *dou* and *gong* is called *dougong* (bracket sets). When they are used under the eaves, they can prop up the projection of the roof, and if they are piled up layers upon layers, the eave projection is even deeper; if they are used under both ends of beams and lintels, they can reduce the span and reinforce them.

The bracket sets came into being very early. On the stone paired gate piers in front of the Han tombs and the brick carvings of the Han underground tombs walls; we can see the bracket sets used in architectures in their early stage. There is a Buddhist temple of the Tang Dynasty (618-907) in Wutai Mountains of Shanxi Province, the main hall of which was built in 857 A.D. and under its roof, we can see bracket sets, neatly arranged, projecting out from the top of columns, so that the eave of the hall is projected out as far as four meters from the wall, and the height of the bracket sets is two meters which is almost half of the height of columns. It clearly

Bracket sets under roof, Han Dynasty picture painted on stone

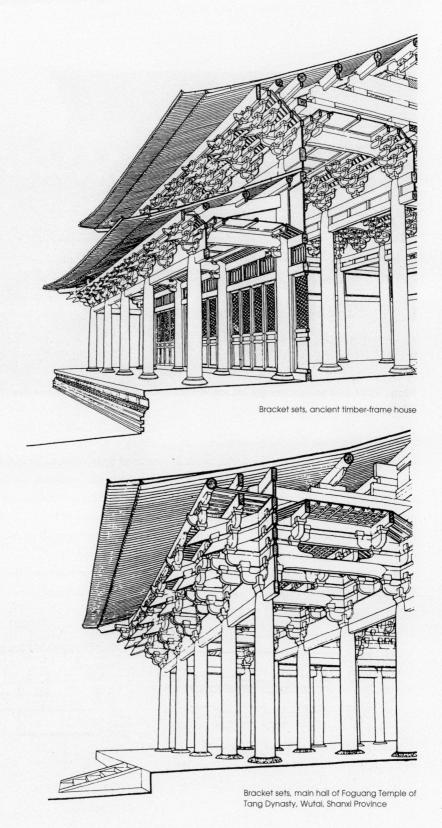

Bracket sets, ancient timber-frame house

Bracket sets, main hall of Foguang Temple of
Tang Dynasty, Wutai, Shanxi Province

Bracket sets, palace architecture, Qing Dynasty

shows the important role the bracket sets play on the roof. Along with the progress made in building materials and technology, clay walls are replaced by brick ones, so that the eaves no longer needed to project that far, and the bracket sets so big and complex. Therefore, on the architectures of the Ming and Qing dynasties (1368-1911), the bracket sets became smaller, but more numerous in number which were densely lined on the beams and lintels. At that time, the role played by bracket sets in house structure has been reduced, but in terms of decoration, their roles have been increased.

Since bracket sets are made of small pieces of wood, and in large numbers, their sizes gradually become standardized; and because the measurements of both *dou* and *gong* are small, it is

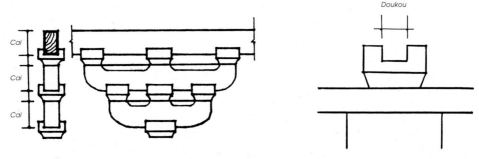

*Cai* of bracket set in Song Dynasty and *doukou* (width of *dou*) of bracket set in Qing Dynasty

comparably easier to unify the basic measurement, which makes it easier to produce them in large quantities on the one hand, and on the other, the measurement gradually become the basic unit for the other component part of the house. In Song Dynasty (960-1279), the depth of *gong* was made the basic unit of height, called *cai* (tenon); in Qing Dynasty (1644-1911), the width of *dou* (mortise) on top of columns was made a unit, called *doukou*. Therefore, the height and width of columns, the depth of beams and lintels, the distance between two columns, etc. are all decided according to the *cai* and *doukou* as the basic units, e.g. the height of a column is how many *cai* or *doukou* are used. For a house to be built, once the measurement of *cai* or *doukou* of the bracket sets is decided, then its width, depth, the size of columns and beams can be exactly calculated out.

The bracket set is really a very peculiar member, it is made of small pieces of bow-shaped and *dou*-shaped wood, but together, they can prop up a very heavy eave, and make the eave projecting out very far. Furthermore, its basic measurement even becomes a constant figure which provides great convenience for the designing and building of Chinese ancient architectures. It is really a splendid creation by the ancient artisans! But after all, it is troublesome to make the bracket sets and use them in actual building work. Therefore, on some ordinary buildings in the locality, especially in the countryside, bracket sets are not used, instead, a timber pole is slanted out from the top of column to prop up a projected roof, which saves both materials and labor. Such a slanting prop which performs the same role as bracket set is called in some areas as propping *gong*, which develops through decoration and transformation into corbel known as "Ox-leg" in Chinese.

Prop-truss under house-eave

Corbelling-table under house-eave

# Timber-frame Structure,
# Merits and Demerits

What are the merits and demerits of the timber-frame structure of Chinese architecture?

First of all, if we make a comparison between the timber-frame structure and stone structure, whose materials are timber and stone respectively, usually coming from mountains and mountain forests, then, timber is much easier to cope with than stone, right from collecting, transporting, processing to building, and saves both time and labor. The famous Khufu Pyramid, tomb of the Egyptian Pharaoh is 146.6 meters high, 230.35 meters long for each bottom line, built entirely with stone. At that time, it took 30 years to complete it with a recruited labor force of one hundred thousand. While the biggest tomb of Ming Dynasty (1368-1644), Changling, tomb of Emperor Yongle, was completed within only four years. The Forbidden City of Ming Dynasty, Beijing, covering a floor-space of 720 thousand square meters, with160 thousand square meters construction area was completed in 13 years, from 1407 when the collection of materials started to 1420 when the project was finished. There is a Cathedral in Florence, Italy, to which a dome is to be built on its octagonal chorus terrace. The work started in 1420, almost the same time when the Forbidden City was constructed. The work on the dome was completed in 1436, and another ten years and more went by before the pavilion on top of the dome was completed. The difference in time needed for building them does not reflect the difference in the technological levels of the artisans. The Khufu Pyramid was built entirely with stones piling up, some of which were as long as six meters. The total amount of stone used for the pyramid was 2.5 million pieces which would be as heavy as six million tons, if each piece weighted 2.5 tons. Then, it would not be strange at all to build it for 30 years by using 100 thousand builders at the time of 3,000 years B.C. when both transportation and lifting means were minimal. The octagonal dome of the Cathedral in Florence is 42.2 meters across, 107 meters high from the base to the pointed tip of the pavilion, built entirely with stone materials. The dome is consisted of two layers of walls, the inner and outer walls, with a space of 1.2 meters to 1.5 meters in between, plus the upper and lower corridors, and the flights of stairs for climbing to the pavilion. The transporting, processing, lifting and assembling of heavy stone pieces, as compared with those of timber, is naturally much more difficult and time-consuming.

Secondly, in timber-frame structure, tenons and mortises are used between the members, e.g. between columns and beams, between the criss-cross beams and lintels, between doors, windows and columns and beams, which is called soft joining in structure. Such joining is tenacious, not easily broken after suffering sudden and violent attacks. Thus, the salient merit of timber-frame structure is its ability in resisting earthquakes. There is a temple pagoda of more than 60 meters high in Yingxian County, Shanxi Province, built entirely with timber. In its history of more than 900 years since its completion in 1056, it has been struck by earthquakes several times, but it is still standing erect today. A violent earthquake hit the ancient city of Lijiang, Yunnan Province in 1996, when the city was applying for the title of "World Cultural Heritage". Many new buildings built with reinforced concrete collapsed, but in the ancient city district, the columns and beams structures of the old houses still stood, only some of the walls were damaged. With some repairing work, the ancient city of Lijiang was successfully listed as the "World Cultural Heritage" by the UNESCO in 1997. Such a phenomenon of "walls falling down but the house stands" fully shows the earthquake-resisting merit of the timber-frame structure.

Thirdly, the timber-frame structure undertakes all the weight of the roof as well as the beam structure, therefore, the walls all around the house and inside it do not sustain any weight, only perform the role of enclosure and partition. Thus, it is much easier to arrange doors and windows on the walls and to partition the space inside. And also, a wider range of freedom in selecting the wall materials is provided.

Brick wall of timber-frame house

Over-head balustrade and screen doors inside a house

In northern China where the weather is cold, the outer wall can be built with clay or bricks, a thicker wall would ensure a warmer temperature inside; in southern China where the weather is warm, the outer wall can be built with hollow bricks and bamboo mats and clay paste; in Xishuangbanna, Yunnan Province, etc. where the weather is hot and humid, the outer wall can be built with wooden planks or weaved bamboo which is good for ventilation and heat dispersing. Whether a house is solid or not is determined by the timber-frame structure itself, but not the thickness of the walls or the kind of materials used for the walls.

With regard to the doors and windows of the house, one is also free to choose where and how many of them are to be installed, so long as not to destroy the system of the timber-frame structure, i.e. you can install doors and windows anywhere between the columns. To ensure peace and privacy, it is natural not to have many doors and windows on the outer walls; while the hall for entertaining guests, doors and windows can be installed in the front and back from floor to ceiling, so that the hall will be bright and airy; for the pavilion or waterside pavilion in the garden, no doors or windows are needed between the columns, they can directly face water or outside space from two or even four sides. Inside the house, partitions can be made by installing screens, balustrades and over-head balustrade, etc. between the columns according to needs. Therefore, out of the same or similar timber-frame structures, we can create various kinds of architectures by changing the doors and windows on the outer walls and the partitions inside the house.

The timber-frame structure has its demerits, of course, the most outstanding one being fire-catching. In the Ming Dynasty, the Hall of Supreme Harmony of the magnificent Forbidden City, the largest one which was just completed in 1420 and used for holding such grand events as the accession to the throne, marriage ceremony of the emperor, etc., was destroyed by the fire next

Hall with screen doors between columns

Bamboo wall of timber-frame house

Pavilion and corridor without doors and windows between columns

Brick wall and gates between columns

Water vats for fire extinction, Forbidden City, Beijing

year. It was rebuilt several years later and was again burnt to ashes for the second time in 1557. Such fire was usually caused by thunder strike, which was a recognized phenomenon at that time, but there was not yet a scientific method to guard against it. The measure taken to put out the fire was to install water vats near the major halls filled with water all the year round, and in winter the vats would have to be heated to keep the water from freezing. However, once the timber-frame caught fire, it burned very quickly, how could the water in the vats be sufficient in putting the fire out? Therefore, the vats were put there just as a kind of ornaments, their roles were just symbolic.

In the tenth year (1860) of the reign of Xianfeng of Qing Dynasty, the Anglo-French Allied Forces invaded Beijing. They looted the imperial gardens in Beijing's western suburbs on a massive scale first, and then set fire to them, making Yuanmingyuan a sea of fire. Dozens of buildings, pavilions, monumental halls and multi-pavilions were burnt down. The only thing that survived was the western-style buildings built with stone in the western building area, so that today, after more than 100 years, those stone columns and walls of the western buildings are still standing in the garden. What happened to the buildings in Yuanmingyuan explains the serious demerit of timber-frame structure, the vulnerability to fire.

Apart from that, it is also vulnerable to humidity and pest. The house must be built on a terrace, and the columns must be put on a stone base, instead of directly putting on the earthen floor, in order to prevent the humidity coming up from the earth below. If the roof is leaking, it would be a big disaster for the house, for the rain water from the roof may seep through the columns and beams, gradually making the timber rotten. In southern China, white ants are rather common, which live on eating wood. They are able to make a column and beam hollow, causing them broken, hence the house would collapse. It is precisely because of the  vulnerability of the timber-frame to fire, water and pest, that the Chinese architectures built in thousands of years constantly met with destruction, so that we  can see very few of them today, e.g. there are only several timber-frame buildings built during Tang Dynasty are still standing. However, a great number of fine ancient architectures e.g. temples, mausoleums and the Coliseums, etc. built several thousand years B.C. that were left behind in some ancient countries like Egypt, Greece and Rome are still in existence. So, the stone structure is far superior to timber-frame structure in terms of solidity and durability.

According to historical documents, the Qin (221-206B.C.) and Han (206B.C.-220A.D.) dynasties built large number of magnificent palaces same 2,000 years ago . In Xianyang, the capital of the Qin, there were 270 palaces, big or small, in an area of 100 kilometers, connected one another by covered corridors, among which, the length of the terrace ruins already excavated from the major palace, the Epang Palace is 500 meters long. All the architectures above ground were made of timber-frame, the wooden columns, beams and lintels. You can imagine what a big amount of timber was used, and most of which were collected from the mountain forests of Sichuan Province. No wonder Du Mu, a poet of the Tang Dynasty once sighed: with the completion of  the Epang Palace, the mountains in Sichuan are bare! At the end of Qin, the palaces in Xianyang were burnt down, but the Han emperors built again huge groups of palaces nearby. In Chinese feudal society of 2,000 years, with the changing of dynasties one after another, palaces were built again and again, how much timber was used, and how many mountain forests became extinct, no one knows. When the Qin and Han dynasties rebuilt the fire destructed Hall of Supreme Harmony, there were no big pieces of timber to be found for several most important columns in the middle of the hall, instead, one big column had to be made of several thinner timbers putting together. From this we get to know, how scarce the timber resources were, and to what extent the natural ecology had been damaged at that time.

No matter how the merits and demerits, the timber-frame structure after all has been chosen as the structure formula for Chinese ancient architecture. In the course of long-time practice, numerous artisans have displayed their entire wisdom and talents in implementing the formula, and created splendid architectural miracles, so that the ancient Chinese architectures have displayed their unique features in the long run of the history of world architecture.

# Chapter 2
# Quadrangles and Forbidden City

The Chinese house with the "bay" as a unit which is the space within four columns is a simple rectangle in plan. It is neither complex in outside appearance, nor big in proportion, and this is true for ordinary people's quadrangles as well as for the feudal emperors' palaces. As compared with the western ancient architecture, a single Chinese architecture is by far less complex and tall. The hall of Supreme Harmony, the biggest hall in the Forbidden City which is the imperial palace for the Ming and Qing dynasties, is a rectangle in plan. It is as wide as 11 bays, but only 2,300 square meters in floor space, and 36 meters high. While the St. Peter's Cathedral in Rome, Italy is 10 thousand square meters in floor space, and 123.4 meters high from the floor to the ceiling of the dome. How can China's simple single building satisfy the different needs of residences, gardens, temples and palaces? Numerous examples can tell us that such a question is not solved by a single house, but by different groups of houses formed by the single houses. Therefore, if we say the art of the western ancient architecture is manifested in the magnificence and beauty of a single building, then, the art of China's ancient architecture is manifested in the grandeur and brilliance of a group of buildings. Thus, following the timber-frame structure, buildings in groups become another important feature of the Chinese ancient architecture.

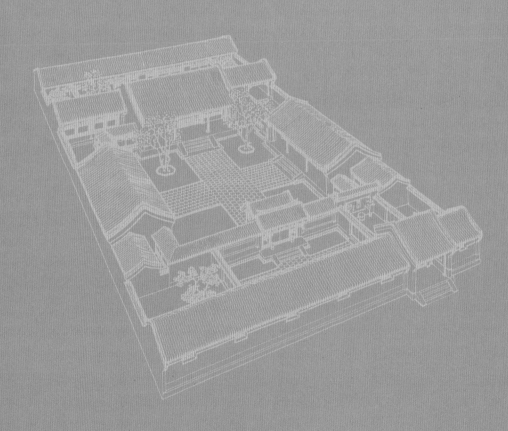

# Regular Quadrangles and the City

What is the form of combination in Chinese ancient architectural group? There is a picture of residence carved on bricks, discovered in a Han tomb which is two thousand years from today. The residence is composed of several houses and corridor houses, forming into two courtyards on the left and right. Seen on the left is the gate and two houses, together with the corridors on both sides, they form into the front yard and rear yard. The house owners are sitting on the ground, and two pairs of chickens and birds are playfully fighting in the yards. Seen on the right is a side courtyard, a kitchen and a well located in front, a watch tower in the rear, and there is also a dog and a servant sweeping the floor. The whole residence is a secluded quadrangle with roofed corridor houses built on all sides which look like the residence of an official or a rich person. The afore-mentioned remains of Fengchu Village of Shaanxi Province are also a regular courtyard architectural group. Such a group of buildings surrounded by houses on all sides are called quadrangles. Judging from a great amount of residences, temples, tombs and palaces left over by history, we get to know the quadrangle is the basic form of Chinese ancient architectural group.

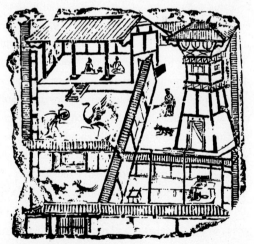

Picture of courtyard residence painted on tomb bricks, Han Dynasty

The reason for this phenomenon, on the one hand, is the merit in function of the quadrangle which provides a peaceful and private space, precisely needed by such architecture; on the other hand, it has something to do with ancient Chinese political ideas. In the feudal society which lasted for as long as 2,000 years, the rulers of each dynasty invariably used "rites" as the fundamental thinking in ruling the country. What is a rite? The rite is the criteria which determines the human relations, distinguishes right from wrong and the regulation from which to formulate virtue and benevolence. The ancient *Book of Rites* records the regulations of all kinds ranging from big matters as politics and military affairs, to small ones of decorations and clothing. It tells people from the principles of formulating the regulations to the detailed rules that in social relations, ordinary people must submit to emperors and kings, the people on lower levels must submit to superior levels; at home, sons and grandsons must submit to their fathers, wives to their husbands, younger brothers to elder brothers. And the heaven, earth, emperor, father and teacher must be respected, obeyed and worshipped by each and everyone in the society. The nuclear thinking and main content of all the ritual system and regulation is a whole set of ideas of hierarchy and hierarchical system, which not only regulates the social ideology and virtue, but also people's life and behavior.

The system and regulation concerning architecture are certainly recorded in the *Book of Rites* and other documents of ritual system. For example, the cities are classified into three categories, the imperial city, capitals of fiefdoms belonging to vassal lords and cities of the imperial relatives in the locality. The city wall tower of the imperial city is a little over 23 meters or 7 *zhang* (a *zhang* = 3.33 meters) high and the width of south-north avenue is 9 Cheriots (enough for 9 cheriots abreast); the wall tower for the fiefdom capital is a bit more than 23 meters and the south-north avenue is 7 Cheriots; and for the third category, the wall tower is only about 16.5 meters, and the avenue 5 Chariots. The ritual system also tells us for the proportion of the house and the utensils used the higher and the bigger, the loftier. Therefore, the emperor's palaces should be the highest, biggest, while the houses for the vassals, officials and ordinary people should decrease from big to small according to hierarchy, and no one is allowed to violate such regulations. This is also true even with regard to the height of tombs and the thickness of coffin timbers. The ritual code also regulates in ancestor worshipping. The most senior ancestor should be placed in the middle in arranging the tablets of ancestors and tomb locations. The rest are placed on the left and right according to seniority. In one word, whether a building is big or small, high or low, being in the middle or not becomes the criteria to distinguish the ranks and nobleness.

It is obvious that the courtyard-type architectural group suits very well the needs of such ritual system. A quadrangle residence is composed of the front, middle and rear yards. As the master of the family, the parents naturally should occupy the center, i.e. the middle yard; and in the middle yard, they naturally stay in the main house on the axis, and their second and third generations stay in wing houses on both sides, while the servants of the family can only stay in the rear yard. The size, height and quality of the houses naturally decreases according to the order of the main house, the wing houses and the houses in the front and rear yards. That is how a quadrangle satisfies the needs of the feudal ethics of the relations between father and son, elder and young brother, husband and wife, masters and servants in a family.

Residences being like that, temples, tombs, palaces take the same pattern. The feudal ritual system enables the Chinese ancient architectural groups to maintain the formula of square and symmetry with a prominent axis. Furthermore, the city which is composed of such different types of architectures also maintains such regular forms. As recorded in ancient documents, the ideal shape of the imperial city is: it takes a square form, each side is nine *li* (about half a kilo) in length, encircled by city walls on all sides, three gates are installed on each wall, nine vertical and nine horizontal streets crisscross the city inside. The center of the city is occupied by the court with commercial area behind it. On the left side stands the temple for worshipping ancestors, and on the right side, the altar for worshipping the god of the land and grain. Such ideal city pattern conforming to the ritual system has all along been abided by all the dynasties, Chang'an ( eternal peace),capital of the Tang Dynasty, Bianliang of the Song and Dadu of the Yuan are all planned and constructed according to this pattern. In such a square and neat city, all kinds of squares and the city center formed by the buildings and roads are nothing other than the serious and regular form. We may also make a comparison of the ancient cities and architectural groups between China and the west. In Athens, the capital of ancient Greece, there was the Acropolis built in the 5th century, B.C. It was an architectural group composed of several temples built on the terrace of a hill slope. At that time, Greece was a free, democratic society ruled by the commerce and crafts slave owners, with highly developed handicrafts and commerce. Every year, a grand event to worship Athena goddess, guardian of the city, would take place, and the procession consisting of many citizens must pass through the Acropolis. Climbing on the hill slope, the first thing they saw was the main gate towering over the steep slope and the bronze statue of

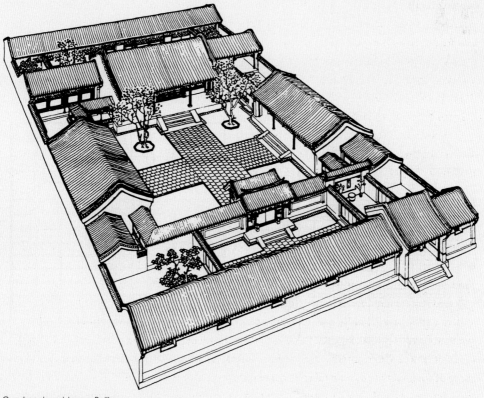

Quadrangle residence, Beijing

Athena gilded with gold. When they were inside the Acropolis, they could enjoy different scenes created by temples scattered freely at different places. The famous Parthenon, situated at the center of this architectural group, is a magnificent and colorful building with gigantic white marbles as open corridors, gilded bronze gate; roofs decorated with colorful flower patterns, and carved eaves, which attracted the attention of the parading processions, making them full of joy. After 14th century, Europe entered the period of the Renaissance; several famous ancient cities in Italy began to build city squares, big or small. The Republic and Imperial Squares in Rome are formed by the House of Lords, the Archive Building and other public architectures. On the seaside of Venice, there is the famous St. Marco Square which is surrounded by a church, the City Administrative Building, the governor's Mansion and a library. These buildings are arranged in a lively and irregular way, and they are the center for people's daily activities, touring and leisure. Apart from the big buildings, there on the square are also the tower, the obelisk, the fountain and the statues, making the square lively with rich scenic spots and cordial atmosphere. So, there is the one kind of the regular architectural groups and the solemn, sacred atmosphere, and the other kind of the irregular, lively architectural groups and an environment catering to people's needs. This tells us that countries and nations in different places, of different political and economic statuses with different culture and ideology must find their expressions on their cities the images of architectural groups.

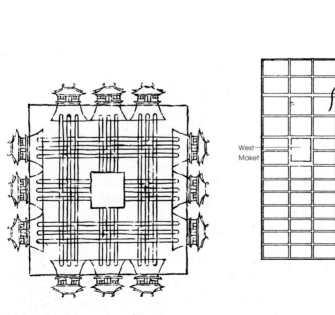

Sketch. Imperial capital, Zhou Dynasty

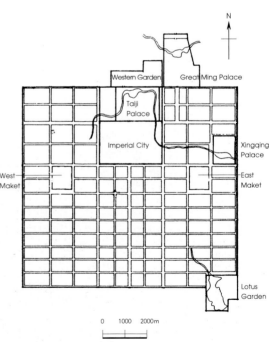

Sketch. Chang'an City, Tang Dynasty

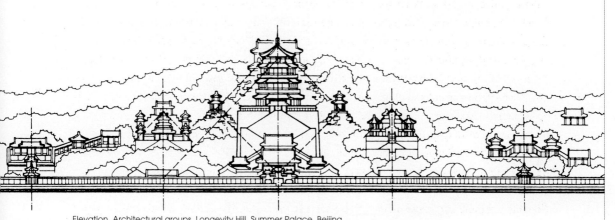

Elevation. Architectural groups, Longevity Hill, Summer Palace, Beijing

Restored elevation, Acropolis Athens

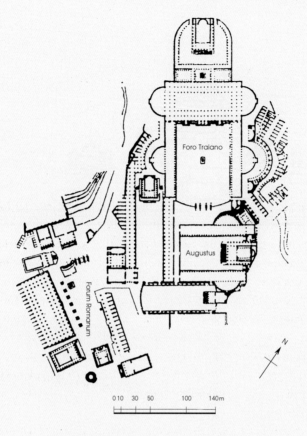

Plan. Republican Square and Imperial Square, Rome

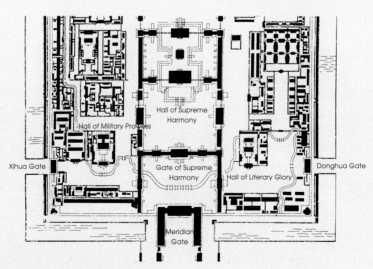

Plan. Gate of Supreme Harmony and
square before Hall of Supreme Harmony, Forbidden City, Beijing

# Planning and Layout of Forbidden City

The biggest quadrangular architectural group in ancient China is the Beijing Forbidden City, the imperial palace used by the two feudal dynasties of the Ming and Qing for 491 years. In history, whenever the emperor of a dynasty seized state power, the first thing he did in construction was to build the palaces for him. The emperors were able to spend large amount of money, use the best materials available, the up-to-date technology and recruit a lot of manpower to build the palaces. As a result, the palaces built at a given time must be the concentrated expression of the most advanced architectural technology and the highest level of architectural art of that time.

Architecture must be embodied with the material function as well as the artistic function. So is the palace architecture naturally. A palace, materially, must satisfy the needs of the emperor in dealing with state affairs, daily life, religious belief and recreational activities, etc., at the same time, spiritually, must show the incomparable authority of the emperor in ruling the country and the highly concentrated power.

Let us, first of all, examine how the Forbidden City satisfies the material function and embody the spiritual needs in the overall planning and the layout of the architectural groups.

To open the map of ancient Beijing of the Ming and Qing dynasties, one can see the central part enclosed on all sides with walls is the imperial city, in which there are the emperor's palaces, the royal family temple, the altar of the land and grain and imperial gardens, as well as the official departments of the dynasty. The palace city, i.e., the Forbidden City is situated to the southeast of the center of the imperial city, but it is right on the central axis of the whole city of Beijing, which is in conformity with the traditional ritual system of observing the center as loftiness. There are three walls in Beijing, which are, from inside out, the wall of Forbidden City, wall of imperial city and wall of Beijing City. This fully embodies the ritual system of a feudal empire.

To open further the plan map of the Forbidden City, one can easily see the front part is occupied by the three big halls of the supreme, middle and preserving harmony, where the emperor holds grand cerebrations on major events, and meets with officials, civilian and military on festival days. There are not only big halls, but a spacious yard and auxiliary halls and corridor halls for keeping equipments for big ceremonies. The spacious yard in front of these halls is not only needed for the civilian and military official waiting to be called upon by the emperor, and for the ceremonial processions on big occasions, but also for the purpose of showing the grand atmosphere of the palace architectural groups. This part is called the front court, because it is for the

1 Gate of Eternal Stability
2 Temple of Heaven
3 Altar of Agriculture
4 Gate of Heavenly Peace
5 Forbidden City
6 Coal Hill Park
7 Bell & Drum Towers
8 Gate of Moral Triumph
9 Gate of Pacified Stability
10 Temple of the Earth
11 Temple of the Sun
12 Temple of the Moon

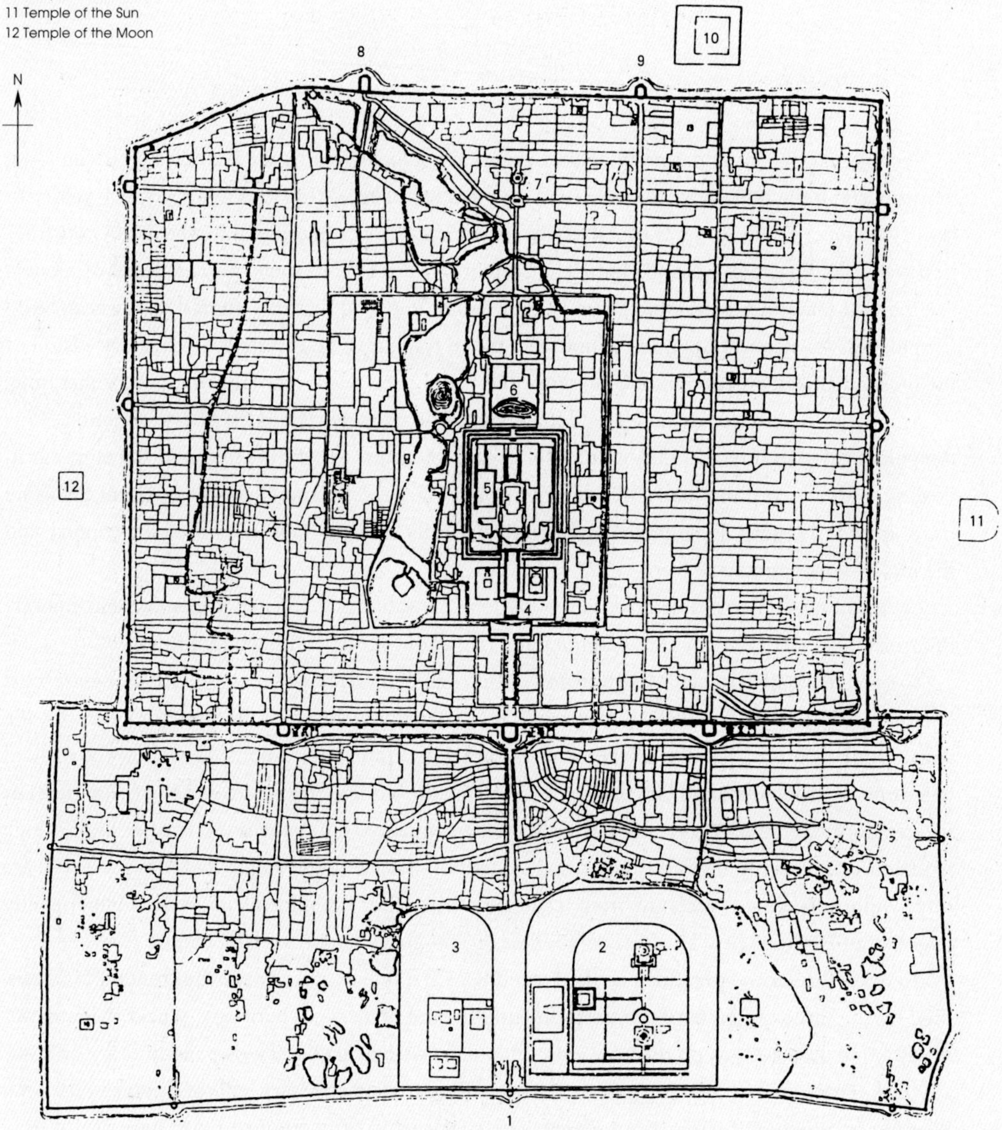

N

0    500    1000m

Plan. Beijing City of Qing Dynasty

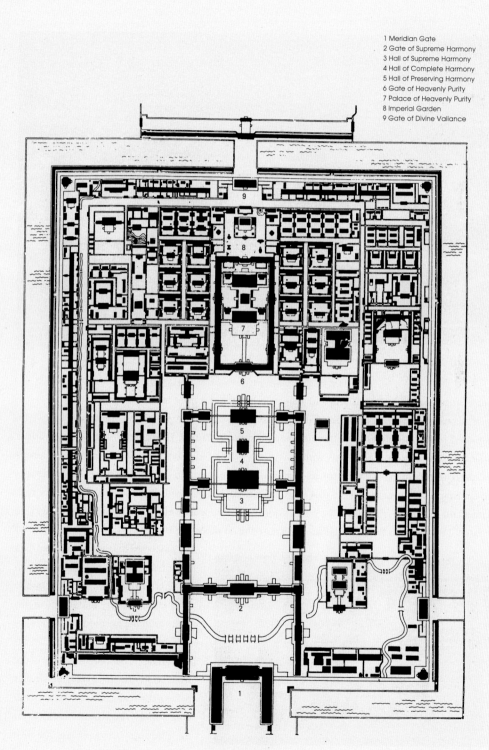

1 Meridian Gate
2 Gate of Supreme Harmony
3 Hall of Supreme Harmony
4 Hall of Complete Harmony
5 Hall of Preserving Harmony
6 Gate of Heavenly Purity
7 Palace of Heavenly Purity
8 Imperial Garden
9 Gate of Divine Valiance

Plan. Forbidden City

Bird's-eye view, Forbidden City

emperor to deal with state affairs and also is situated at the front part of the palace city.

The rear part of the Forbidden City is arranged with buildings for the emperor's daily life. Situated in the middle are the three halls of Heavenly Purity, Union and Earthly Tranquility, where the emperor lives and deals with day-to-day state affairs; on the east side are the residences of imperial concubines and the son as the would-be emperor; on the west side are the residences of the Empress Dowager and the past emperor's concubines; besides, there are buildings for religious and sacrificial purposes, the garden for the emperor as well as a large amount of service houses. This part is called "rear palace", because the emperor and his family live in the rear part of the palaces. This part covers less than half of the palaces, but contains much more buildings than the front court.

Architectural groups, the rear palace, Forbidden City

It is noteworthy that all the architectures in the Forbidden City are invariably quadrangles, one group after another. The three big halls in the front court, the three halls in the rear palace, the residences of the imperial concubines, the would-be-emperor, the Empress Dowager and the past emperor's concubines are all quadrangles, big or small. So many quadrangles are arranged together according to order, connected by lanes in vertical and horizontal directions, and surrounded on all sides by high city walls, with a gate on each wall, a corner tower at each corner for observation and protection. Outside the walls there is a moat. So, that is a complete and solid Forbidden City, composed of numerous quadrangles. The city occupies an area of 720 thousand square meters, with 160 thousand square meters for buildings, so far the biggest palace architectural groups in the world.

It is noteworthy still to see that the major palaces and gates are all on the same axis including the three halls in the front and rear, and their gates: the gate of supreme harmony and the gate of heavenly purity, and the front and back gates of the Forbidden City: the Meridian Gate and the Gate of Divine Valiance known as Shenwumen in Chinese. Furthermore, this axis extends further southward and northward. From the south, the Gate of Eternal Stability or Yongdingmen Gate, southern gate of Beijing outer wall, to Zhengyangmen Gate of the inner city wall, to the Gate of Heavenly Peace which is the gate of imperial city, to Duanmen Gate, and then Meridian Gate; further north from Shenwumen Gate, through the Longevity Pavilion situated in the center of Jingshan Hill, to the Gate of Earthly Peace which is the north gate of imperial city, until it reaches the Drum Tower and Bell Tower. This axis is as long as 7,500 meters from Yongdingmen Gate in the south to the Bell Tower in the north. It is situated in the center of Beijing, which fully demonstrates the unity and authority of the feudal imperial power.

Corner tower, Forbidden City

Palace wall and moat, Forbidden City

# Architectures in Forbidden City

We have mentioned before that the construction area in the Forbidden City is 160 thousand square meters and the Chinese houses made of timber-frame are consisted of the basic unit "bay". If we calculate with bays, someone says that there are 9,999 and a half bays in the Forbidden City. The half bay refers to the Wenyuange Storied Pavilion for keeping books which is six bays wide, but one of them is only for the staircase and very narrow, thus it is considered a half bay. Actually, this assumption of 9,999 and a half is only to show that there are many houses, the actual counting is over 8,700 bays. In face of nearly 1,000 big or small buildings, we can only select the major ones on the axis to explain what material and spiritual functions are embodied with the buildings.

## Meridian Gate

Meridian Gate is the main gate of the Forbidden City, also the place where the emperor issues edicts, orders the army to start an expedition and to be presented with prisoners of wars by the victorious army, thus, it is the most important gate of the Forbidden City. The Gate is built on a high wall terrace, with a big hall of nine bays wide sitting in the middle, hip roof with double eaves. On both wings, there is hall each, 13 bays wide, protruding southward, culminating in a square hall at the end. The wall terraces and buildings on three sides encircle a square in front, the whole gate tower being in the shape of ⊓, called "paired gate piers". The shape of the roof and the paired gate piers belong to the highest grade among roofs and gates. Below the city wall terrace, there are three gate tunnels, and on the north ends of the right and left terraces, there is a side door each. The middle gate in front is reserved exclusively for the emperor himself , with the exception of the empress who may enter this gate when she is going to marry the emperor, and after the imperial examination, the first three on the accepted list may exit the palace through this gate. In daily life, the east gate is for the civilian and military officials and the west gate for princes, dukes and imperial relatives. As for the side doors, they only open in time of holidays and festivities when there are many officials and relatives going in and out, or when the emperor holds imperial examinations. On such occasions, the civilian and military officials use the east and west side doors respectively, and for the scholars from different provinces, those who have got the odd numbers on the list of enrolment use the east side door, those with even numbers, the west. It is evident that the installment and use of the five gate tunnels also follow the hierarchy of ritual system.

Meridian Gate, Forbidden City

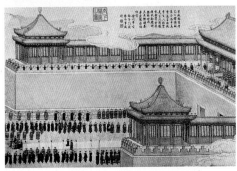

Presentation of prisoners of war in front of Meridian Gate

Reverse side of Meridian Gate

## Gate of Supreme Harmony

The Gate of Supreme Harmony is the gate of front court, an entrance of a group of buildings inside the Forbidden City, so it can only be less important then the Meridian Gate. The gate sits on a white stone terrace, nine bays wide, with a gable and hip roof, the form only next to hip roof and double eaves. On the left and right in front of the gate, there is a bronze lion each, guarding the gate, since lion is the king of beasts. This pair of bronze lions squat on the high stone bases with mouths open, eyes glaring, and a totally powerful image which adds menacing power to the gate.

In front of the gate, there is a long but narrow square on which runs a river called Gold Water Stream with five stone bridges spanning it. There is no natural waterway inside the Forbidden

City, then why there appears a stream in front of the gate? The early human beings can not exist without mountains: there are wild beasts in mountain forests, the primitive humans depended on beast skin for keeping warm, beast meat to fill the stomach; gradually they knew how to get fire, with it to get warm, cook food and to make pottery and there were fire-wood provided by the forest; when they walked out of the caves, there was timber to build houses with. And water was even more important for their life and production. Through practice, the humans came to realize that the heaven, earth, mountain and water were the environment for their existence, and the ideal environment would be a place backed by a mountain and facing a river. In the long history of development, an idea, a theory gradually evolved out of the longing for an ideal environment, that an environment pattern has become a public acknowledgement for achieving peaceful and harmonious life. In the vast countryside, such acknowledgement has become systemized and deified through the teaching of geomancy (*fengshui*), or geomantic influences, so that if there were no such natural environment, then a man-made one should be created in order to achieve tranquility and auspiciousness. The Gold Water Stream in front of the gate is made according to this teaching. During the construction of the Forbidden City, the water of the moat was diverted into the city from the northwest corner and made it flow by the front of the gate. Furthermore, the earth dug from the moat was piled up into a hill behind the Forbidden City, called Jingshan. In this way, the imperial palace fits into the auspicious environment of facing water and with mountain backing. Naturally, the auspiciousness is only significant psychologically

Gate of Supreme Harmony

Entering the Gate of Supreme Harmony, you will find in front a very open and wide square, and the Hall of Supreme Harmony is situated to the north of it. It is the place where the Emperor holds big ceremonies on the occasion of accession to the throne, marriage, birthday and banquets, and accepts congratulations from civil and military officials on major holidays. Behind it, is the Hall of Middle Harmony where the Emperor rests and prepares for going to the Court. Behind this hall is the Hall of Preserving Harmony where the Emperor holds imperial examinations and banquets for high officials. These three big halls consist of the center of the front court, and also the center of the whole Forbidden City. The Hall of Supreme Harmony naturally occupies more important position, thus, its proportion is the biggest in the city. It is 11 bays wide (60.06 meters), 35.03 meters high, the widest and highest among all the ancient architectures still in existence all over China. Its roof naturally is of the highest class: hip roof with double eaves. These three halls are constructed on a common 3 layer stone terrace as high as 8.13 meters. The ancients admired the theory of "high terraces and beautiful palaces", meaning, the higher the terrace, the palace is more magnificent and nice-looking. So, a three-layered terrace is adopted here, built entirely with white marble. The terrace is surrounded with balustrades fully covered with carvings. Such three-layered terraces in Beijing, apart from this one, can only be seen in Ling'endian Hall of Changling of the Ming Tombs, the Circular Altar and the Hall of Prayer for Good Harvest of the Temple of Heaven, and the main hall of Imperial Ancestral Temple. That is to say, it can only be used for the halls of the Emperor's palaces in life time and after-life world, and for the halls of worshipping the Heaven and ancestors. The importance and sacredness of it is very evident here.

Wedding ceremony of Qing Emperor being held before Hall of Supreme Harmony

Hall of Supreme Harmony

Three big halls of Supreme, Middle and Preserving Harmony, Forbidden City

Inside view of Hall of Supreme Harmony

Hall of Preserving Harmony

Three-layered stone terrace under three major halls of the front court, Forbidden City

Besides, on the terrace in front of the Hall of Supreme Harmony, four objects are arranged and displayed: bronze turtle, bronze crane, bronze measurement and stone sundial. Both turtle and crane are symbols of longevity. The measurement is a tool for measuring, unified all over the country. The sundial is very ancient, a round stone plate carved on its outer circle even marks of lines, and a long needle stuck in the center. With the sunlight, the shadow of the needle would be

Bronze incense burners before Hall of Supreme Harmony

Bronze turtle before Hall of Supreme Harmony

Bronze crane before Hall of Supreme Harmony

Bronze measurement in stone tower

Stone sundial

seen on the marking indicating time. To install these objects in front of the big hall is meant to symbolize an ever lasting unified country and a stable peaceful society. There are also bronze stoves lining on the several layers of terraces for burning fragrant sandalwood. Whenever there were big ceremonies, with grand guards of honor lining the square, colored flags flying, smoke out of burning fragrant wood dancing, drums and bells ringing, the civil and military officials were praying best wishes in unison for the Emperor, such atmosphere could be rather contagious.

## Gate of Heavenly Purity and Three Halls of Rear Palace

The Gate of Heavenly Purity is the gate of the rear palace, which is inferior to the Gate of Supreme Harmony in ritual system. That is why it is only five bays wide, although it is also a palace-type gate. The stone terrace below is lower than that under the Gate of Supreme Harmony. The roof is gable and hip roof with a single eave, belonging to a class lower than that of double eaves of the Gate of Supreme Harmony. There is also a pair of bronze lions guarding the gate, but they are not to compare with the other pair both in terms of size and spirit. Nevertheless, the Gate of Heavenly Purity is, after all, an important gate on the axis, so two screen walls in the shape of Chinese character eight (八) are added to both sides of the gate. They become one with the gate as a group, adding importance to the gate.

There are also three halls in the rear palace. In the front is the Hall of Heavenly Purity, the bedroom of the Emperor and Empress, and sometimes, the Emperor deals with the day-to-day state affairs and meets with big officials here. The Hall of Union is behind, the place for the Empress to receive congratulations from royal relatives. The northernmost one is the Hall of

Earthly Tranquility; the residence of the Empress, and in Qing Dynasty, the bridal chamber was also in this hall for the Emperor to get married. These three halls are also built on a common terrace, but only one layer instead of three. The roof of the Hall of Heavenly Purity is also hip roof with double eaves, since it is for the emperor to live, but it is only nine bays wide instead of 11. There is also a square in front of it, but its area is far smaller than that before the Hall of Supreme Harmony. In a word, the rear palace is a grade lower than the front court in terms of the shape of halls, the size of courtyard and the height of terrace. This is the requirement by the traditional ritual system which can not be violated.

Inside view of Palace of Heavenly Purity

Gate of Heavenly Purity

Palace of Heavenly Purity

Rear palace, Forbidden City

# Decorations of Architectures in Forbidden City

The planning and layout of an architectural group and the shape of a house can demonstrate its material function as well as its spiritual function. However, they can only give people a certain kind of feelings, either lofty, magnificent, mysterious feelings, or tranquil, secluded and joyous feelings in terms of the environment, scenery and the overall image. If the architecture should further demonstrate certain ideas and thinking, or to emphasize the afore-mentioned different kinds of feelings, then, the architectural decorations must be adopted.

The meaning of architectural decoration is very rich. The treatment of colors and material feeling, the creation of images of a particular part of the buildings, e.g. roof, house-body, terrace, the beautification of part of buildings and members, paintings and sculptures on the buildings, etc. all belong to the category of decoration.

## Color of Forbidden City

If you step into the Forbidden City on a clear, fine day, the first thing you may feel is the colors of the environment. Yellow roofs are here and there under the blue sky; red walls, red doors and windows of the palaces contrast with the blue and green paintings under the roofs; under the white terrace is the grayish black brick floor. The colors of blue and yellow, red and green, black and white form strong contrast. The rich and brilliant colors fully demonstrate the magnificence, loftiness and wealth of the imperial palaces. Why these colors are chosen for the architectures of the Forbidden City? Why the roofs are all yellow and the house bodies are all red?

In ancient China, it was a universal acknowledgement that the world and everything in it was composed of the five elements: metal, wood, water, fire and earth. And then, there were several fives: the directions on earth were classified into five; east, west, south, north and center; the constellation in the sky was composed of five palaces: east, west, south, north and middle; the colors were divided into green (blue), yellow, red, white and black; the sound was divided into five gamuts: *gong, shang, jue, zhi* and *yu*. And then, the ancients made a step further to establish a regular relationship of collocations between the five elements and the five directions, colors, palaces and sounds. For example, between the palaces, directions and colors, to combine the east constellation resembling a dragon with the east color which is green, then we have green dragon for the east; to combine the west constellation resembling a tiger with the west color which is white, then we have white tiger for the west; to combine the south constellation resembling a rosefinch with the south color which is red, then we have red rosefinch for the south; to combine the north constellation resembling a tortoise (also called *wu*) with the north color which

Color of palace architecture, Forbidden City

Yellow glazed tile-roof of palace architecture

Dark green colored paintings, red doors and red windows of palace architecture

is black (or *xuan*), then we have *xuanwu* for the north. Therefore, green dragon, white tiger, red rosefinch and *xuanwu* become symbols of the constellations of the four cardinal directions in the sky, and also symbols of the four directions on earth. Hence, dragon, tiger, rosefinch and tortoise become the divine animals, the images of which are widely adopted in decorations. Among the five colors, apart from the east green, west white, south red and north black, the middle is yellow. Yellow is the color of earth, and earth is the fundamental thing among myriads of things. Especially in China which has all along been an agricultural farming society, earth is of even greater significance. Since ancient times, yellow color has been regarded in China as the original color, the color above all colors, the center of the five colors and ultimately, the most beautiful and lofty color. The yellow robe becomes the exclusive garment for the Emperor, the road for the Emperor is placed in the middle of several parallel roads and called yellow road. The yellow color has been associated with the Emperor.

The red color is one of the five colors. The mankind came to know the red color very early. The Sun is red, which brings warmth to them. When they learnt how to get fire through drilling wood, they began to eat cooked food, instead of raw meat, an important step forward for mankind, and the fire is red. The archaeologists have found shells and animal teeth dyed with red in the caves of Zhoukoudian, outside of Beijing, inhabited by the primitive man. Careful studies have been made about them to know that they could be the ornaments of the primitive man. This shows they not only knew red color, but also used it to show what was beautiful. In ancient China, red dress represented the festival costume for women; among the people, red color represents solemn, happiness and celebrations. When people get married, red quilt, red pillows and red furniture are used; when a baby is born, eggs dyed in red are offered to family members, called happiness eggs; on the occasion of birthday cerebration for an old man, a red screen with a big character, meaning longevity is hung high up; during New Year holidays, red couplets are pasted on the doors, etc. In the Ming Dynasty, it was a rule that the memorial presented to the Emperor must be in red, called red book; in the Qing Dynasty, those memorials read and approved by the Emperor must be issued by the Court with red brushes, also called red book. So, in Court, as well as among the people, red color represents happiness, auspiciousness and joyfulness. Therefore, the yellow and red colors used as the principal colors on the architectures of the Forbidden City are by no means accidental, but a matter of course.

Apart from the cultural connotation and symbolism contained in the yellow and red colors, they also show their own visual effect as colors. In the study of colors, colors are divided into warm and cold colors, and the yellow and red belong to warm colors, and the yellow, as compared with the red, is brighter and more prominent. Dark blue and green belong to cold colors. If the warm and cold colors are put together, then a sharp contrast is shown, the respective color becomes more vivid and prominent than a single color shown alone. The Ming Dynasty put an end to the rule of the Mongols of the Yuan Dynasty (1271-1368) and unified China, and restored the rule of the Han people in the entire country, so the Emperor wished to display his power and prestige by demanding a magnificent and beautiful palace. In order to achieve this goal, apart from the afore-mentioned efforts in designing and layout, different combinations of skylines and the creation of architectural images, efforts should also be made to fully adopt the method of contrast in architectural colors. Under the clear blue sky of Beijing, it is absolutely suitable to use the bright yellow glazed tiles; on the vermilion red walls, doors and windows, it is just right to use dark green colored paintings; on the grey black bricks, a shining white terrace is most needed. The blue sky and yellow tiles, red buildings and dark green paintings, white stone and black floor are colors just comparable to each other, which produce very strong color effect. The magnificence and brilliance of the colors have fully brought about the imposing air and power of the feudal empire. So the colors used here truly play a prominent role of decoration.

## Decoration with Dragon Designs

The images of dragon can always be seen on Chinese architectural decorations, especially in palace buildings of the Forbidden City, they are everywhere. What is a dragon? When we examine the images of dragon, we see the head, the tail, the legs and claws, and its body is covered with

Jade dragon unearthed in Inner Mongolian Autonomous Region

Dragon design on pottery

Dragon design on eave tiles of Warring States Period

scales. In a word, it has a body of an ordinary animal. But in China, it is not the kind of animal in the material world, but rather, a divine animal created by the ancients by mixing the body parts of various kinds of animals. People gave the dragon many abilities of a deity: it is all capable of going up to heaven and down into the sea, and it can bring instantly strong wind and big flood. It can bring both fortune and disaster to human world. Therefore, we can say that dragon represents a kind of mythological image by the ancients, or the deity respected by man, or the incarnation of some supernatural power unknown or uncontrollable by the primitive people. Through a prolonged historical development, dragon for the Chinese has become a kind of mark in ancient China similar to a totem. That's why the Chinese descendants of Yan Di (Flaming Emperor) and Huang Di (Yellow Emperor) all call themselves as the posterity of the dragon.

Emperor's dragon throne

Emperor's dragon robe

Dragon design on beams

The images of dragon as a divine animal appeared very early on ancient Chinese arts and handicrafts and daily utensils. A jade dragon discovered in the Inner Mongolian Autonomous Region dates back to 5,000 years ago. They also appeared on the pottery found in Banpo Village of Shaanxi Province 6,000 years from today. A great many of them have been found on bronze wares belonging to the Warring States period (475-221B.C.)  On architectures, we have found them on the eaves tiles of the Warring States period.

When did the relation between the dragon and feudal emperor take place? According to historical records, when Liu Bang, first emperor of the Han Dynasty seized power in 206 years, B.C., he
tried to prove that he was the descendent of the dragon, and called himself the son of dragon,
because he was from an insignificant background. From then on, all emperors invariably regard
themselves as dragons, and son of heaven. Since the descendants of Yan Di and Huang Di are the
posterity of the dragon, it is only natural for the dragon, and son of heaven to rule the people, thus,
the dragon becomes the symbol of the emperor. The garments of the emperor, embroidered fully
with designs of dragon are called dragon robes; the armchair for the emperor, carved fully with
dragons is called dragon chair; the utensils for food and tea used by the emperor are also decorated with dragon designs. The Forbidden City being the emperor's palace is of course decorated
with a great number of dragons. There are dragon designs on the balustrades of the white stone
terrace and stone steps; golden dragons painted on the beams and lintels and ceiling; carved wooden
dragons on the doors and windows; dragon designs are even on the small rings attached to the
doors and windows. In the Hall of Supreme Harmony, designs of dragon can be seen on the
outside beams and lintels, doors and windows; on each of the six golden columns inside the hall,
a giant dragon coils; the hall ceiling and caisson are covered with dragon designs; the imperial
armchair and the screen behind it are also covered with wood carved dragons. Someone has calculated that inside and outside the hall, on upper and lower levels, there are altogether 12,654
dragons. The figure may not be very accurate, but this is really a place for dragons, once entering
the hall, you may feel as if you have come to a world of dragons.

Since the dragon is a divine animal created by Man, its postures may not be restricted by that of
natural animals, which makes it convenient for decoration purposes. One can apply or create the
images of dragon on different parts and members of architecture. One can use a long dragon to
coil the column; one may create a dragon sitting in the center of the little space on the ceiling,
called sitting dragon; one may make the dragon creeping along the beams and lintels, called
creeping dragon; if two creeping dragons are made facing each other with a treasure ball in between,
then it is called two dragons playing with a pearl; in the caisson situated in the middle of the
ceiling, there is a coiled wood-carving dragon gilded with gold, with the dragon head facing the
floor, a treasure ball in its mouth, which is called coiled dragon, a magnificent key decoration. But
it is difficult to use the whole image of dragon on some members, e.g. both *zhengwen* of the main
ridge on the roof, or ends of the ridge; the bases for the rings on doors; the drainage openings
protruding out from the terrace, etc. On these places, it is always suitable to use only the dragon
head to decorate. Since the whole image of dragon is not there, these heads are called sons of
dragon, which is really a subtle name. Therefore, in the Forbidden City, there are not only decorations with dragons, but also with sons of dragons. These sons have got their names, and also their
respective features according to the different locations they occupy. For example, the first son is
called chiwen, positioned on both ends of the main ridge of the roof, its image is the head of a
dragon, with its mouth open to the end of ridge, so it is good at looking afar and swallowing; the
second son is called pushou, the knocker bases on the doors with door rings in their mouths, its

Carved dragon on stone pillar head of balustrade, Forbidden City

Dragon design on copper wrapping at door

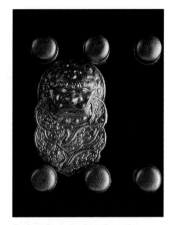

*Pushou* (knocker base) on door

image is an animal face which keeps the door shut, so it likes to be at leisure; the third son is a stone carved animal head on the terrace for drainage, when it rains, the water on terrace would drain through its mouth, so, it likes water; the fourth son is called *bixi*, i.e. the tortoise under the stele, since it has a heavy stele on its back, so it likes heavy things; the fifth son is the animal head

Wood carved dragon on caisson ceiling

*Zhengwen* (Zoomorphic Ornament) on palace architecture

Stone carved animal heads on terrace

Animal head on incense burner leg

on the legs of incense burner, with its mouth open at the leg, it likes smoke because the incense burner produces smoke. There are still more sons, of whom there is no fixed order. As the saying goes: "the dragon has nine sons, each shoulders its responsibility", which means the dragon has many sons, they are of different uses and images in different places. Therefore, the so-called dragon son does not mean anything in terms of biological significance; rather it is a sociological phenomenon. Since the ancients have invented the dragon, they can naturally invent the dragon's family, including the sons and grandsons of the dragon.

Tortoise under stele

## Demonstrations of Hierarchy System

The system of hierarchy being the nucleus of Chinese ritual system is naturally manifested in the decorations of the Forbidden City. We can see nine carved dragons on the big stone steps both in front and behind the three big halls in the front court; on the glazed screen wall in front of Ningshou Palace, there are nine glazed dragons; on the gates of palaces, there are nine studs vertically and another nine horizontally. Why so many nines? This phenomenon is by no means accidental. The Chinese ancients hold that everything in the world belongs to either *yin* or *yang* (negative or positive). For examples, the heaven is *yang*, earth is *yin*; the male is *yang*, female is *yin*; the odd number is *yang*, even number is *yin*; the front is *yang*, back is *yin*; etc. The *yin* and *yang* are opposite to each other, and at the same time, inseparable from each other, such is the recognition of the objective world by the ancients, a viewpoint of the universe. In terms of the Forbidden City, the master of the palaces is the Emperor who is *yang*. The Emperor's palaces are decorated with dragons, as to how many dragons to be used in a particular place, naturally, the biggest number of the odd numbers, which are *yang* numbers, should be chosen. Among the odd, *yang* numbers, one, three, five, seven, nine, nine is the biggest number. That's why there are nine dragons on the steps and the pass exclusively for the Emperor and on the glazed screen wall in front of the palace; and the 9 by 9 = 81 studs on the palace gate have also become the special

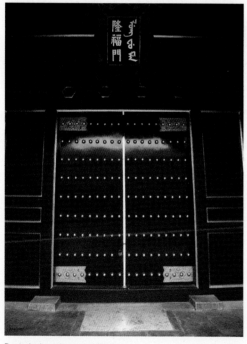

Door studs, palace architecture

Carved dragons on imperial pass behind Hall of Preserving Harmony

Nine-dragon Screen Wall, Forbidden City

Animals on roof ridge, Hall of Supreme Harmony

marks. For the important big halls such as the Hall of Preserving Harmony, the little animals on the roofs are also numbered nine, but on the Hall of Middle Harmony, seven, and on the pavilion, waterside pavilion and storied buildings in the Imperial Garden, the number reduced to five, or three. Such obvious or obscure numbers are indications of the hierarchy set by ritual system on the one hand; but on the other hand, they are also embodied with rich cultural connotations. However, such connotations are not easily understood without further explanations. They are not like the colors of the Forbidden City which produces direct decoration effect through people's eyesight, nor like the stone and wood carvings which demonstrate concrete decoration content.

# Construction of Forbidden City

Immediately after the Emperor Yongle of the Ming Dynasty, named Zhu Di ascended to the throne, he decided to move his capital from Nanjing to Beijing. At that time, Beijing as the capital of the former Yuan Dynasty, Dadu, was still kept intact as a city, but the palace city in the imperial city had been destroyed. So the Forbidden City of the Ming Dynasty was built anew on the location of Yuan palace city.

In the 5th year (1407) of Yongle,the emperor ordered the Forbidden City to be built. For such a major project, the first thing to do was to make the overall planning and architectural designing. The planning and designing included: on the spot survey of the terrain, geology and environment; designing, drawing and making models of buildings according to the requirements of the palaces set by the Court both materially and spiritually, which were subjected to the examinations by several levels of the Court, and finally got the approval by the Emperor; and then, estimation of the necessary materials and manpower needed for the construction, which were to be counted in terms of money and grains, and after these were ratified, the construction officially began.

First of all, it was imperative to collect materials. For Chinese timber-frame buildings, timber is the key material; moreover, for building palaces, the timber material must be good in quality, big in size and large in quantity. At that time, they mainly came from Zhejiang, Jiangxi, Hunan, Hubei and Sichuan provinces. After being cut from the mountain forests, they were usually flown into the Yangtze River through the local waterways, and then through the south-north Grand Canal, they were finally transported to Beijing. In this way, it took a long time, sometimes three years for the timber materials to reach Beijing, and furthermore, they had to be sun-dried before being stored for using.

Beside timber, a large amount of other materials such as bricks, tiles, stones and limes are needed. Bricks are needed in many places: the city walls of the palace, building walls, the floors both outside and inside of the buildings, and their sizes and quality requirements are different in different places, the total amount of which was estimated to be more than 80 million pieces. It was impossible to make all those bricks in the capital area, e.g. the bricks for the floor inside the halls were made in Suzhou area of Jiangsu Province, called "gold bricks", because they required the refined clay of that area to make the adobe. There was a set of strict requirements from the adobe making, sun-drying, baking in kiln to the ratifying and transportation of such bricks. They are square in form, hard in quality and can give metallic sound when being hit, so they are called "gold bricks", (in Chinese, metal and gold share the same character). The glazed bricks and tiles are also needed in large quantities and various kinds, requiring complicated methods. For the sake of convenience, kilns were built to produce them in the capital area. The present-day Liulichang in the southern part of the city and the Liuliqu in the suburb are all the sites for the kilns. Of building materials, the stone material is the most difficult to collect. A kind of white marble is needed for the terraces, balustrades and steps of the palaces. Such stone is produced in Quyang County of Hebei Province, some 200 kilometers from Beijing. It was not easy at all to transport heavy stone materials for such a long distance at that time. The wise artisans invented the method of making the on-land boat moving on ice, i.e. to dig wells along the road, and fetch the water from the wells to spray on road in winter, thus, an ice road is made, then put the on-land boat on the ice road with the stone materials on it, and pull the boat along. Behind the Hall of Preserving Harmony, there is a big piece of stone used as the imperial pass with steps, which is 16 meters long, 3.17 meters wide, 200 tons or more in weight. In order to transport it, according to historical records, more than 140 wells were sunk, the laborers pulling the on-land boat formed a line as long as half a kilometer, the boat moved at a speed of 2.5 kilometers a day, as many as 20 thousand laborers were mobilized, and the total cost was 110 thousand taels of silver. Later, although a big cart of 16 wheels was invented for that purpose, pulled by many donkeys, the speed was only 6.5 *li* (two *li* makes a kilo) a day.

The work for accumulating materials like this dragged along for nearly ten years before the work on the worksite began on a large scale. At that time, about 100 thousand artisans and several hundred thousand laborers were recruited all over the country, and an all-round construction was unfolded on the worksite of 720 thousand square meters: building palace walls, making and assembling timber-frames, constructing house walls and roofs, laying indoor floors, installing doors and windows, painting and carving beams and lintels, processing and carving stones, etc. After several years, the Forbidden City was finally completed in the 18th year (1420) of Yongle. Just imagine a scene of those years: all the civil and military officials and envoys from different places, entering the Meridian Gate, crossing the Gold Water Stream, entering the square through the Gate of Supreme Harmony, they saw colored flags flying everywhere; and then, going through the formidable guards of honor, walking past the long stone slab road, climbing up the three layered terraces, where drums and bells were ringing with smokes dancing around; and then, entering the Hall of Supreme Harmony, seeing through the gold columns coiled with dragons, and finally, they saw the feudal Emperor sitting upright on the imperial chair high up. Such an environment was really imposing and menacing. It was precisely through the changes of the airy shapes of the architectural groups, the creation of building images and decorations of various kinds, the builders of the Forbidden City fully satisfied the requirements of it both materially and spiritually, which shows the high technical and artistic level of architectures in the Ming Dynasty and demonstrates the superior technologies of the ancient artisans. As of today, the menacing power of the Forbidden City of those days is no longer existing. What it remains is the precious heritage which embodies the fine architectural culture of ancient China. In 1987, it was enlisted as the "World Cultural Heritage" by the UNESCO, becoming the cultural treasure of the world.

# Chapter 3
# Sacrificial Offering and Altars and Temples

For the human beings of the very early stages, their existence was very much depended on the heaven, earth, mountains and rivers. As the old saying goes: "The weather is unpredictable", or, "wind and rain are not to be controlled", which means that the mankind was unable to predict or dictate the weather. Heavy rain would give rise to mountain torrents, making the rivers flooding; and if there is no rain for a long time, there would be a drought; and sudden strong wind can also destroy the houses and kill people. The primitive people did not understand these natural phenomena, nor master and change them. They can only fear and hope. Naturally they were awe-struck by the heaven, earth, mountains and rivers. This is the social reason for Man's worship of nature, or their primitive belief. After China entered the agricultural farming society, the people's farming production deepened their dependence on the mountain, river and weather. The land, mountains, forests and rivers are the bases for their production, and the change of weather has a direct bearing on their production. If there is sufficient wind and rain, there will be a good harvest; if there is flood or drought, then there is nothing to harvest. The changes in the nature directly affect the harvests of crops and the fortune of people. Thus, the worship of the heaven, earth, mountains, and rivers become intensified, and developed into sacrificial offerings to the heaven, earth, sun, moon, mountains and rivers.

# Birth of Altars and Temples
# for Sacrificial Offering

Sacrificial offering is a kind of worshipping activities in the form of showing and offering material objects. In China which is for ruling the country with ritual system, such worshipping is naturally regulated in the scope of the ritual system. Therefore, the ritual system has formulated clear regulations for such worshipping from its significance, principle to the ritual ceremonies. The ritual system holds: the reason for the emperor to offer sacrifices to Heaven and Earth is because they are the parents of the emperor, and to worship them is to show the emperor' filial piety. So, to worship the Heaven and Earth has become the important political activities of all the Chinese dynasties. It is also regulated in the ritual system that even during state mourning, meaning the emperor or his mother has died, then all the worshipping for the ancestors or gods must stop, but for the Heaven and Earth it has to continue. Since the emperor is the son of the Heaven and Earth, he can worship the Heaven and Earth, mountains and rivers, and the four directions, etc., according to the ritual system, while the vassals and other officials below them can only worship the mountains and rivers, but not the Heaven and Earth. So, to worship the Heaven and Earth is the privilege of the emperor. If anyone else should do that, he would be considered as violating the rules, and furthermore, whatever he does would have no effect at all.

As the Heaven, the Earth, the Sun and the Moon are all gods of nature, all the places for worshipping activities are located in the suburbs which are far away from the noises of the city, and seem closer to the universe. In such circumstances, one can show more respect in a solemn mood. So, all the activities for worshipping the Heaven, the Earth, the Sun and the Moon are called suburban worshipping. According to the ancient theory of *yin* and *yang*, the Heaven means *yang*, the Earth means *yin*; and the South means *yang*, the North means *yin*. So the Heaven worshipping is located in the southern suburb and the Earth worshipping in the northern suburb. And because the Sun rises in the east and the Moon is born in the west, so the Sun worshipping is located in the eastern suburb, and the Moon worshipping in the western suburb. In this way, the *yin* and *yang* are corresponding to each other, and the Heaven, the Earth, the Sun and the Moon have got their rightful places, reaching an overall balance. When Emperor Yongle made the planning for Beijing City he ordered the altar of the heaven to be built in the south while the altars of the Earth, the Sun and the Moon were built respectively in the north, east and west under the reign (1522-1566) of Emperor Jiajing of the Ming Dynasty. Among them the one in the south is known as the Temple of Heaven, the largest and most important of the kind.

# Temple of Heaven, Beijing

The Temple of Heaven is the place where the emperor holds rites of worship and offers sacrifices to Heaven. According to the ritual system, it is located in the southern suburbs of Beijing. During the middle period of the Ming Dynasty, the city was enlarged by adding an outer wall in the south which enclosed the Temple of Heaven into the city. The temple was built in 1420, the same time when the Forbidden City was built. It covers an area of 273 hectares which is four times that of the Forbidden City.

The front gate of the temple is on the west, facing the avenue inside the Yongdingmen Gate which is the axis of Beijing City. Thus, it provides convenience for the emperor to come to the temple from the Forbidden City. Entering the western gate on the right side, there is a group of buildings called Zhaigong (Abstinence Hall) where the emperor lives before he presents himself at the rites of Heaven worship. The main buildings for the actual ceremonies are located to the east of the Temple, which is arranged according to the south-north axis. The southernmost one is Yuanqiutan (Circular Mound) where the emperor holds ceremonies to worship Heaven. It is consisted of three layers of circular stone terraces, with balustrades on each layer, and outside of it are

Yuanqiutan (Circular Mound), Temple of Heaven

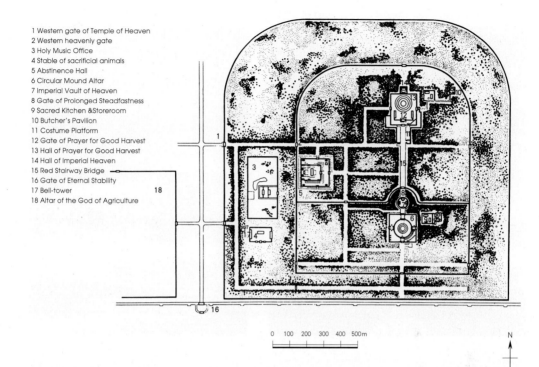

1 Western gate of Temple of Heaven
2 Western heavenly gate
3 Holy Music Office
4 Stable of sacrificial animals
5 Abstinence Hall
6 Circular Mound Altar
7 Imperial Vault of Heaven
8 Gate of Prolonged Steadfastness
9 Sacred Kitchen &Storeroom
10 Butcher's Pavilion
11 Costume Platform
12 Gate of Prayer for Good Harvest
13 Hall of Prayer for Good Harvest
14 Hall of Imperial Heaven
15 Red Stairway Bridge
16 Gate of Eternal Stability
17 Bell-tower
18 Altar of the God of Agriculture

0 100 200 300 400 500m

N

Plan. Temple of Heaven, Beijing

*Zhaigong* (Abstinence Hall), Temple of Heaven

Bird's-eye view, Temple of Heaven

Huangqiongyu (Imperial Vault of Heaven),
Temple of Heaven

Qiniandian (Hall of Prayer for Good Harvest), Temple of Heaven

two low walls, the inner and outer wall. To the north is a group of buildings called Huangqiongyu (Imperial Vault of Heaven), of which the main hall is a small round hall for keeping the tablet of the Heavenly Emperor. There are wing halls on both sides of the main hall, and this group of buildings is encircled by a round wall. To the north of Huangqiongyu, i.e. at the northern end of the axis, there is another group of buildings called Qiniandian (Hall of Prayer for Good Harvest) where the emperor prays for good harvest every summer. Qiniandian is the main building which is a round hall with a roof of three layers of eaves, and under the hall there is a three-layered white stone terrace. This hall is located to the north of the square, with the Gate of Praying for Good Harvest in front and wing halls on the right and left, and surrounded on all sides by a wall. Apart from these groups of main

Inside view of Huangqiongyu

Red Stairway Bridge between Huangqiongyu and Qiniandian

structures, there are the places for the music and dance personnel to live and for keeping the animals as sacrifices within the western gate. There are also several groups of houses to the west of the Circular Mound and beside the Qiniandian for killing animals, making food as sacrifices for worshipping as well as for storing tools and costume. The number of buildings can satisfy the emperor's needs for Heaven worshipping and praying for good harvest. Then how can they meet the spiritual and artistic requirements needed for worshipping activities?

First, the architectural environment, on a land of 273 hectares, apart from the several groups of architectures, almost the entire remaining land are covered with pines, cypresses and other evergreen trees. The big area of green forests makes the Temple of Heaven an entirely different environment as the Forbidden City. The latter is magnificent with a menacing air, while the former is solemn with a sense of sacredness. On the axis of worshipping architectures, between the Heaven worshipping in the south and the praying for good harvest in the north, there is a passage known as Red Stairway Bridge for pedestrians which is as long as 300 meters, 30 meters wide, built of stone-slabs in the middle and gray bricks on the sides. The passage is four meters above ground, flanked by the forests of pines and cypresses. Walking on it from the south to the north, looking towards the blue sky with the sea of green trees around you, you would feel as if you were walking, step by step, towards the embrace of the sky above, which is exactly the sensation one desires to get in the environment of worshipping Heaven.

Floor of Yuanqiutan

Second, the method of symbolism is used in various architectural formations. The ancients think the sky is hollow, so it is round; the earth is in square shape, so it is square. "Heaven is round and Earth is square" is the recognition of the ancients towards the natural celestial body. Also, the Heaven is above and the Earth below, so the outer and inner walls of the Temple are all shaped round on top and square below. In architectural shape, the Circular Mound is in round, while the surrounding parapet walls, one round, one square.; both the Imperial Vault of Heaven and the Hall of Prayer for Good Harvest are round from the terrace to the hall bodies to the roofs.

In colors, since the sky is blue, so the Imperial Vault of Heaven and the Hall of Prayer for Good Harvest, the main hall and the wing halls alike, are covered with blue glazed tiles; the Circular Mound itself is built of white stones, while the surrounding short walls are also covered with blue glazed tiles. The overall colors of the Temple of Heaven are the blue and white architectures standing out of a vast area of green forests, seemingly pure and solemn.

In numbers, both in decorations and members of the buildings, the biggest number nine among the odd numbers are widely used. The Temple of Heaven belongs to the imperial architectures, therefore, the studs on the gates are arranged nine vertically and nine horizontally, totaling 81, as the decoration. On the Circular Mound, there are nine steps between each of the three layers of terraces. On the top one, there are nine rounds of stone slabs not including the round stone in the center, the first round is paved with nine stone slabs, the second round, 18 slabs, the third round, 27 slabs, until the 9th round, 81 slabs. The terraces are enclosed with standing stone slabs, on the top floor; there are nine slabs on each side, totaling 36 slabs, on the second floor, 18 slabs each side, on the third floor, 27 slabs each side. But, on the Hall of Prayer for Good Harvest, the symbolic number of nine is no longer to be seen, instead, there are numbers concerning agricultural production, because it is the place for the emperor to pray for good harvest. In the round hall there are three rings of pillars, the inner ring is composed of four big pillars, symbolizing the four seasons of the year; in the middle are 12 pillars for 12 months, the outer ring is composed of another 12 pillars, symbolizing 12 time-periods of a day; and the 24 pillars of the middle and the outer rings also symbolizing 24 solar terms of a year. In China which has a long history of agricultural farming, the season, the time and the solar terms indeed have a direct bearing on the harvests of agricultural production.

Concerning the creation of the environmental atmosphere and the symbolic decorations, some can be perceived directly, e.g. the green trees and buildings in blue and white colors can produce a solemn and sacred atmosphere. But the symbolic meanings of the numbers are difficult to be discovered and understood. Nevertheless, all these brilliant creations have embodied the wisdom of the ancient artisans who have left behind a treasure of architectural culture for the mankind. In 1998, the Temple of Heaven was enlisted as "World Culture Heritage" by the UN Educationdal, Scientific and Cultural Organization.

# Altar of the Land and Grain, Beijing

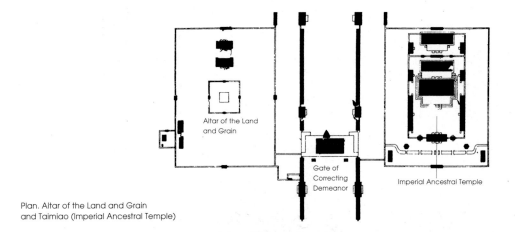

Altar of the Land
and Grain

Gate of
Correcting
Demeanor

Imperial Ancestral Temple

Plan. Altar of the Land and Grain
and Taimiao (Imperial Ancestral Temple)

In the long-lasting agricultural farming society of China, the respect and worship of the land and grain are very much emphasized. Since it is impossible to worship the vast land, the only thing to do is to worship the God of land, called *she*, likewise, there is the God of grain, called *ji*. So, when the ancients worshipped *sheji*, they were worshipping the land and grain. Such worshipping ceremonies, much like the other worshiping of the Heaven, Earth, Sun and Moon are often held on the open air terrace, that is why the *shejitan* (Altar of the Land and Grain) was built exclusively for such purposes.

The Altar of the Land and Grain is built within the Imperial City at the same time with the Forbidden City. It is composed of three major architectures of the Altar of the Land and Grain, Baidian and Jimen, which form the central axis, covering an area of more than 360 *mu* of land. Baidian is for the emperor to rest or keep away from the wind or rain during the worshipping activities. The Altar is the place for holding worshipping ceremonies which is an earth terrace in the form of a square, symbolizing the square earth. Each side of the square is 15 meters wide, one meter above the ground. On the terrace, there are earth in five colors, and according to the theory of *yin* and *yang*, the green earth is put on the east, red one on the south, white one on the west, black one on the north and yellow one in the middle. The five colors of earth are all contributed by different areas of the country, indicating that all the land belongs to the emperor, and the emperor has a unified country. The terrace is surrounded on all sides by a pararet on which four colors of glazed bricks are pasted corresponding to the four directions: green for the east, red for the south, white for the west and black for the north, and in the middle of each short wall, there is the stone arch. The altar, wall, stone arch and the Baidian in the north have formed a complete group of worshipping architecture.

Altar of the Land and Grain

Parapet round the Altar of the Land and Grain

# Mountain Worshipping

The earlier human being's life can not be separated from the mountains: the grass in the mountain forest can be used to feed the animals, the forest can give rise to clouds and rains to moisturize the land, so, they become attached to the mountain forest, feeling awesome and respectful and gradually form the habit of mountain worship. But the mountains in the country are too numerous to worship each one of them, then, after choosing for a long time, several famous mountains are selected as their representatives. As early as the Spring and Autumn and Warring States period (770-221B.C.) Taishan (Mt.Tai) was already the famous mountain for the emperors to worship. Afterwards, five mountains were decided according to the theory of the five elements: the Eastern Mountain, Taishan of Shandong Province; the Southern Mountain, Hengshan of Hunan Province; the Western Mountain, Huashan of Shaanxi Province, the Northern Mountain, Hengshan of Shanxi Province and the Central Mountain, Songshan of Henan Province. Being the leaders of the mountains. They became the objectives for worshipping by the successive dynasties. Therefore, there were temples built for that purpose at all the five mountains.

Among the five mountains, Taishan Mountain is the most famous, because it is the first one to receive the worshipping by emperors. Many emperors came personally to the mountain to hold worshipping ceremonies starting from the Spring and Autumn period. Emperor Wu of the Han Dynasty came here seven times altogether to hold grand ceremonies in person, so that such worshipping became a major political activity for the successive feudal dynasties. The Dai (Mt.Tai) Temple at the foot of the mountain is the place for worshipping the mountain god. This temple should have been built very early, because from the Tang Dynasty afterwards, there have been major repairs or rebuilt by all the dynasties. The existing architectures were built after the Yuan Dynasty. The scale of the group of the architectures is very large. In front of the temple, there is a group of buildings consisting of the archway, the temple gate and halls, etc. as the prelude to the temple. The big yard of the temple is behind it with the main hall, Tiankuangdian, sitting on the central axis. The hall is nine bays wide, 48.7 meters in depth, with the hip roof and double eaves on top. That is the place for worshipping the god of Taishan Mountain. There are two gates in front of the temple and a bedroom palace behind. Several dozen steles carved with important records of the worshipping activities and the temple itself have been preserved in the big yard. The big yard resembles a small imperial palace with high walls all around and watch towers on the four corners.

The temples at the other mountains are also on a large scale. The Central Mountain Temple in Dengfeng City, Henan Province and the Southern Mountain Temple in Hengshan of Hunan Province all cover an area of 100 thousand square meters; the architectural groups are composed of several courtyards one after another. The big halls are usually nine bays wide, sitting on big stone terraces, with stone balustrades around them. In the middle of the stone steps there is the carved stone passage exclusively for the emperor. Although the emperors do not necessarily come here in per-

Taishan (Mt. Tai), Taian, Shandong Province

Main hall, the Dai Temple

son to worship, these are the important places for the royal court to worship the mountain gods, so their architectural form are only next to the imperial palaces and tombs in the hierarchy.

The Taishan Mountain is the most famous among the five mountains, but it is not as high as the Northern Mountain Hengshan, or as steep as the Western Mountain Huashan, or as beautiful as the Yellow Mountain of Anhui Province. However, it has been an important place for emperors of successive dynasties to hold big ceremonies of worshipping mountain god. As a result, it has always been attracting a great many men of letters to tour this place, leaving behind many related articles and carved calligraphy pieces. Therefore, Taishan Moutain is endowed with far richer cultural connotations than the other mountains, and it has been enlisted by the U.N. Educational, Scientific and Cultural Organization as the "World Culture and Nature Heritage".

Central Mountain Temple, Dengfeng City, Henan Province

Thousand-year-old cypress in the Central Mountain Temple

# Ancestor Worshipping

During the prolonged feudal society of China, the patriarchal clan system has always been the basis of the feudal autocracy. The nucleus of the patriarchal clan system is to contain the people with the familial blood relations, and to formulate the hierarchy of the old and the young, and the respected and despised. On the state level, the emperor passes the throne and the state power to the eldest son; on the family level, the patriarch passes the family assets and family power to the eldest son; only under special circumstances, those powers are passed on to the other sons or grandsons appointed by the emperor or the patriarch. In a word, the imperial power or family power are bestowed by the ancestors, therefore, under the hereditary system of the emperor, there exists a peculiar relationship of Chinese feudal society which does not distinguish between the state and family. A prevailing patriarchal ideology of emphasizing blood re-

Main hall, Ancestrial Temple, Beijing

Ancestrial Temple, Beijing

lations and respecting the ancestors is born in the society from top to bottom, and this ideology is materialized by the ritual system into actual practices which gradually become the tradition of ancestor worshipping. The ancestral temple of the royal court and the family temples among the people are special places for ancestor worshipping, the actual objects symbolizing the ancient patriarchal clan society.

Taimiao (Imperial Ancestral Temple) is the place where the emperors worship their ancestors, so it is of the same importance as the places where they worship the heaven, earth, sun, moon and the gods of earth and grain, and it also should be arranged in the centre of the capital. During the city planning of the capital, it was clearly pointed out according to the ritual system, that "court infront, market back, ancestral temple left and *sheji* altar right", meaning, the ancestral temple and the *sheji* altar should be arranged on the left and right of the imperial palace. The layout of Dadu of the Yuan Dynasty and the Beijing city of the Ming Dynasty was exactly like this. This Taimiao of Beijing belonging to the Ming and Qing dynasties is the only one kept intact among all the ancestral temples of all the Chinese dynasties.

Taimiao of Beijing is situated to the eastern side of the Tiananmen and Duanmen, within the Imperial City, but in front of the Forbidden City. There are two walls surrounding it. Large areas of cypress trees are planted outside of the first wall, which produce a very solemn environment. The buildings for worshipping purposes are located within the second wall, consisting of the main hall, the residence hall and Taimiao which form the axis. The main hall is for the emperor to hold worshipping ceremonies; the residence hall is for enshrining the soul-tablets of ancestors; the Taimiao is for enshrining the soul-tablets of the emperor's early ancestors. Before the Qing entered Beijing, there were several kings back in northeast who were conferred posthumously upon the titles of forerunner emperors whose soul-tablets are enshrined in the Taimiao. When the emperor worshipped his ancestors at the end of every year, the soul-tablets kept in the residence hall were moved into the main hall for the purpose of holding grand ceremonies. The main hall originally was nine bays wide, just next to the Hall of Supreme Harmony in hierarchy, but the roof is hip roof with double eaves, and there is a stone terrace of three layers, the top grade in hierarchy. During the Qing Dynasty, the main hall was reconstructed into eleven bays wide, raising the status to a new high. However, the three layer terrace is not as high as that under the Hall of the Supreme Harmony, and the courtyard in front of the main hall is not as big as the square in front of the Hall of Supreme Harmony, therefore overall, it is not as magnificent as the latter.

Cypress forest, Ancestrial Temple,Beijing

# Ancestral Hall of the People

The Ancestral Hall is a place for the common people to worship their ancestors. According to the ancient ritual system, only the emperors and the officials of various ranks can build temples to worship their ancestors, while the common people can only do so in their homes. It was not until the Ming Dynasty, were the people allowed to build ancestral halls for worshipping purposes. In the Qing Dynasty, ancestral halls appeared in great numbers, especially in those villages, people were gathered according to blood relations, sometimes; there were several ancestral halls in a village.

## Function of Ancestral Halls

The primary function is to worship the ancestors of course, and through this, to reach the objective of respecting the ancestors and unifying the family clan. As a clan, in order to safeguard its overall interests and to increase its cohesive power, there must be corresponding clan rules and regulations apart from the spiritual role played through ancestral worshipping. They are the criteria for people's thinking and doing set according to the ritual system and moral standard of the feudal society. For example, there are ten prohibitions formulated by a family clan: Owing or resisting paying the money and grains which should be paid or returned is prohibited; destroying or laying waste the graveyard is prohibited; violating father and elder brothers is prohibited; violating the respected and the elderly is prohibited; the secret appointment of heir in violation of ritual code is prohibited; abusive language and physical fighting are prohibited; hiding thieves and bandits are prohibited; raping is prohibited; indecent language and doings are prohibited. Some family clans have formulated articles for punishment: there is the difference of seniority among brothers, if the younger brother is not obedient to the elder brother, the former should be hit 30 times with a plank; if the elder bullies the younger, the former should be hit ten times; to embezzle the funds, grain or objects of the clan should be punished for light cases, and hit for serious cases, apart from paying back what have been taken; to instigate the daughter-in-law not to show filial piety to the husband's father and mother, or to sow discord among the wives of husband's brothers, should be hit severely, etc. These rules and regulations are recorded in the clan genealogy book, and sometimes, carved on a stone tablet to be erected in the ancestral hall for everyone of the clan to abide by. The one who enforces these rules and regulations is the chief of the clan of course, and the place for that is the ancestral hall. Some clan rules contain such distinctive article, if violated; one would be locked up in the ancestral hall for a month after receiving 40 hits with the plank. From these prohibiting codes and punishment articles, one sees clearly that the role of the clan has far exceeded ancestors worshipping and clan gathering, actually, the clan has become the basic political structure in the countryside, managing the behavior of the people, even the public affairs of the village, marriage and death ceremonies and popular activities are carried on through the clan. If the clan is the basic grass-root organization of the feudal patriarchal clan system, then the ancestral hall is its basic grass-root court and political institution.

Every family clan has a genealogy book which records the names and their relationship of this clan generation after generation, and deeds of those members who have attained great achievements, and also major events concerning the local production, construction and folkways. Therefore, the genealogy is the history of a family clan, and for the continuation of the clan, the genealogy should be renewed periodically. For such major event concerning the family history, it is up to the clan chief to hold a meeting in the ancestral hall to make a decision and appoint a person to write the manuscript, and a special ceremony is to be held to announce the beginning of the renewing work.

It is also necessary for the clan to run schools to educate their posterity, and to arrange the farmland belonging to the entire clan, using the rent of the land in education and other public welfare affairs of the clan. The administrative organ for such matters is in the ancestral hall, and the school is also near it, and sometimes, right in it. In Guangzhou of Guangdong Province, there is a general ancestral hall of all the families bearing the Chen surname in the province in which there is a school exclusively for the clan people, therefore the ancestral hall is also called Chen Clan Academy. In the vast countryside the ancestral halls are usually the political centers of the villages, and they usually occupy the key positions of the entrance of the village or the village center.

## Shape of Ancestral Hall

Although the ancestral hall has several functions, the major one is ancestral worshipping, so the arrangement of buildings is made according to its need. Their shapes are taken after the quadrangles just like the commonly seen residence buildings and palaces, putting the main gate and the hall on the axis, wing houses on both sides so that a courtyard is formed, and the size of the ancestral hall is decided by the number of yards included.

The Zhuge Village of Lanxi City, Zhejiang Province is inhabited by the descendants of Zhuge Liang, Prime Minister of Shu-Han of the Three Kingdoms period (220-280). In the center of the village, there is the Prime Minister Hall, the general ancestral hall of the Zhuge clan, in which the soul-tablet of Zhuge Liang, ancestor of the

Ancestor worshipping, Prime Minister Temple

Wood carving on beam, Prime Minister Temple

Prime Minister Temple, Zhuge Village of Lanxi,
Zhejiang Province

Stage, General Ancestral Hall of the He Clan

Elevation. Roof of stage

Zhuge clan is enshrined. There is a gate-house in front, a hall in the middle, a residence house in the rear, and wing-houses on both sides, forming two yards, the front one and the back one. In addition, there is a bell tower and a drum tower on the right and left side of the residence building. On the occasion of the winter solstice and tomb festival, every year, the clan people would come here to worship their ancestor, Zhuge Liang. During the worshipping ceremony, a place for burning incense is set before the soul-tablet in the residence house and also in the middle hall, and in front of that , a table of sacrificial objects is arranged, offering pig, cattle, goat, chicken, fish, as well as rice, steam bread, tea, wine, paper flowers, etc. The person presiding over the ceremony must be the one of high ranking, high learning and high prestige chosen from among the clan people. It is a grand ceremony, carrying on according to a set rule. Amid the music of drums and instruments, the clan people repeatedly kowtow before the soul-tablet, offering wine and food. After the ceremony, food and cakes are distributed among the elders of the village to indicate the respect for the elderly.

The Guodong Village of Wuyi County, Zhejiang Province is inhabited by the He clan, in which there is also a general ancestral hall of the He clan. This hall is also composed of the gate, the middle hall, the residence house in the rear and the wing-houses on both sides, forming two courtyards. The middle hall is for ceremonial purposes, and the soul-tablets of all the ancestors of the He clan are

General Ancestral Hall of the He Clan, Guodong Village of Wuyi, Zhejiang Province

83

enshrined in the residence house. During the spring and autumn ceremonies every year, the screen-door between the middle hall and the residence house is open to ensure a larger place. In front of the soul-tablets, a table is set for offering the candles, pig, goat, wine and cakes, etc. The participants should be those people in the clan who are fairly knowledgeable. During the ceremonies, the chief person would lead everyone to kowtow before the soul-tablets, offering wine, food, burning paper money. After the ceremonies, the clan people would dine together to celebrate the occasion. From the above two ancestral halls, we know that apart from the halls and houses on the axis which are for ancestral worshipping, the wing-houses and other auxiliary houses can be used for meetings and other activities of the clan people. The Chen Clan Ancestral Hall in Guangzhou is larger than average because it is also a school. Apart from the front and back yards, there are three houses in its east and west respectively, totaling 18 halls and wing-houses, forming 6 courtyards, covering a floor space of 13,200 square meters. There is one thing different with the Guodong Village ancestral hall and the Zhuge Village hall that there is a stage between the gate and the middle hall, which is for the clan people to watch operas. Why a stage in the ancestral hall? This is because the ancestral halls are for the activities like ancestral worshipping, business discussion, solving disputes among clan people etc. which are serious matters, and involves only a few people. In order to educate more people and give the roles of the ancestral halls into full play, many places combine the ancestral worshipping with the festive activities like the Spring Festival celebrations in addition to the dinner together and releasing of cakes, etc. after the ceremonies. On such occasions, there are also riddles-guessing, sweet-cakes releasing and opera singing specially for the clan people. Aside from those bad elements, everyone, from the aged to children, can participate. In this way, the villagers can receive education and at the same time enjoyment, and the relations among the clan people and villagers are strengthened, and the objective of respecting the ancestors and uniting the clan people is better achieved. Therefore, such stages are rather common in many countryside ancestral halls in Zhejiang, Jiangxi and Shanxi provinces.

## Ancestral Hall Decoration

Since the ancestral hall is the center and symbol of a clan, apart from its material function, it must be able to show the glory and richness of the clan in its images, which makes the ancestral hall architecture more elaborate and decorative than that of residences and shops, etc. The He Clan Ancestral Hall of Guodong Village is larger than any building of residence in the village. The roof of its stage is decorated with fish and flower patterns, under the eaves there are wood carved corbels, and the ceiling is full with painted flower patterns. All this makes the stage the most exciting place when performances are going on, and even during ordinary times, the most beautiful center of the ancestral hall.

In Zhuge Village, beside the Prime Minister Hall, there are more than ten sub-halls belonging to different pedigrees. They are all larger than residence buildings in size; in addition, the gates are

Main gate, Chen Clan Ancestral Hall

Stone balustrade, Chen Clan Ancestral Hall

Chen Clan Ancestral Hall, Guangzhou, Guangdong Province

decorated into an archway using carved bricks. The middle hall of the Prime Minister Hall is five bays wide, with 16 stone pillars surrounding it, using single pieces of stone, on which the beam, the *dou* and *gong* (mortise and tenon) are all made of wood, full of wood carvings as decoration. The four pillars in the middle are made respectively of the timber of cypress, Chinese catalpa, tung and Chinese toon, putting the four Chinese letters together to mean a hundred children sharing the Spring, symbolizing the prosperity and auspiciousness of the family clan.

The Chen Clan Ancestral Hall is famous for its decorations which are not only wide spread, but also in various categories. Standing outside the gate, one sees two colored pictures of gate gods on the black lacquer doors

Balustrade decorated with metal members

and the carved blocks of stone on both sides of the gate (gate piers); several large size brick carvings on the walls beside the gate. After entering the gate, one sees all kinds of different decorations from the beams to the windows and doors, to the bases for pillars inside the house; and from the ridge to the wall to the balustrades, pillars and steps on the terrace from outside of the house. Beside the wood carving, stone carving and brick carving commonly seen in the ancestral hall, one sees a lot of lime sculpture, pottery sculpture, glass flower, bronze and iron casting, etc. Wood carvings are mainly found on the beams, doors, and windows of halls. Stone carvings are found on the balustrades, steps and pillar bases, and also on the stone columns and stone beams in the hall. The decorations on the stone columns include simple lines on the four angles of a rectangular one and carved animals and flower patterns on the surface of the column. The stone pillar bases here are different from those in other places. The role of a pillar base is to protect the pillar from the humidity coming up from the earth and transfer the weight of the house evenly on the ground, thus, it is larger in diameter than the pillar. But, here in the ancestral hall, the bases are often smaller which seems instable but graceful. Brick carv-

Gate pier, Chen Clan Ancestral Hall

Stone pillar base, Chen Clan Ancestral Hall

ings are seen in many places, at the ends of eaves and outer walls, and even on the brick walls, there are carved pictures. There are three large-size brick carvings respectively on the walls beside the gate and the outer wall of the main hall among which a picture showing the heroes of the Outlaws of the Marshes (Liangshanpo) in a Chinese classical novel getting together in the Hall of All Men Being Brothers or Juyiting in Chinese. There are more than 30 figures scattered in the

Wood carving decoration on gate of Chen Clan Ancestral Hall

Large-size brick carving on wall of Chen Clan Ancestral Hall

hall and pavilion, each is different from the other in posture, costume and even facial expressions. The roof of the hall, the balustrades are clearly shown, including the decorations on the four margins. The artistic level of the sculpture is so high that everyone marvels at it.

Shiwan of Guangdong ceramic is famous for its pottery production since ancient times. Putting glaze on pottery, members of different colors can be baked. Such pottery members are widely used in Guangdong, Hong Kong and Macao. They are also used on the roof, forming colored

House ridge decoration of Chen Clan Ancestral Hall

house ridges. The 11 ridges of the Chen Clan Ancestral Hall are all decorated with such ceramics showing human figures and animals in various colors, which produce very strong decorative effect. Carving on glass is a traditional folk art in Guangdong and Fujian provinces, which is also used in the Chen Clan Ancestral Hall. The windows of the main hall and wing-houses are often assembled with blue glass carved with white pictures of plants and flowers which are pleasant to the eye. Those wing-houses are suitable places for the youngsters of Chen clan to read and write. It seems too heavy and strenuous to decorate the ancestral hall from inside out and from the upper to lower places, but it does reflect the wishes of the Chen clan for family prosperity and good fortune of the descendants.

After going through ancestral hall decorations in various places, we know that their content is very comprehensive. There is the combination of dragon and phoenix, meaning auspiciousness; of carp, fish and dragon, meaning after persistent self-cultivation, a carp can suddenly change into a dragon one day; there are the images of a crane, a deer, a bat, a lotus, a peony, a pomegranate, a design of the Chinese letter meaning long life ( 卍 ), a design of a coin, etc. all indicating longevity,

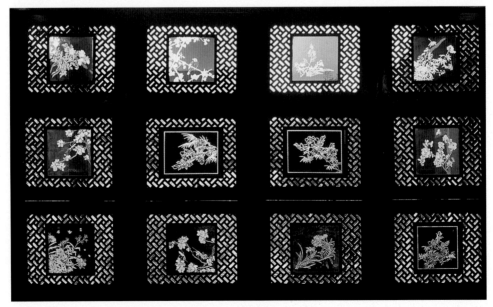

Glass carving on windows of Chen Clan Ancestral Hall

multiple sons and fortune and auspiciousness; there is the combination of a lute, a chess, a book and a painting, indicating the high aspirations of scholars; there is even a large-size picture telling a traditional legend, using the combination of human figures, animals and plants. A large clan is bound to produce, in the long history, officials, merchant landlords and many people engaged in physical labor. To convey the overall ideas and interests of the clan in a common ancestral hall would surely require a rich content in decoration. It is natural that in certain areas or in a particular ancestral hall there are some unique decorations. For example, the bedroom chamber of the Prime Minister Hall in Zhuge Village is for enshrining the tablet of Zhuge Liang, there are no figures and animals as decoration on the corbels of this chamber like those corbels in the Middle Hall, instead, an imitation antique shelf fits into the wood carving, on which little bonsais of flowers and rocks are placed. In this way, the picture decoration is simple, but elegant both in content and style, which exactly suits the personal interests of Zhuge Liang. Another example, Guangzhou has been an important port city in history, where commerce developed very early, which enabled the local people becoming knowledgeable, but at the same time, commercial utilitarianism was bound to

House ridge decoration with buildings and figures

House ridge decoration with two dragons, Chen Clan Ancestral Hall

Wood carved characters and flowers in ancestral temple

Stone and wood carved flower and
grass decoration in ancestral temple

Stone and wood carved flower and
grass decoration in ancestral temple

Wood carved characters and flowers in ancestral temple

Wood carving in ancestral temple

Wood carving in ancestral temple

influence their ideas and interests. That's why there is a scene of busy street on the main ridge of Chen Clan Ancestral Hall, in which there are all kinds of stores, with officials, merchants and ordinary people wandering in and out, and the patterns symbolizing wealth can be seen in many places as decorations.

To compare the overall decorations of ancestral halls in different areas with that of palace architectures, of course the former is by far the less elaborate, delicate and perfect. But in terms of decorative images and content, the former is much richer and varied than the latter. Because the decorations used on palaces can also be used on ancestral halls including the dragon which is the symbol of the emperor. It is true that the Court forbids the dragon to be used on civil architectures, but, because the dragon has long since become the totem of the whole nation, so the dragon designs do appear on ancestral halls in defiance of the government restrictions. On the contrary, the folk decorations and designs often used on ancestral halls, e.g. Guangzhou towers and pavilions, the eight scenes of Guangzhou appeared on Chen Clan Ancestral Hall and the chicken, duck, pig, rabbit, fruit and vegetables often appeared on countryside ancestral halls can not be seen on palace decorations.

The open-air altars for worshipping the heaven, earth, sun and moon, and the temples for worshipping ancestors and mountain gods have a combined name: altar and temple architecture. Since these worshipping activities are important ceremonies required by the ancient ritual system, the altar and temple architecture is also called ritual system architecture, which occupies an important position in Chinese traditional architectures.

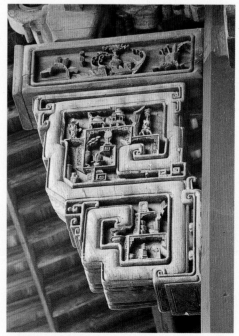

Antique shelf decoration on truss leg, Prime Minister Temple, Zhuge Village, Zhejiang Province

91

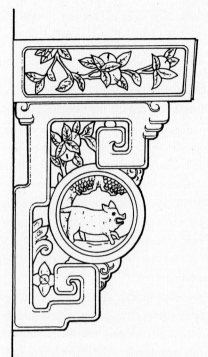

Decorations with pig, rabbit and ox in
countryside ancestral temple

# Chapter 4
# Tombs

Everything in the world has its soul; this is the acknowledgement of the objective world by the ancients, when the scientific knowledge is not yet perceived. The soul, according to them, can exist, independent of the objective entity, while the latter can disappear, the former is eternal. It is the same with human beings: the death of a man means only the death of his body, but his soul will never disappear, which has only left the obvious and positive world for another world to live on, this world is called "netherworld". Therefore, in order to live a life better than that in the positive world, the dead person must wear good clothes and good ornaments, bringing all kinds of fine personal belongings, even servants into the underground building which is called "netherworld building". This is the social reason for Chinese ancient system of rich burial.

The all-powerful emperor is naturally interested in pursuing this rich burial system. The emperors of all dynasties, without exception, lay emphasis on the construction of mausoleums. Many emperors, once ascending to the throne, start to build his palaces and at the same time his mausoleum. The construction of palaces for the living and dead emperor always occupy an important position in the construction of the government.

# Qin and Han Tombs

In 221 years, B.C., Emperor Qinshihuang unified the whole of China, becoming the first emperor of a unified dynasty in Chinese history. He built palaces in his capital, Xianyang in a big way, and at the same time, began to build his mausoleum until his death. The gigantic and magnificent palaces were burned down as early as the time when the Qin Dynasty ended, but the Mausoleum of Emperor Qinshihuang buried deep underground has been kept intact. In the past, we only know from reading documents that the underground tomb is very elaborate: there are carved pictures on the walls, markings of the sun, moon, stars, and rivers, lakes and seas on the ceiling and floor respectively, the rivers are even filled with mercury; the tomb chambers are full of pearls and precious stones; bows and arrows are installed on the doors to protect the tomb. In

Terracotta figures, Tomb of Emperor Qinshihuang

recent years, the scientific exploration by archaeologists has proved that there is indeed mercury in the underground tomb. But aside from that, what is to be seen is only the tomb in the shape of a pyramid with a square base and top above ground. However, since the terra-cotta figures have been found and excavated, our knowledge of the Mausoleum of Emperor Qinshihuang become more concrete. They are soldiers and horses baked with clay, serving as the defending army for the mausoleum. Among those already excavated are nearly a thousand terra-cotta figures, a hundred horses and several dozens of chariots, and among the soldier figures, there are archers, infantry, cavalrymen and chariot men, and many of them are holding weapons. These are discovered at some 1,000 meters east of the mound and the excavation work is still under way. There are reasons to believe this defending army should be rather big. Since the underground tomb chamber has not been opened, we have no way of knowing its actual situation. However, judging from the large size of the defending army and the technology in making them, from the artistic level of those unearthed bronze and jade articles made prior or after the Qin Dynasty, we can believe that this mausoleum which was built with a force of 700,000 men is unprecedented both in size and in technology.

The Han Dynasty inherited the system of the Qin in building mausoleums for the emperors. The tomb chamber is buried deep into underground, while on the ground; a high mound is piled up with halls built for worshipping purposes. Several Han Dynasty mausoleums scattered around Xianyang area nowadays are of the same type.

None of the emperors' mausoleums of the Han Dynasty have been formally excavated. formaeey archaeologists have excavated a considerable amount of the Han tombs in many places. The underground chambers are built with brick and stone in the shape of a rectangular, using long stone slabs or hollow bricks for the floor, the ceiling and the four walls. These stone or brick materials are 1.50 meters long, 0.6-0.8 meter wide and 0.2-0.3 meter thick, which are stuck to the walls and ceiling one after another with the side facing the chamber carved with all kinds of

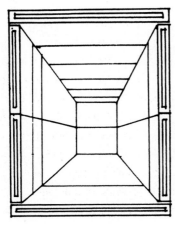

Han tomb structure

Han tomb structure

Animals and Hunting

Appreciating animals' plays

Trotting horse

Painted pictures on bricks and stone in Han tombs

designs, therefore called pictured stone or bricks. The designs can be human figures and the images of animals like horse, tiger, phoenix and birds, or pictures composed by men, animals, buildings depicting the scene of labor, daily life and leisure, e.g. the owner of the tomb goes hunting, sightseeing and holding a banquet, farmers sowing, harvesting, boiling salt, as well as some legendary story scenes. These designs are carved with very fine strokes on the surface of the stone and bricks, producing very clear images, which vividly conveys the then social life and environment. Because of the difficulty in making such bricks and stone materials and the size of which limited the size of the chamber, so gradually, they were replaced by the vault structure made of bricks. The walls are built with smaller bricks; the vault is put on top, the width of which far exceeds the large size brick or stone slab. The decoration of the chamber is to whitewash the surface with lime, and then, colored paintings made on it. Such decorations are far better than before both in image and in color.

Gaoyi gate piers of Han Dynasty, Ya'an, Sichuan Province

The ground structures of the Han tombs have been mostly destroyed with only a few stone gate piers left in front of some tombs. The gate pier resembles a stone tablet with a house roof on top, usually in a pair, situated to the front of the tomb, therefore the landmark of the entrance of the tomb. In Xianyang of Shaanxi Province, there is a tomb of the famous general, Huo Qubing, belonging to the Western Han period (206B.C.-25A.D.). He led the army to fight against the Huns for six times, winning repeated battle honors and died in battle at the age of 23. In order to mark his merits, Emperor Wu of the Han Dynasty built a tomb for him near the Emperor's Mausoleum. As of today, we can still see a series of stone sculptures in front of the tomb, including battle horse, sleeping ox, sleeping elephant, crouching tiger and stone fish, etc. These stone sculptures, with simple formation and vivid image, display high artistic level of our early sculptures.

In some comparatively elaborate Han tombs, we can find, apart from the coffin of the owner, there are also many burial objects, among which, the daily necessities such as bronze mirrors, lacquer ware, potteries, etc., and also jade, gold and silver articles as ornaments, male and female terra-cotta figures and pottery models of houses. These objects are meticulously done, some are peculiar and deft in shape, and some are colorful and graceful. They can reflect the life of the people at that time, and also serve to testify the traditional fine art of ancient China.

From the ground, underground situation and the remains available today, we get to know the set form of the Han tombs is like this: it is composed of a sacred way and buildings above ground, and underground chambers. In front of the sacred way there is a pair of gate piers at the gate of the tomb. There are stone sculptures of men and animals lined at the left and right side of the sacred way. Behind it are the ground architectures of the tomb. And then there is the tomb chamber buried underground, in which there are coffin and burial objects. So, it can be said that in the Han Dynasty, the basic form of the ancient tombs had already taken shape.

Stone carved animal in front of the tomb of General Huo Qubing

Stone carved animal in front of the tomb of General Huo Qubing

Tomb of General Huo Qubing, Xianyang, Shaanxi Province

# Tang and Song Tombs

The Tang Dynasty is a powerful one in the middle period of Chinese ancient feudal society. It built its capital Chang'an according to a strict plan, including the magnificent palaces, and also, gigantic mausoleums. It is a pity; however, the old Chang'an has long been destroyed together with the palaces, only some mausoleums of emperors have survived. The Tang imperial mausoleums inherited the tomb system since the Han: sacred way in front, with stone sculptures of men and animals lined on both sides, and the above-ground halls, the only difference is that these things are longer, bigger and more numerous. The biggest difference between the Tang imperial mausoleums and those of the Qin and Han lies in the choice of the form of tomb above ground, the latter bury the tomb chamber deep into underground and pile the earth up into a pyramid shape on the ground as the tomb body, while the former select natural mountain as the tomb body and build the tomb chamber under the mountain, therefore, they are by far more magnificent in outside look than their predecessors, the most typical one being the Qianling Mausoleum of the Tang Dynasty.

Situated in Qian County of Shaanxi Province, Qianling is the tomb for Emperor Gaozong of the Tang and his Empress Wuzetian buried together. They were buried in it in the year of 684A.D. and 706A.D. respectively. The mountain chosen for the tomb is called Liangshan which has three peaks, among which the northern one is the highest, the two peaks in the south are lower, and they are situated on the east and west side of the northern peak, resembling human breasts, hence the mountain is also called "Breast Mountain". The north mountain is used as the body of the Qianling tomb, tunnels

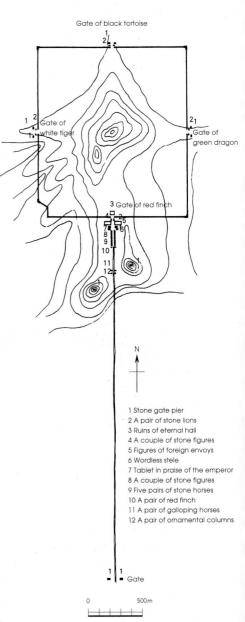

Plan. Qianling Tomb of Tang Dynasty, Qian County, Shaanxi Province

1 Stone gate pier
2 A pair of stone lions
3 Ruins of eternal hall
4 A couple of stone figures
5 Figures of foreign envoys
6 Wordless stele
7 Tablet in praise of the emperor
8 A couple of stone figures
9 Five pairs of stone horses
10 A pair of red finch
11 A pair of galloping horses
12 A pair of ornamental columns

Imperial tombs of Song Dynasty,
Gongyi, Henan Province

Sacred way of Qianling Tomb and two peaks in the south

Sacred way of Qianling Tomb and Northern Peak

were dug so that the chamber is built under the mountain, called underground palace. Tomb walls are built all around the northern peak, one door on each wall, and corner towers on the four corners. Inside the south gate, there are halls for worshipping purposes. The sacred way is built south of the south gate between the breast peaks. On both sides of the way from south to north, there lines a pair of ornamental pillars, flying horses, phoenixes respectively, five pairs of stone horses, ten pairs of stone statues of men and a pair of stone steles. There are storied pavilions on the breast peaks as gate piers, serving as the end of the sacred way. To aid more royal airs, the sacred way is extended three kilometers south by building another paired gate piers. Therefore, it is more than four kilometers from this gate piers north until one reaches the underground palaces under the northern peak, which is naturally more magnificent than the man-made earth mound. The underground palaces have not been excavated until today, and the worshipping halls have been destroyed. However, we can indeed feel the magnificence of the Tang Dynasty at its zenith from the mountain environment selected for Qianling and the sacred way.

The imperial tomb system of the Song Dynasty is different from the previous dynasties. According to the royal court regulations, the mausoleum is built after the emperor passes away, and it must be completed within seven months including the burial. Therefore, although in term of the tomb system, it is also composed of the sacred way, stone statues and animals, the tomb body and the underground palaces, it can not be a match for that of the Tang both in scale and magnificence. However, all the eight royal mausoleums of the Northern Song Dynasty (960-1127) are built in Gongxian County (now Gongyi City), not too far from the capital, Bianliang (now Kaifeng City); thus, the Song sets a precedent of concentrating the imperial mausoleums in one place, which greatly influence the imperial mausoleum construction of the following dynasties.

During the Song Dynasty, along with the development of handicraft industry and commerce, some merchants and landlords in urban and rural areas became richer and richer. They not only spent a lot of money building elaborate residences, but also built their tombs. Over the years, the archaeologists have excavated quite a few such tombs among which a comparatively typical one is the Baisha Tomb No.1 in Yuxian County (now Yuzhou City), Henan Province. It was built in the second year (1099) of the reign of Yuanfu. The underground chamber is divided into two rooms, the front one in square shape, the

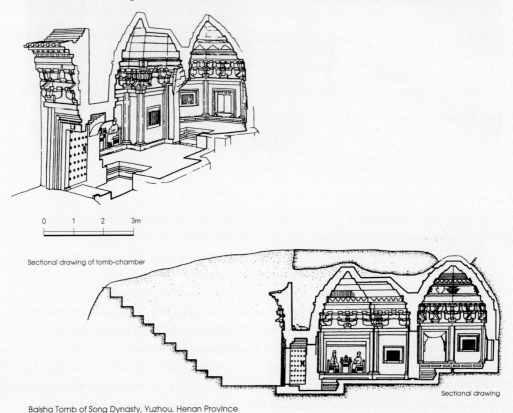

0　1　2　3m

Sectional drawing of tomb-chamber

Sectional drawing

Baisha Tomb of Song Dynasty, Yuzhou, Henan Province

rear one, in hexagonal shape. It is built entirely with bricks, but imitating the form of timber-frame structure: there are pillars, beams and lintels on the wall, bracket sets on the beams and lintels, on the bracket sets layers upon layers of bricks projecting the roof which is the ceiling of the tomb. All the walls of the two rooms and the surface of all the members of the roof are decorated with colorful paintings. On one wall in the front room, there is the painting showing the husband and wife sitting opposite each other enjoying a banquet, which vividly portrays their life before their death.

Another example is a tomb belonging to a landlord by the name of Dong in Houma of Shanxi Province, built in Jin Dynasty (1115-1234). The underground chamber is in square form, each side is only 2.2 meters long, built entirely with bricks. In this small chamber, all the building members on the four walls are shown by way of brick carving, from the terrace below, to the door and window in the middle, to the octagonal roof propped up by bracket sets on top. Furthermore, all these members are covered with brick carvings showing the images of all kinds of people in action: the tomb owner, servants,

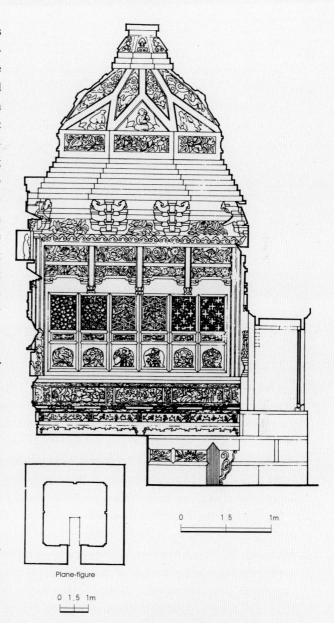

Plane-figure

0 1.5 1m

Tomb of Mr.Dong, Jin Dynasty, Houma, Shanxi Province

warriors, dancers, etc. and decorations of plants, flowers and geometry shapes. These two tombs are not big, but the living conditions and life scenes of the owners are shown through the colored paintings or brick carvings in the tombs, from which we know that in the Song Dynasty, the development of social life had influenced the style of architecture from the magnificence in the Tang to the detailed richness of the present.

# Thirteen Tombs of Ming Dynasty

1 Ancestral mountain peak
2 Main mountain peak
3 Protective mountain peak
4 Worshipping mountain peak
5 Water-flow in front

Sketch. Ancient *fengshui*

After he ascended the throne, Zhu Di, Chengzu of the Ming Dynasty was getting ready to move his capital from Nanjing to Beijing, and at the same time he ordered his subordinates to look everywhere for a suitable place for building his mausoleum. The Chinese ancients came to know through their own experiences that their existence had to depend on the mountain, river and earth, and also learned how to choose the environment suitable for living. The ideal environmental model for living is a place facing water, with the backing of a mountain and surrounded on three sides by mountains. This understanding acquired through practices gradually became the theory of *fengshui* (geomantic influence). In ancient China, this theory gave guidance to almost all the choosing and deciding the places for building houses. For royal palaces which are always built in the capital cities, it is different to find the mountain-river environment. When the Forbidden City was built in the Ming Dynasty, the river and hill had to be made by man power in order to create a geomantic (*fengshui*) situation. But the royal mausoleums are always built outside the cities, which provide a great freedom in choosing a *fengshui* treasure land in the great natural environment.

A place north of Changping District, Beijing, on the south side of Tianshou Mountain was chosen as the location of the Ming Tombs. The Chinese ancient *fengshui* theory laid emphasis on the mountain-river environment in selecting the locations for villages and houses; especially the mountain which is also called dragon, looking for the dragon in *fengshui* just means looking for the mountain. To look for the mountain, first of all, one must look at the origin of the mountain range, which is the highest place inhabited by the ancestors, according to the ancients. Then, one should try to find the mountain nearby along the mountain range from the far distance to the nearer places. To judge a good mountain one must see its overall image, weather it has many peaks with ups and downs as if it is galloping. Only such a mountain is suitable to serve as the backing of a village. Apart from the backing of a big mountain, there should be smaller mountains on the sides so that they can form a situation of surrounding the village from three sides which is able to keep off the evil wind from outside. Besides, across the big open area in front, it is best to have a distant mountain opposite the big mountain at the back. According to the *fengshui* theory, this kind of environment can keep wind and air, suitable for the human beings. So the positive residences for the living and the negative residences for the dead should all be built in such a environment, which is the flat land at the foot of the mountains on three sides.

Beside the mountains, there must be water. It is the best that the water flows from the mountains on the left and right forming into a river which passes by the village and houses in front. The *fengshui* theory holds that the air which is suitable for human being's existence disperses with wind, but halts with water. Therefore, with little streams on the left and right, a river in front, plus the mountains on three sides, such a place is really the *fengshui* treasure land which keeps wind and air, an auspicious land.

The place chosen for the Ming Tombs is just such a piece of land. The Tianshou Mountain

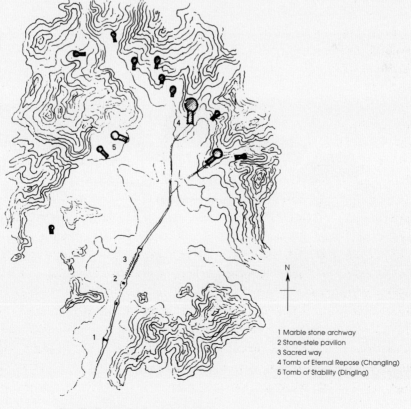

1 Marble stone archway
2 Stone-stele pavilion
3 Sacred way
4 Tomb of Eternal Repose (Changling)
5 Tomb of Stability (Dingling)

Plan. The Thirteen Tombs of Ming Dynasty

range snakes along from the northwest. It is a branch of the Yanshan Mountains which is again a branch of Kunlun Mountains and Taihang mountains. The Kunlun Mountain is the famous Chinese mountain, the ancestor of Chinese mountains, as the ancients called it. The Tianshou Mountain snaking along from the Kunlun Mountain is of sacred significance. And the Tianshou Mountain itself is full of peaks, coming along from the west to the north, then east, southeast like a dragon, covering dozens of kilometers, forming a big curve on three sides. On the south is an open area, with a few peaks facing north. Right at the foot of the curved Tianshou Mountain, there is a patch of flat land, on which, the mausoleums not only have peaks as their backing, but also enjoy the streams from the mountains passing by from the front. Today, we can see rivers passing by eight mausoleums. From the beginning of the 15th century to the middle of the 17th century, a total of 13 emperors built their mausoleums here, that is from Chengzu's Changling to Chongzhen's Siling, the last emperor of Ming, which enables the foot of Tianshou Mountain becoming a large area of royal mausoleums. They are more concentrated than the Song mausoleums in Gongxian County (now Gongyi City). Each of the 13 mausoleums is independent, though they share the same entrance gate, which makes them a whole body of royal tombs, currently called the Thirteen Tombs of the Ming Dynasty.

The general entrance of the Ming Tombs is located between two little hills opposite to each other to the south of Tianshou Mountain. At the forefront of the entrance is a stone archway which

Stone archway of the Thirteen Tombs of Ming Dynasty

Stele pavilion and ornamental pillar of Ming Tombs

is consisted of six square pillars and five bays. There are beams between the pillars, on which 11 roofs are propped up by rows after rows of bracket sets. Below the pillars, there are six bases filled with carved lions, and there are also colored stone carved designs on the beams. This stone archway, totally imitating a timber-frame archway, is upright and dignified, showing the evident style of the Ming architecture which is simple but imposing. Opposite the far away main peak of Tianshou Mountain in the north, it stands on a flat land in an open space, serving as the main gate of all the Ming Tombs. Going through the big red gate and stele pavilion after entering the archway, one arrives at the sacred way on both sides of which there are 18 pairs of stone statues of men and animals including civil officials, army generals, horses, elephants and camels, etc. At the northern end of the sacred way is Lingxing Gate. It is 2.8 kilometers from the stone archway to Lingxing Gate, which is the entrance series for the whole mausoleum area. Going through Lingxing Gate, one sees a large patch of riverbed flat land near the Tianshou Mountain, where there is a main road leading directly to Changling, and several smaller roads leading to the other 12 mausoleums.

Changling is the tomb of Emperor Yongle, Zhudi, which is the earliest in time, largest in size, and occupies the most important position, among the 13 tombs. It has the main peak of Tianshou Mountain as its backing, and Mangshan Mountain in the east, Huyu Mountain in the west, looking southward; there is the Baoshi Mountain near the north gate of the Changping District seat. There are streams in the mountains on the sides, which form a river in front of the tomb. Therefore, this is the best treasure land according to the theory of *fengshui*. The tomb is consisted of the gate, the Ling'enmen Gate, the Ling'endian Hall, Memorial Shrine on a High Square and the Treasure Top, which are arranged on the central axis from the south to the north, forming three courtyards. The Ling'endian Hall and the Treasure Top are more important, the former being the place for worshipping purposes and the latter is where the emperor's tomb chamber located, buried underground.

The Ling'endian Hall to Changling is tantamount to the Hall of Supreme Harmony to the Forbidden City. It is 9 bays wide, although not as numerous as 11 bays of the Hall of Supreme

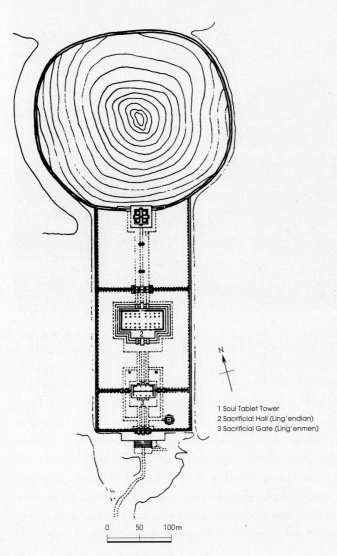

1 Soul Tablet Tower
2 Sacrificial Hall (Ling'endian)
3 Sacrificial Gate (Ling'enmen)

0    50    100m

Plan. Changling Tomb of Ming Dynasty

Harmony, it is as wide as 66.75 meters, six meters wider than the latter. The roof is also of the highest grade: hip roof with double eaves. The hall is also sitting on a three-tiered stone terrace with balustrades all around it. The pillars, beams and lintels, and bracket sets are all made of the most precious *nanmu* wood, among which the biggest pillar is 1.17 meters in diameter. Although the highest architectural grade is used on the roof and terrace of the Ling'endian Hall, the building materials are of best quality. After all it is the palace belonging to the dead emperor, so there are no wing halls around it. The terrace is not high enough, nor a big square in front. So overall it is by far less magnificent and imposing than the Hall of Supreme Harmony. This hall of Emperor Yongle after his death and the Hall of Supreme Harmony which he built and used in his lifetime are currently the two largest buildings left over by the ancient capital of Beijing. On the

Ling'endian Hall of Changling Tomb

*Nanmu* structure of Ling'endian Hall

axis between the Treasure Top and the Memorial Shrine, there is the inner red gate, an archway with two pillars and stone offering table, etc. Looking at the mausoleum as a whole, the Ling'enmen Gate and Ling'endian Hall belong to the front court, the inner red gate and further on belong to the rear part. So in building tombs, the traditional form of front court and rear residence is also followed.

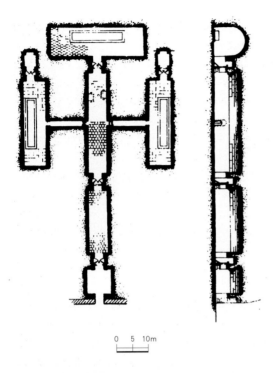

0  5  10m

Plan and section. Underground palace of
Dingling Tomb of Ming Dynasty

Underground palace of Dingling Tomb

The underground palace has not been excavated as of today. But in 1956, our archaeologists excavated that of Dingling which is the tomb of Emperor Wanli. His reign is the longest among all the Ming emperors, totaling 48 years. He personally went to the Tianshou Mountain to choose and decide the location for his tomb which was built in six years. According to historical records, after the tomb was completed, the emperor went personally to the place to inspect. When he saw the towering halls on the ground and the underground palace was very solid, built solely with stone, he was so overjoyed that he ordered a banquet to be held right in the underground palace to cerebrate the completion of the work together with his officials, which is rarely seen in Chinese history. Nowadays, the underground palace is on display: it is composed of the front hall, the middle hall and the rear hall, and a wing-hall on each side of the middle one, built totally with stone materials, and it covers a total area of 1,195 square meters. The middle hall contains the thrones of the emperor and his two empresses, in front of which, there are five objects for offering purposes and a big oil vat for the eternal lamp. The rear hall is the main hall of the underground palace which contains the stone coffin bed. On the bed, there are three coffins of the emperor and empresses, and many wooden cases full of burial objects.

These objects include articles for daily use by the emperor and the empresses like hats, clothes, pillows, quilts, basins, bowls, etc., and all kinds of articles for burial ceremonies, totaling more than 3,000 pieces, among which, quite a few are the masterpieces of that time. For example, the four crowns of the two empresses, one shows 12 dragons and 9 phoenixes, the second one, 9 dragons and 9 phoenixes, the third one, 6 dragons and 3 phoenixes, and the last one, 3 dragons and 3 phoenixes. It can be said that each of the crowns is meticulously done and splendid in craftsmanship. Every crown is decorated with a lot of pearls and precious stones, e.g. the one with 6 dragons and 3 phoenixes is inlaid with 128 rubies and sapphires and decorated with 5,400 pearls. Another example is the empress' garment, embroidered with a hundred boys, engaging in all kinds of activities in about 40 groups of pictures. Some are exercising, wrestling, others are kicking the shuttlecocks, flying kites, lighting firecrackers, playing hide and seek, and still others are picking fruit on a tree, etc. This garment vividly portrays the naivete and liveliness of children. The blank spots between the pictures are embellished with the designs of ancient coins and "as you wish" which is of symbolic meaning, and flowers of the four seasons: peach, peony, lotus and plum. The embroidery boasts bright colors and meticulous methods, displaying the refined technological and artistic level of the Ming Dynasty embroidery.

It takes a great amount of manpower, materials of timber and stone, and bricks and tiles to build the 13 imperial mausoleums at the foot of the Tianshou Mountain. Like the *nanmu* pillars in the Ling'endian Hall of Changling, those with the diameters more than one meter are usually 100 years old, moreover, they are grown in those provinces of Sichuan, Yunnan and Guizhou. It is recorded in the Ming history how difficult it was to go into the forests of deep mountains to gather such giants: "a thousand men can't manage a freshly felled tree"; and for those men, "out of 1,000 who entered the mountains, 500 survived when coming out". Large quantities of stone materials are also needed for the stone archway, several kinds of stone gates, stone offering table, stone terrace, stone balustrades and stone statues of men and animals on the ground, and the palace made of stone underground. For example, a stone elephant along the spirit way, together with its base would require a large stone of 30 cubic meters. To transport these wood and stone materials from the places of their origin to the tomb area is farther away than the Forbidden City and therefore it requires more manpower and animals. The construction cost of a single Dingling was more than 8 million taels of silver which was tantamount to the total amount of the farmland tax of the entire country for two years at that time. This figure does not include those valuable burial objects, e.g. that crown with more than five thousand pearls and precious stones, among which, one ruby alone costs 500 taels of silver.

# Eastern and Western Tombs
# of Qing Dynasty

In 1644, following its troops entering the Shanhaiguan Pass from the Northeast; the Qing Dynasty began to exercise its rule over the whole of China. At that time, the first emperor Shunzhi was only 6 years old. He died at the age of 24, but during the 18 years of his reign, this young emperor went personally to those places around Beijing to make investigations in order to choose a place to build his tomb. Finally, a piece of treasure land in Zunhua City, Hebei Province to the east of Beijing was selected as the area for tombs, called the eastern tombs. This area is 125 kilometers away from Beijing. It has the Lurui Mountain as its backing, protected by Daoyang Mountain on the east and Huanghua Mountain on the west, the Malan River and Xida River zigzag

Stone archways, Western Tombs of Qing Dynasty, Yixian County, Hebei Province

Western Tombs of Qing Dynasty backed by big mountains

through it, and in front, there is the Jincheng Mountain. So, this is really a *fengshui* treasure land which keeps well the wind and air. Starting from the Xiaoling Tomb of Emperor Shunzhi, there are altogether 15 built in this area for five emperors and their empresses and concubines. The Xiaoling Tomb is located in the middle, flanked by the other tombs. The gigantic stone archway and red gate serves as the big gate for the whole area, so there is everything needed in the Eastern Tombs area.

Emperor Yongzheng, the 3rd emperor of the Qing Dynasty originally should be buried in the Eastern tombs together with his father and grandfather, and had initially chosen the site for his tomb. But, after making investigations with the officials and *fengshui* masters, he thought that the earth of the site is mixed with sand and stones, and the mountains nearby were not adequate, so he went to other places to look for the treasure land. Finally, he found an area in Yixian County, Hebei Province, which was 125 kilometers west from Beijing. This place is backed by the Taining Mountain on the north, protected also by mountains on the east and west, and the Yishui River flows by it in front. Emperor Yongzheng made the decision to build his tomb in Yixian County, which is located to the west of the capital, therefore called the Western Tomb. Starting from his tomb, there are four more tombs for emperors and also tombs for the empresses, imperial concubines, princesses, totally 14 tombs in the Western Tombs area. The three big stone archways and the red gate also became the entrance for the whole area of the Western Tombs. A wall connecting the big red gate extends 21 kilometers to the east and west, encircling all the tombs in the area, making the whole Western Tombs.

Now, let us see two typical tombs.

**Yuling in Eastern Tombs Area**  It is the tomb of Emperor Qianlong, the 4th emperor of Qing Dynasty. He ascended to the throne at the age of 25, and descended from it after 60 years, because he did not wish to surpass Emperor Kangxi, his grandfather who was in the reign for 61 years. After that, he acted as the emperor "above an emperor" for three more years, and died at the age of 89. Among all the emperors in Chinese feudal society, his life was the longest, and he was in power the longest. During his reign, the Qing Dynasty was politically stable, economically developing, financially rich, or his reign was one of the zenith of the dynasty. His tomb occupied an area of 462 thousand square meters, and the construction work lasted for more than ten years. Also buried here were his two empresses, three imperial concubines, and finally the emperor himself . The underground palace has been excavated, but owing to the tomb robbery many years ago, all the burial objects have been robbed clean, only the chamber was left unharmed, so that today we still have the underground palace.

The underground palace is consisted of the bright hall (soul tower), corridor and the golden vault, covering a distance of 54 meters, totally built with stone. The four walls of the tomb chamber, the ceiling and the doors are all decorated with Buddhist carvings. There are four stone gates in the chamber; all the eight doors are made of stone, 3 meters high, 1.5 meters wide and 0.19 meter thick,

Carved statue on stone gate, underground palace
of Yuling Tomb belonging to Emperor Qianlong

Carved statue on stone wall,
underground palace of Yuling Tomb

so each door weighs about three tons. On the front of each door is carved a standing bodhisattva, and on the walls of the corridor, the stone statues of the four heavenly kings. The golden vault is the major chamber of the underground palace, the place where the six coffins were stationed. On the ceiling of the vault are three carved big Buddhist flowers, the center is composed of a Buddhist statue and Sanskrit, surrounded by 24 petals. On the stone walls at the both ends of the vault are carved Buddha statues and eight treasure designs. On the walls of the vault are carved Buddhist scriptures in Sanskrit and Tibetan scripts, of which there are 647 characters in Sanskrit and 29,464 characters in Tibetan. All these Buddhist statues, treasures and scriptures are carved meticulously in the same style and balanced layout. Emperor Qianlong was a loyal adherent of Buddhism in his lifetime, and he decorated his tomb chamber into a Buddhist hall.

Dingdongling in Eastern Tombs Area   Dingdongling is the tomb of Empress Dowager Ci Xi. According to the Qing rules, those empresses who died after the emperor should be buried separately by the side of the emperor's tomb. The two empresses, Ci An and Ci Xi both died after the Emperor Xianfeng, so their tombs were built east of the emperor's tomb, Dingling, thus, called Dingdongling. The two tombs of Ci An and Ci Xi are built side by side in the east and west, exactly following the same pattern. There are stele pavilion and Longenmen Gate at the front, the Longendian Hall and wing-halls in the middle, and in the rear part are the bright tower, treasure

Longendian Hall of Dingdongling Tomb, Eastern Tombs of Qing Dynasty

Stone carving showing phoenix above dragon in Dingdongling Tomb

top and the underground palace, forming a complete architectural group. Empress Ci An died in 1881, and was buried there. Empress Ci Xi dealt with state affairs behind a screen when Emperors Tongzhi and Guangxu were in reigns, and she was more powerful than the emperors. When she was 60, she ordered to dismantle the ground structures of the Dingdongling tomb and have them rebuilt. The work was completed after 14 years when her life came to an end (1908). The pillars, beams, doors and windows are all built with precious *nanmu* and yellow-flower pear wood, and the beams are all decorated with the designs of dragons, clouds and flowers, and gilded with gold. The pillars are also covered with gilded coiling dragons and lotus flowers originally, but it is a pity they all come down. The walls of the hall are inlayed with carved bricks covered with gold leaf, forming auspicious pictures of fortune and longevity in Chinese characters. The stone terrace under the hall is also covered with carvings. The balustrades surrounding the terrace are carved with phoenix on the head, dragon on the poles, forming the scene of the dragon looking up at the phoenix, and on the slabs between the poles, there are also carvings showing the phoenix in front and the dragon at the back. In the middle of stone stairway, there is a picture showing the phoenix is above and a dragon in the clouds chasing the phoenix. If one compares this with the carvings on the stone balustrades of the Forbidden City, showing two dragons playing with a pearl, and the imperial passage showing nine dragons in the middle of stone steps, one is clear that the stone carving showing the phoenix above the dragon is by no means accidental. It reflects a special period of history when the Empress dowager dealt with state affairs behind a screen during the two reigns of emperors, and her desire for power knew no bounds.

Although the imperial tombs of the Qing Dynasty are divided into eastern and western tombs, they inherited the rules and forms of the Ming imperial tombs in emphasizing the environment, or *fengshui*. Each of the tombs is independent, but they share a common entrance, forming a whole imperial tombs area. Beside the eastern and western tombs, in its capital Shengjing (nowadays, Shenyang City of Liaoning Province) before Qing entered Shanhaiguan Pass, there are two tombs, Fuling and Zhaoling belonging to Emperor Taizu, Nurhachi and Emperor Taizong, Huangtaiji.

In addition, in Xinbin County of Liaoning, the native place of the Qing rulers, there is a tomb called Yongling, belonging to the father of Nurhachi, founder of the Qing Dynasty, and several preceding ancestors. The above 11 imperial Qing tombs and one ancestors tomb located in Hebei and Liaoning provinces, plus the Ming Xiaoling in Nanjing, the 13 tombs of the Ming in Beijing and Ming Xianling in Hubei, form the total tombs of the Ming and Qing dynasties. With their rich historical and cultural values they have been listed as "the world cultural heritage" by the UNESCO.

Zhaoling Tomb, Shenyang, Liaoning Province

Stele pavilions of Yongling Tomb, Xinbin County, Liaoning Province

# Chapter 5
# Buddhist Architectures

Buddhist architecture belongs to the religious architectures. In ancient China, there were mainly the three religions of Buddhism, Taoism and Islamism, among which Buddhism was the prevailing religion with many believers. Therefore among religious architectures, the Buddhist architecture is the most numerous.

Buddhism came into being in ancient India, with Sakyamuni as its founder. Originally he was a prince of the Kapilavastu kingdom. It is said that this prince walked out of the palace into the society to experience the life of the common people, and saw that the human beings were suffering from the pains of birth, old age, illness and death. So at the age of 29, he decided to bid farewell to his wife and son and go out of the palace to seek the ways to relieve human beings of their pains. At one evening six years later, he finally got totally enlightened and became a Buddha. From then on, he toured many places to recruit disciples and to explain the truth he had come to understand. Furthermore he organized his teaching team and founded Buddhism. According to estimation, this was between the 6th to 5th centuries, B.C. The Buddhist theory holds that the actual world is a "boundless sea of sufferings" which is filled with the bitterness of the birth, old age, illness, death, parting with relatives, no guarantee for life, desire can not be fulfilled, etc., and all these sufferings are due to all kinds of man's desires, and all these desires are produced through man's vision, hearing, sniffing, tasting and touching. Therefore to do away with the sufferings of the human world, one has to break away with the desires and painstakingly cultivate himself until the end of his life before he can arrive at the ideal realm of no desire and no pains.

Buddhism was introduced into China at a time in the Han Dynasty. Because its teachings were closely connected with the everyday life of the people, it was quickly accepted by the people, and it also received support and assistance from the rulers. The court organized special people to translate Buddhist sutra and teach Buddhist teachings. By the Southern and Northern Dynasties (420-589), the development of Buddhism in China reached the first high tide. According to records, there were 2,800 monasteries with more than 82,700 monks and nuns in Liang state in the south; in Northern Wei, more than 30,000 monasteries and two million monks and nuns. During the Tang Dynasty, Buddhism reached its zenith in China, with several emperors as its faithful followers. In Changan, the capital, there was a special institute for translating Buddhist scriptures, famous teachers were invited from abroad to train large numbers of venerable monks and scholars. Official monasteries were built in many places and monks were treated with courtesy. As a result, Buddhism has not only developed in China, but also spread to Korea, Japan, Vietnam and other places. Through the promotion of the successive courts and the practice of the believers among the people, the foreign Buddhism gradually merged with the Chinese traditional culture to form the Buddhist culture with the Chinese characteristics. The Buddhist architecture also became an important part of China's ancient architecture.

# Grottoes

A grotto is a cave dug into a cliff, which is a form of India's early Buddhist architectures. There are two forms of grottoes: one is a small cave in square shape, gate in front, within the cave, there are little niches arranged in parallel on three sides, which are for the monk to sit in and cultivate himself; the other cave is much bigger with a pagoda built in the center of the rear part, the place in front of the pagoda is for disciples to get together to pay respects to the Buddha. The merit of such grotto temple is that it is cool inside, which suits the hot weather in India. Also, grottoes are situated in remote areas; the quiet environment is good for cultivation. Besides, it is easier and cheaper to dig a grotto.

Buddhism was introduced into China through the ancient Silk Road which was a road of commercial trade, and at the same time, a road of cultural exchange. Buddhist architecture was introduced into China together with Buddhist scriptures, so there appeared some grottoes along the Silk Road. The earliest grotto found up to now is the grottoes in Xinjiang, dug at the end of the 3rd century and the beginning of 4th century. These grottoes have a pagoda pillar in the center and the Buddhist images on wall paintings showing distinctive Indian style. The other earlier grottoes are at Dunhuang which is located to the west of Gansu Province. Dunhuang was the juncture of the south and north silk reads, the pass between China and the western regions, so it became the commercial center since the ancient time, and Buddhism followed commerce here very early. For

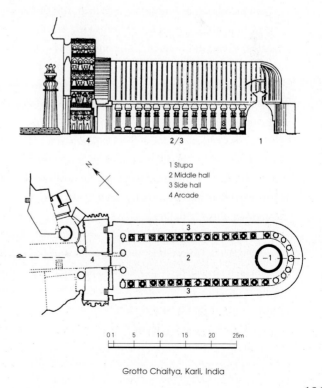

1 Stupa
2 Middle hall
3 Side hall
4 Arcade

Grotto Chaitya, Karli, India

Mogao Grottoes, Dunhuang, Gansu Province

those merchants trudging along for years in the vast desert, it is only natural that they would ardently pray to the Buddha to guarantee their safety. Owing to the needs of religion and the favorable economic conditions, the building of grottoes was carried on continuously from the Southern and Northern Dynasties in the 5th century to the Yuan Dynasty in the 14th century. Grottoes of different historical periods are found in Dunhuang, making it the largest and most persistent grottoes in ancient China. In the numerous grottoes, apart from Buddhist statues, colored paintings cover almost everywhere, including the ceilings, four walls and terraces, displaying all kinds of Buddhist stories, environmental scene of temples and secular life in different places, and a great amount of decorative flower patterns, enabling Dunhuang grottoes to become the art treasure house of ancient China.

With the spread of Buddhism to the interior of China, grottoes also appeared in the Yellow River basin, among which, the following were more famous: Maiji Mountain Grottoes in Tianshui of Gansu Province, Yungang Grottoes in Datong and Tianlong Mountain Grottoes in Taiyuan of Shanxi Province, Longmen Grottoes in Luoyang and Gongxian Grottoes in Henan Province, and Xiangtang Mountain Grottoes in Handan of Hebei Province, etc. Chinese Buddhism was prevalent during the Northern Wei period (386-534) and the Yungang and Longmen grottoes are two important grottoes of this period.

Yungang Grottoes are located in Datong, Shanxi Province, which was once the capital of Northern Wei. The work on the grottoes began in around 460 A.D. and ended in 524 A.D., lasting around 60 years. Altogether there are 252 grottoes and niches dug into the Wuzhou Mountain slopes extending as long as one kilometer. In these big or small grottoes and niches, one can see different kinds of sculptured statues of Buddhas, Bodhisattvas and close disciples, see Buddhist architectures and decorations. There are Buddhist statues in Indian style, and also those with Chinese characteristics; one can see architectures in western style in the form of stone steles, and also those stone sculptures showing Chinese timber-frame halls and storied buildings. The Yungang Grottoes describe the process of how the Buddhist culture, after being introduced into China, gradually becomes Chinese Buddhist culture.

Longmen Grottoes are located in Luoyang, Henan Province. The work on the grottoes started when Emperor Xiaowen of the Northern Wei moved his capital from Datong to Luoyang. In the following four to five hundred years since 500 A.D., through the Tang, Song and Jin dynasties, 2,345

Grottoes in Maiji Mountain, Tianshui of Gansu Province

Yungang Grottoes, Datong of Shanxi Province

Inside view of Yungang Grottoes

Chinese traditional architectural image of Yungang Grottoes

grottoes were constructed all together in which there were a hundred thousand stone statues and more plus 3,600 stone tablets. The biggest one is the Vairocana Buddha in Fengxian Temple. The work on this statue started during the reign of Emperor Gaozong of the Tang Dynasty and completed in 675 A.D. In order to seize power by utilizing Buddhism to create public opinion, his empress Wuzetian laid special emphasis on the construction of the Fengxian Temple, she even contributed her own property to it. After the work was completed, she personally attended the opening ceremony. The statue is 17.14 meters high, and the head alone is four meters; on its sides there are two disciples, two bodhisattvas, two heavenly kings and two vajras, which are as high as ten meters. In order to contain this group of statues, they have to cut the mountain slope to make an open air ground of 41 meters deep and 36 meters wide, and only after that can the statues be made. Under the technological conditions at that time, the mountain cutting alone lasted three years and nine months, and more than 30 thousand cubic meters of stone were produced.

In order to make the statues more divinely impressive and more attractive to the vast believers, they are made bigger and bigger so that no grottoes can hold them, so at the Fengxian Temple, the statues are made standing in the open air on the mountain slope. This practice further developed in the Tang Dynasty with the emergence of the giant Buddha at Lingyun Temple in Leshan of Sichuan Province. The giant Buddha is carved out of the natural rock of the Lingyun Mountain which is facing the Minjiang River. So the Buddha uses the mountain as his back, with feet on the riverside.

Fengxian Temple, Longmen Grottoes, Luoyang of Henan Province

It is 71 meters high in total, and its shoulders, 28 meters, its nose, 5 meters and more. There is saying to this effect: "the mountain is a Buddha, and the Buddha is a mountain". The whole image of the Buddha can only be seen from the river, so that is the biggest Buddha in the world today. The work on the giant Buddha started on the second year (713) of Xiantian and completed on the 19th year (803) of Zhenyuan of the Tang Dynasty during the reigns of four emperors for a total of 90 years. Originally, the statue was colorfully decorated all over, and shielded by a 13-storey building. In the Ming Dynasty, the building was burned down and the Buddha was left standing by the river side in the open air.

This giant Buddha and the Mogao Grottoes, Yungang Grottoes and Longmen Grottoes have all been successively listed as "the world cultural heritage" by the UNESCO.

Giant Buddha, Leshan, Sichuan Province

125

Giant Buddha, Lingyun Temple, Leshan of Sichuan Province

# Buddhist Temples and Halls

In ancient China, the main form of Buddhist architecture is not the grottoes, but many Buddhist temples. It is said that in the 7th year (64 A.D.) of Yongping reign of the Eastern Han Dynasty (25-220), Emperor Ming sent special envoys to the western regions to seek Buddhism. When they came back together with venerable monks and Buddhist scriptures and sculptures on horsebacks from Tianzu, they were first put to stay in the Honglusi which was specially for housing foreign guests, because there was not special Buddhist architecture yet. The next year, a new building was put up for them, which was called a temple, because those venerable monks were guests from the west, and also because those horses carrying the Buddhist scriptures and sculptures were white ones, so the temple was also called the White Horse Temple, which should be the first Buddhist architecture in China. The Honglusi and the White Horse Temple were all Chinese traditional quadrangles, in which the monks began their Buddhist activities. They enshrined the statue of Buddha in the front hall of the middle of the quadrangle, and the back hall became the place for studying Buddhist scriptures, and the wing-houses and the back yard were for the monks to stay. The quadrangles can satisfy the needs of Buddhist activities, so they have provided a suitable place for Buddhism, and the traditional quadrangle group of architecture became the basic form of Chinese Buddhist temples.

Along with the development of Buddhism and the increase of Buddhist activities, the size of temples become bigger and bigger. The gate, the hall for enshrining heavenly kings, the Mahavira for enshrining the Buddhas and bodhisattvas, the preaching hall, the scripture building are main buildings of the temple, so they are arranged according to the order of Buddhist rules on the central axis; the houses on the sides and around the main buildings are for the guests and the monks to live in. In large temples, there are the drum and bell towers for hanging a drum and a bell on the left and right sides of the front yard, and on the axis or on its sides, smaller hall are added for enshrining bodhisattvas. Facts have proved that the enlargement of the size of the temple do not and need not break the pattern of quadrangles. The existing, well preserved complete temples are all architectural complexes of quadrangle style, for example, Baoguo (National Protection) Temple and Tiantong (Holy Children) Temple of Ningbo, Zhejiang Province, Longxing Temple of Zhengding, Hebei Province and Shanhua Temple of Datong, Shanxi Province.

The traditional quadrangle architectural complex can satisfy the needs of Buddhism, and the buildings in the complex can also provide suitable places for enshrining Buddhist statues and for

Bird's-eye view, Baoguo Temple, Ningbo of Zhejiang Province

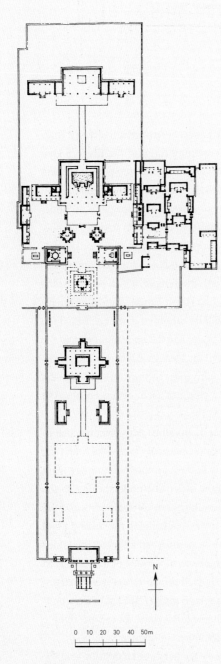

Plan. Longxing Temple, Zhengding of
Hebei Province

indoor Buddhist activities, therefore, the traditional Chinese architecture of halls have also become the major form of the Buddhist temple halls. The Foguang Temple hall of Wutai Mountain, Shanxi Province, built in the 11th year (857) of Dazhong of the Tang Dynasty is one of a few largest Tang temples discovered today. It is 7 bays, or 34 meters wide, 17.66 meters deep, in rectangular form. Inside the hall along the back wall, there stands a terrace five bays wide on which statues of Buddhas, bodhisattvas and disciples added up to 30 and more are enshrined. In front of the terrace, or about half of the hall space is for holding Buddhist activities. In the big hall of the Tiantong Temple of Ningbo, Zhejiang Province, several Buddhist statues are enshrined. The floor of the hall is filled with cushions for the disciple to knell down, and the Buddhist streamers hanging there fills the hall with religious mysterious air.

Like the Buddhist statues in the grottoes, those in the Buddhist hall become bigger and bigger. Since they can not be moved out of the hall into the open air, for they are mostly made of clay or timber, the only way out is to build bigger halls to suit the big statues. There is a Dule Temple in Jixian County of Tianjin, built in the Liao Dynasty (907-1125). In its main hall is enshrined a statue of the Goddess of Mercy which is 16 meters high. A single storey hall can

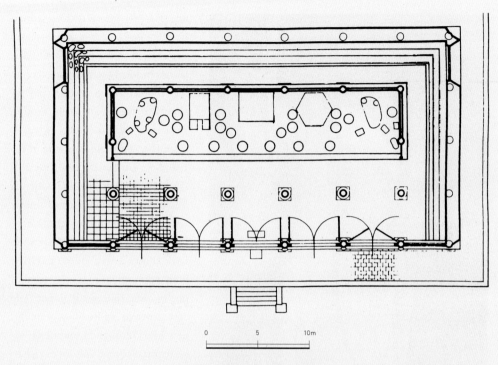

Plan. Main hall of Foguang Temple

Foguang Temple, Wutai of Shanxi Province

Inside view of Goddess of Mercy Pavilion,
Dule Temple, Jixian County of Tianjin

Inside view of Buddhist Hall of Tiantong (Holy Children) Temple, Ningbo
of Zhejiang Province

not possibly house it, so a storied building is built for it, which shows two stories on the outside but three stories inside. Disciples can climb to the second or third storey to pay respects to the Goddess. In Puning Temple of Chengde, Hebei Province, there is an even bigger statue of the Goddess of Mercy enshrined in Dasheng Storied Pavilion which is 22.28 meters high, made of timber frame. Thus, the form of the Storied Pavilion is also special: the outside look shows a five storey pavilion with a pyramidal roof composed of one big and four small slopes. The emergence of big Buddhas promotes new breakthrough in traditional architectural forms, and gives rise to more colorful architectural images.

China enjoys a vast expanse of land, and Buddhist temples are scattered all over whose environment may be rather different. In face of special topography, it is sometimes difficult to stick to the quadrangular form. For example, there is a temple in Hunyuan County, Shanxi Province, which is built on the cliff of Hengshan Mountain. It is by no means some additional buildings on the mouth of a grotto, but entirely a temple architectural complex composed of several halls. It differs with an ordinary temple in that it is not built on the ground, but looks like hanging on the steep cliff. A small portion of its weight rests on a few pillars standing on the cliff, but the

Little Putuo Temple, Erhai Lake, Dali of Yunnan Province

greater portion is on the timber beams stuck into the cliff. On these beams, pillars are placed, then beams and lintels are structured, and then the roofs are put on. Looking from afar, it seems the whole architectural complex is hanging on the cliff of Hengshan Mountain, hence the name, the "Hanging Temple". Another example, on a small island on Erhai Lake of Dali, Yunnan Province, there is a Buddhist temple which is actually only a Buddhist hall, and the hall covers almost the whole island. There is only a narrow passage around the hall, so that once people step out of boat and land on the island they can enter the hall. The local people take this Buddhist temple as the sacred Buddhist land, Putuo mountain in the sea region of Zhoushan, Zhejiang Province, and call it "Little Putuo". These non-quadrangle Buddhist temples usually have their own special forms, so many of them become the unique scenes of that region.

Hanging Temple, Hunyuan of Shanxi Province

Dashengge Pavilion of Puning Temple, Chengde of Hebei Province

# Buddhist Mountains

Buddhist mountains are mountains with many Buddhist temples. These mountains have been developed because of the temples, and the Buddhist architectures constitute the main scenic spots in the mountains. The Buddhist mountains come into being after going through a long process.

In the early stages, the Buddhist monks did not participate in productive labor, they lived on begging for alms. But changes took place when this system was introduced into China which was based on agricultural economy. The monks in those major temples in the cities could relay on the government or those rich disciples, but in the vast rural areas, it was impossible for them to live on without engaging in agricultural production. Therefore, during the Southern and Northern Dynasties when Buddhism was prevalent, Buddhist temples began to own their own land for agricultural production, and begging was no longer the main means of living. This situation was more common in the Tang Dynasty, for Buddhism reached the zenith of its development at that time. There emerged a great amount of temples all over the country and the number of monks suddenly increased in a big margin, and the land owned by the temples also resulted in a big increase. Under this circumstance, in order to achieve further development, and not to compete with the others for the land in the cities, temples began to move to the mountain and forest areas far from the cities. These areas can provide not only mountain, river and land to ensure their means of living, but also the quiet environment for them to sit and meditate, for their self-cultivation. Thus, many temples appeared in the mountainous forests, and after prolonged development, four famous mountains with concentrated temples came into being, they are: Emei Mountain of Sichuan, Wutai Mountain of Shanxi, Putuo Mountain of Zhejiang and Jiuhua Mountain of Anhui. They are called the Four Great Buddhist Mountains.

Located in the middle part of Sichuan Province, Emei Mountain is a famous beautiful mountain with peaks upon peaks all in green, and deep, dark gullies. Its main peak, Wanfoding (Myriad Buddhas Top) is 3,099 meters above sea level, and the next highest peak, Jinding (Golden Top), 3,075 meters. Gullies crisscross in the mountain, the sound of stream flowing can be heard here and there, and everywhere one sees the luxuriance of grass and trees. The Tang poet Li Bai, who toured almost all the beautiful mountains in his lifetime, gave the Emei Mountain very high appreciation in his poem: "There are many fairylands in the country, but none can be compared with the beauty of Emei". As early as in the Han Dynasty, there began to appear some simple temples, when it came to the Tang and Song dynasties, more and more big or small temples were built.

Qingyinge Pavilion, Emei Mountain

Baoguo Temple, Emei Mountain of Sichuan Province

Those far-sighted monks chose the mountain foot and the lower mountain area for building Baoguo Temple, Fuhu Temple and Huayan Temple; the areas half way up the mountain for Wannian Temple, Qingyin Pavilion and Xianfeng Temple, etc. These major temples of the Emei Mountains were built, either close to the mountain rocks or striding over water, or in the form of quadrangular complex, or standing alone by itself, but all in the midst of mountainous forests, merging into the natural environment. Furthermore, the monks also built small temples on top of Wanfoding and Jinding, by utilizing their heights, so that one can look at the mountains down below, nearby or in the distance, or in fine weather when the sunshine is at a certain angle, one might be able to see on the sea of clouds colored ring of light, a rare natural view named by the monks as "Buddha halo", the light coming from Bodhisattva Samantabhadra. This "auspicious light of Jinding" not only shows the mysterious aspect of Buddhism, but has become one of the four unique scenes of the Emei. To enable many disciples to see the Buddha halo, the monks, through the efforts of several generations, built a stone paved road in the mountain from the foot to the top, it passed by several temples on the way where one can enjoy different scenes of the mountain.

The Putuo Mountain is situated on a small island to the east of Ningbo, Zhejiang Province, which is part of the Zhoushan Archipelago. It is said that in the Tang Dynasty, the Japanese monks obtained the statue of Bodhisattva Avalokitesvara, after paying respects to the Buddha in Wutai Mountain. On their way back to Japan, they encountered strong wind near the Putuo Mountain and were unable to advance further. So they left the statue on the island, and the Putuo

Fayu Temple, Putuo Mountain, Zhejiang Province

Mountain became the place only for enshrining the Bodhisattva. The terrain of Putuo is higher in altitude in the northwest and lower in the southeast with mountain peaks one after another, the highest peak, situated to the north shore, is 291.3 meters above sea level. The mountain runs to the southeast, with flat land and basin connecting each other along the way, and the mountain is rocky, with strange rocks spreading everywhere. The three big Buddhist temples:Huiji, Fayu and Puji are built respectively on the mountain top, mountain flat land and mountain foot. In addition, there are several dozen nunneries scattered on the flat land and basin. From the foot of the mountain, there are two passes going through the mountain from south to north, linking all the temples and nunneries together. Along the passes, those strange rocks are used to create scenic spots concerning Buddhism, like, "two tortoises listening to Buddhist teaching", "the rock resembling the letter heart", etc. On important sections, the passes are paved with stone slabs on which are carved lotus roots and flowers symbolizing Buddhism every three or five steps. In those years, it was these lotus passes that the disciples followed to go to the temples, stopping to kowtow on the passes every three or five steps. Right here, the temples, nunneries, mountain passes and stone scenic spots are merged into one, or, the temples are no longer restricted within their walls but spread to the surrounding natural forests, while the natural forests are merged into the Buddhist culture.

Busy Buddhist activities in the mountain forests have promoted the interchanges between the mountainous area and the outside world. With more and more disciples coming and going, the

Stone scenery in mountain pass, Putuo Mountain

Stone scenery in mountain pass, Putuo Mountain

Nunnery in Putuo Mountain

Buddhist Temple, Wutai Mountain, Shanxi Province

Mountain pass in Putuo Mountain

temples have to establish guest-rooms, dinning-rooms and selling stalls for candles and articles for the netherworld. With the increase of Buddhist activities in numbers and in scale, these commercial undertakings were moved from inside the temples to the outside, and then from small to big, gradually forming Business Street in the mountain. Some even became small towns with the temples as their center. Such business street can be seen in Emei, Putuo and Wutai mountains.

With Buddhist temples entering the mountain forests, not only the temples have gained development, but also help develop the mountain forests. The Chinese people's tradition of paying respect to mountain gods has close relations with their belief in the Buddha at heart. No matter whether worshipping the mountain gods or the Buddha are all for the purpose of seeking fortune and happiness, long life, getting rid of harm, and realizing all kinds of personal wishes. Now, people swarm into the mountain forests, they not only can pay respect to mountain god, but also the Buddha by lighting incense sticks and candles in front of him and telling him their own wishes, and also tour the beautiful scenery. As an old saying goes: "Once there is an immortal in the mountain, then it is sacred, regardless of the height." Here, the immortal could be the mountain or the Buddha, or both. The mountain can be famous because of the temples and the temples prosperous because they are in the mountain. This is the reason why the Buddhist Mountains enjoy lasting prosperity, and this is also their special value.

# Buddhist Architectures of Tibetan Buddhism and Southern Buddhism

## Tibetan Buddhist Architecture

In the 7th century, during the rule of Songtsan Gampo of the Tubo Kingdom, the Esoteric sect of Buddhism directly introduced from India began to gain the upper hand in Tibet, and by the later part of the 10th century, the Tibetan Buddhism with its special features came into being, which is commonly called Lamaism, and the monks in temples are called lamas.

The Esoteric (Tantric) sect is one of the sects of Buddhism, which is very strict about every step of its activities, and its organization and internal management are also strict. Apart from the one who is responsible for the overall affairs of the lamasery, there are others in charge of the study, debate, examination, discipline, investigating the violation of regulations and leading others in chanting the sutras, etc. respectively. For a long time, Tibet has been practicing the policy of combining the politics with the religion, so, those lamas with titles in the lamasery can also play the roles of officials, and the chief manager can even participate in the important meetings of the local government. There are many festivals to the Lamaism, e.g., the Praying meeting in the first month, Buddha's birthday in the fourth month, the Xuedun (Tibetan opera) Festival in the sixth month, the Wangguo Festival (wishing for good harvest) in the seventh month, etc. These festivals are always combined with the local traditional festivals, thus they last long, attracting many participants. In Tibet where almost everyone believes in Lamaism, those Buddhist festivals are actually for the whole people. The numerous factors: integration of politics with religion, everyone a lama, grand cerebrations and long lasting festivals, enable the Buddhist temples becoming large in size and multi-functioned. In a lamasery, apart from the main hall, pagoda, Buddhist script house and lama dormitory, there are office rooms, private living quarters, gardens and streets, so a big size lamasery is like a small town.

There are distinctive special features to the temples of Tibetan Buddhism. First of all, in layout, emphasis is not lay on the axis or the neat quadrangular form, but on the actual mountain situation, because Tibetan plateau is full of mountains; secondly, with regard to a particular building, a combination of the traditional timber-frame structure of the Han region and the local stone pillbox style is used; thirdly, in decoration of the outside and inside building, the style of the palaces and temples of Nepal is used; thus, the special style of Tibetan temples is created. Two representatives are the

Double deers and Dharmacakva harmacakra, roof of Jokhang Temple

Jokhang Temple, Lhasa, Tibet Autonomous Region

Dazhao (Jokhang) Temple and the Potala Palace in Lhasa.

The construction of Jokhang Temple began in the 7th century when Songtsan Gampo welcomed and married Princess Chizun from Nepal and Princess Wencheng of the Tang Dynasty. The two princesses were all devout disciples, bringing with them Buddhist scriptures and statues to Lhasa. The Jokhang Temple was built for the special purpose of keeping those scriptures and statues, and it is said that Princess Wencheng chose the site and Princess Chizun presided over the construction work. The temple was enlarged through the three dynasties of the Yuan, Ming and Qing and became its present look. Its construction floor space is 25,100 square meters and plus, its main hall is built with a stone outer wall and traditional timber-frame structure of the Han nationality, the roof of which is paved with golden tiles and on the ridges are golden Dharani column and Dharmacakra which glitter under the dark blue sky peculiar to Tibet, showing the unique enchantment of Tibetan temples. The eaves of the inner corridors of the hall are decorated with crouching animals and lions with human heads rows after rows special to Tibet. The walls of the corridor and the hall are covered with murals depicting Tibetan Buddhism and also the picture showing Princess Wencheng entering Tibet and the Jokhang Temple being constructed. Those murals are life-like in bright colors, but always using the black color as the background, making them profound and mysterious. They are of great value not only in art but also in historical records.

The Potala Palace is situated on the Red Mountain of Lhasa City, built for commemorating the

Mural painting, Potala Palace

Roof, Jokhang Temple

marriage of Songtsan Gampo and Princess Wencheng in the 7th century, but it was destroyed by lightening and war later. The present palace was rebuilt and enlarged since the 17th century. This is a large-size palace temple which combines politics with religion. The whole palace is composed of four parts: the White Palace, Red Palace, Xue at the foot of the mountain and the Dragon King Pond. The White Palace is the largest which is the palace for Dalai Lama, the supreme leader of Tibet. It also houses the hall where lamas chant the sutras, their residences and the school for training lama officials. In the red palace, there are halls of stupas for the successive Dalai Lamas and all kinds of Buddhist halls. At the foot of the mountain, Xue contains the local government organs, prison and workshops serving the palace. The Dragon King Pond is the rear garden of the palace. The Potala Palace is built following the shape of the Red Mountain, layer upon layer, covering almost the entire mountain, with a height of 117.9 meters. The outside appearance is built totally after the local form of pillbox citadel, with walls made entirely with stones, 13 stories high. The eaves are decorated with a kind of grass peculiar to Tibet. But the roof is made according to the gable and hip roof style with timber-frame structure. On the roof are paved copper tiles gilded with gold, and the ridges and wall tops are decorated with golden bells and pagodas. In shaping the whole palace, the symmetrical balance along the axis is not the goal; the effort has been made only to follow the natural ups and downs of the mountain and to suit the actual needs from the inside. Therefore, although some parts may be higher or lower they fall into one whole palace which is very imposing and magnificent.

Potala Palace, Lhasa, Tibet

White Palace of Potala Palace

Eaves of Tibetan temple decorated with grass

144

Door frame decoration of Tibetan temple

Pillar head decoration of Tibetan temple

We can easily find out from the Jokhang Temple, Potala Palace and other Tibetan temples that apart from the difference to the Han temples in architectural layout and individual images, their decorations are also unique with local features. The overall effect of decorations is emphasized. The big stone wall and its edges are decorated with the local grass; the golden roof and its decoration under the blue sky give these temples a sense of magnificence. In coloring, the red and the white are popularly used, because, the clouds and snow mountains in Tibet are white, the milk products which the Tibetan people depend on are white, while the beef and mutton are red. When the local government holds banquets, white banquet is prepared in ordinary times, which takes milk and cheese as the main food; red banquet is given when celebrating a victorious war, which takes beef and mutton as the main food. Thus, the red and white colors represent wealth and auspiciousness. Besides, decorations are also made on the door, window, indoor pillars and walls. These temples, with their overall images and the decorations both inside and outside, display a unique Tibetan style of magnificence, heaviness, thickness and coarseness, which is a very distinctive feature among the Chinese ancient Buddhist architectures.

## Architecture of Southern Buddhism

In about the middle of the 7th century, a certain upper vehicle Buddhism was introduced into the southern part of Yunnan Province inhabited by the Dai nationality from Burma (Myanmar), this was called Hinayana Buddhism. At that time, temples were not yet built; the spread of Buddhist sutras was from mouth to ear. It was not until the latter part of the 16th century that the King of Burma sent here a delegation of monks, bringing with them Buddhist sutras and statues. Then Buddhist temples and pagodas began to be built in Jinghong area, and Hinayana Buddhism was spread to Dehong and Menglian and other area, covering the whole area inhabited by the Dai nationality in Yunnan Province, to the extent that everyone was a believer, and there is a temple in every village.

The form of temples here is influenced by their counterpart in Burma and Thailand, but also shows the local architectural features, thus, they are special. In layout pattern, there is no axis and symmetrical balance. A temple takes the Buddhist hall as the center, surrounded by small sutra-chanting hall, pagoda, temple gate and residences for the monks in a casual way, only fixing a small covered corridor between the gate and the Buddhist hall. In temple image, the Buddhist hall is very high because the statue inside is very tall, here, the method adopted is to make the roof big and high, not following the Han temples in building the hall into several storied pavilion. The local artisans can make multi-fold treatment to the roof. First of all, divided the huge roof into several

Inside view, main hall of Buddhist temple, Xishuangbana, Yunnan Province

Main Hall, Hinayana Buddhist Temple

layers from the top to the bottom and several sections from the left to the right with prominence given to the central section, so that the big roof has changed into a combination of several small roofs, therefore the heaviness of the big roof is much lessened. Secondly, decorate almost all the ridges with little animals and grass, one ridge after another, and in the center of the main ridge, a small pagoda is built as decoration, so the ridges of different altitude and direction are formed into colored ribbons in the air, vividly and nice looking. Roofs of this kind are not only used on the Buddhist halls, but also on the smaller buildings of temple gates and sutra-chanting halls. There is a Buddhist temple called Jingzhen in Jinghong area, the sutra-chanting hall of which is not big, but its roof is a complex structure composed of dozens of small overhanging gable roofs. The whole roof is octagonal in shape, and there are ten layers from bottom to top, so there are 200 and plus small ridges in total, and furthermore, every ridge is decorated with little something, so that the roof resembles a beautiful flower in full blooming. So, in this area, the roof of temples is the important part to be decorated. We have talked about the palace architecture in the Forbidden City where the big roofs are made into different varieties of hip roof, gable and hip roof, over-hanging gable roof and flush gable roof, so that they become the part which boasts the unique feature of Chinese architecture. But in comparison, the Buddhist temples roofs in Dai nationality area are more vivid, rich and colorful. The Buddhist temple architecture, judging from its overall layout, architectural image and decoration, displays a special ingenious and graceful style, just like the residence buildings and other architectures here.

Closer look of sutra-chanting hall of
Jingzhen Buddha Temple, Jinghong
area, Yunnan Province

# Chapter 6
# Buddhist Pagodas

Pagoda is a special Buddhist structure. After Sakyamuni, the founder of Buddhism became Buddha, he went to various places to preach Buddhism until he reached the senior age of 80 when he got seriously ill on the way and died on a suspension bed in the forest. His disciples cremated his body and found many sparkling and transparent hard pearls which were called sarira. According to Buddhism, only those who have gained enlightenment through self cultivation and become Buddhas can they produce sariras after their bodies are cremated, so, sarira is a treasure representing the Buddha. The disciples carried those sarira to various places and buried them underground, and piled up a clay mound on top of them, which is called "stupa" in India Sanskrit. So, the stupa is in reality a memorial object for burying the sarira of the Buddha which become the worshipping object of disciples. Stupa was translated into Chinese as *Tabu*, simplified as *Ta* (stupa). Pagoda becomes a special Buddhist architecture.

# Chinese Pagodas

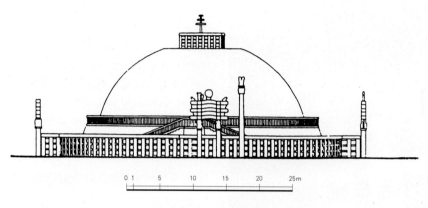

Great Stupa of Sanchi, India

Such "stupas" were introduced to China together with Buddhist sutras, but the mound shape did not prevail in China. Since pagoda is an object symbolizing Buddha, a memorial object worshipped by Buddhist disciples, it must have a lofty, magnificent image according to Chinese traditional psychology, and this image in China is the multi-storey pavilion. Among those burial

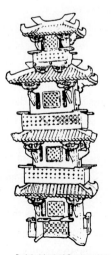

Burial object of Gaotong Han tomb, Shandong Province

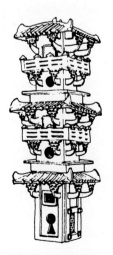

Burial object of a Han tomb, Wangdu, Hebei Province

Burial object of a Han tomb, Shanxian County, Henan Province

Watch towers, burial objects, Han Dynasty

Storied pavilion in Grotto, Datong, Shanxi Province

objects unearthed from the Han tombs, there is a modal of a pavilion: a three or four story building, every storey has protruding eave and balcony, on the top is a roof with four slopes, and there are flower patterns carved on the door, window and balcony balustrades which make the pavilion look very beautiful. Thus, the Chinese style of pagodas came into being by combining Chinese storied pavilion with the incoming India stupa: the lower part is the storied pavilion, the stupa style roof is placed on top, called Tacha, and such is the image of the early Chinese pagoda of pavilion style. Such pagoda is worshipped by the disciples as the symbol of Buddha, so it is placed in the center of the Buddhist temple, just like the stupa is in the center of an India Buddhist grotto, serving as the major architecture of a Buddhist temple. After Luoyang became the capital of Northern Wei in 495 A.D. a great many of temples began to be built in the city. According to the records in the book, *Records of Jialan of Luoyang* (a special book about temples in Luoyang), there was a famous temple in the city called Yong'an Temple, in the center of which was a pagoda of storied pavilion style built with timber-frame structure. It was 9 stories high, totaling a thousand *chi* (about 300 meters). It was a quadrangle in shape, each of the four sides in every floor had three doors and six windows, the red color doors are installed with gold-color studs and golden knocker bases, a *tacha* 30 meters high was standing on the top of the pagoda. On the tip of *tacha* was a gold treasure vase, below which were 30 layers of gold basins, and there were four iron chains connecting the *tacha* and top of the pagoda. There were also gold bells hanging to the eaves of each floor, the sound of them could be heard five kilometers away when wind blew. Such a high wooden pagoda could be seen 50 kilometers away. The description of the architectures by the ancients was probably exaggerated, especially regarding measurements which were largely perceptual, but, the magnificence and beauty of this pagoda can certainly be imagined. There were some visitors from Persia who claimed to have toured many countries. After seeing the pagoda, they marveled at it by saying: grand building and marvelous craftsmanship, the only great pagoda in the whole of the Buddhist world. But this wooden pagoda was destroyed by fire in 534 A.D. The only wooden pagoda survived until today is the Sakya Pagoda of Fogong Temple in Yingxian County of Shanxi Province, commonly called Wooden Pagoda of Yingxian County. It was built in the second year (1056) of Qingning reign of the Liao Dynasty, some 900 years ago. It is a five-story wooden pagoda, 67.31 meters high, in octagonal shape, totally made of wood. It is still standing in the temple after almost a thousand years, and going through several earthquakes. On the bottom floor of the pagoda, there is a whole-body statue of Sakyamuni, 11 meters high enshrined on the Buddhist dais in the center of the floor. On the other four floors, there also enshrine statues of Buddhas and Bodhisattvas big or small. Originally, pagoda is for burying Buddhist sarira, after statues of the Buddha were created, the concrete statue is naturally more attractive to the disciples than the sarira pagoda, thus, there were Buddhist statues enshrined in the Wooden Pagoda of Yingxian County. After the statues entered the halls, there emerged Buddhist halls specially for enshrining Buddhist statues, then the hall replace the pagoda to occupy the central place, while the pagoda was moved to the other positions of the temple nearby the hall or in another courtyard, called pagoda yard. However, it is still the symbol of the Buddha, attracting the disciples with its imposing image.

Wooden Pagoda in Fogong Temple, Yingxian County, Shanxi Province

Big Wild Goose Pagoda, Xi'an
of Shaanxi Province

Kaiyuan Temple Pagoda,
Dingzhou of Hebei Province

Twin Pagodas of Arhat Courtyard,
Suzhou of Jiangsu Province

The timber-frame storied pavilion is magnificent in shape and tight in structure which is able to resist the damage of earthquake, but vulnerable to fire, especially the high wooden pagodas are easily struck and burnt by lightening. So, in the Tang Dynasty when Buddhism was on the rise and prosperous, wooden pagodas were replaced by brick and stone ones, but their outside look still resembled the wooden ones. Brick and stone are not afraid of fire; so many pagodas built with them have survived until today. Especially the bricks are easily collected, made and built with than stone, thus, the ancient brick pagodas are more common than stone ones, among which

Bao'en Temple Pagoda, Suzhou

Longhua Pagoda, Shanghai

Glazed Pagoda, Xumifushou Temple

the more famous ones are: Xuan Zhuang Pagoda of Xingjiao Temple in Xi'an, Shaanxi Province, built in the Tang Dynasty, Big Wild Goose Pagoda in Xi'an, the Twin Pagodas of Arhat Courtyard in Suzhou, built in the Song Dynasty, the pagoda in Kaiyuan Temple in Dingzhou of Hebei Province, etc. In southern part of China, there are pagodas built with bricks inside, but decorated with wooden eaves and balustrades outside. Such pagodas built in combination of bricks and timber are not only good for fire prevention, but also maintained the look of wooden storied pavilion, even in the case of fire destruction, only the wooden eave structure is burned, which can easily be reconstructed. For examples, the Longhua Temple of Shanghai and the Bao'en Temple of Suzhou all belong to this category. The

Stone Pagoda of Kaiyuan Temple, Quanzhou of Fujian Province

White Pagoda, Zhakou, Hangzhou of Zhejiang Province

155

Top of stupa for Master Minghui, Pingshun, Shanxi Province

Stupa-top in Qixia Temple, Nanjing, Jiangsu Province

Pagoda-top of Songyue Temple, Dengfeng, Henan Province

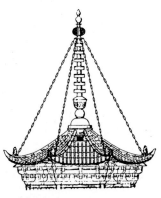

Top of stone pagoda in Kaiyuan Temple, Quanzhou, Fujian Province

White Pagoda at Zhakou, Hangzhou, Zhejiang Province

Different types of pagoda-pinnacles

Raised eaves, Buddhist pagoda of northern China

Raised eaves, Buddhist pagoda of southern China

Longhua Temple of Shanghai was built in the second year (977) under the reign of Taipingxingguo of the Song Dynasty. It is in octagonal shape, seven stories high, totaling 40.55 meters. The body of the pagoda is built with bricks, the eave and the balcony balustrade with timber-frame structure, with the eaves protruding out very far, and the ridge rose up high, and there are bracket sets both under the eaves and the balconies. The walls of every floor are decorated with wood pillars and beams, the door on each of the four sides is open to the balcony, and the balustrades on the balcony are decorated with relief flower patterns. The pagoda is not high, but dignified, with the distinctive style of the southern architecture, graceful and beautiful.

There are also pagodas built with bricks but with glazed bricks or tiles inlayed or glued to the outside, thus becoming glazed pagodas, e. g. those in the Sumeru (*xumi*) Fushou Temple in Chengde of Hebei Province and in Xiangshan (Fragrant Hill) of Beijing. There are much less pagodas built with stones, of which, the Twin-Pagodas of Kaiyuan Temple in Quanzhou of Fujian Province are big ones, and the White Pagoda at Zhakou of Hangzhou, Zhejiang Province, is a small one.

In summing up, we can see a phenomenon, the Chinese style pagodas created through the combination of Chinese traditional storied pavilion and the stupa introduced from India have undergone changes in their forms both of the storied pavilion and the stupa in the development of such pagodas in China. Originally, three or four story pavilions increased to seven, nine or even more than ten stories, and in overall planning, from the bottom to top, every floor is smaller than the previous one, so that the outside line of the pagoda is a slant or curved line; at the same time, also from the bottom to top, the height of every story is lower than the previous one, so that the Buddhist pagoda looks higher and more imposing. The stupa on top of the pagoda is no longer a simple basin upside down, but it is made higher, and additional wheels and treasure crown bearing Buddhist significance are added to it. While in shaping, they could be sturdy or pointed in line with their combination with the pagoda body and top, so that they become an inseparable part of the whole pagoda. Besides, the storied pavilion style pagoda, no matter whether they are built with timber-frame or bricks or stone, still maintain the different architectural styles of the northern or southern China, for example, the protruding of the eaves seems milder in the north, but steeper in the south; the spike on top of the pagoda is sturdier in the north, but more pointed in the south. In a word, after long time practice and incessant creative work by the artisans, Chinese Buddhist pagodas are no longer the simple piling up of the storied pavilion and the stupa, but a new type pagoda by the merging of the two.

# Different Types of Pagodas

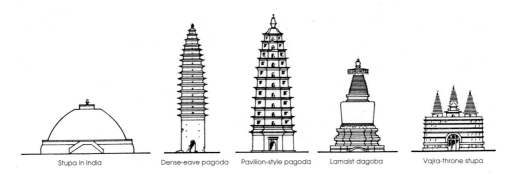

| Stupa in India | Dense-eave pagoda | Pavilion-style pagoda | Lamaist dagoba | Vajra-throne stupa |

Different types of Buddhist pagodas

China is a country with a long history, vast expanses of land and multiple nationalities, so, apart from storied pavilion type of pagodas, there are other types of Buddhist pagodas:

## Dense Eaves Pagodas

Storied pavilion type pagodas, but the pillars, beams, protruding eaves, doors and windows supposedly made of timber on the outside are all bricks. Inside the pagoda, there is the staircase leading to the top, also made of bricks, in some cases, the staircase and the steps are made of wood. Such brick pagodas gradually underwent changes in outside appearance, mainly, making the bottom story high, and all the other stories lower, so that those eaves seem piling up one after the other, and the pagoda is divided into three parts of the body, the closely arranged eaves and the pinnacle. Such pagoda is called Dense Eaves Pagoda which is a new type Buddhist pagoda evolved from the storied pavilion type pagoda.

The earliest such pagoda survived until today is the Songyue Temple Pagoda in Dengfeng of Henan Province. It was built in the fourth year (523) of Zhengguang reign of Northern Wei. It is 41 meters high, with 12 sides on its outside, but an octagon shape on its inside. There are only two stories on the body, a low terrace beneath it, and above the body are the 15-story dense eaves, and on top, the pinnacle made of stone. What is strange is that this 12-side dense eaves pagoda has never been seen again in the whole of China. There are a number of such dense eaves pagodas left over from the Tang Dynasty, e.g., the Little Wild Goose Pagoda in Xi'an (built in 707), Qianxun Pagoda of Chongsheng Temple in Dali of Yunnan Province (built in 824-839) and Fawang Temple

Songyue Temple Pagoda,
Dengfeng of Henan Province

Little Wild Goose Pagoda,
Xi'an, Shaanxi Province

Qianxun Pagoda, Chongsheng Temple,
Dali of Yunnan Province

pagoda in Dengfeng of Henan Province. These pagodas are usually built with bricks, square in plan, hollow in the center from bottom to top, the floors and staircases are made with timber-frame. There is even a legend concerning the Little Wild Goose Pagoda: the earthquake in 1487 ripped it apart from top to bottom, and the widest part of the breach is one *chi* ( one third of a meter), but another quake in 1521 closed the breach and the pagoda was in one piece again. This pagoda has suffered from more than 70 quakes, strong or weak, in its history of more than one thousand years, which destroyed its top two floors. Out of the original 15-story dense eaves, only 13-story have remained which have been repaired and consolidated, and now, it still maintains its damaged image of 13-story pagoda.

During the Song, Liao and Jin periods, this kind of dense eaves pagodas were prevailing in the north, but they are different in form from their Tang counterparts, among which, the Tianning Temple Pagoda is a typical one. It was built in the Liao Dynasty, octagonal in plan, and solid inside, below the pagoda is a terrace in combination with the Sumeru seat, upon which sits the pagoda body; each side of the pagoda has corner pillars, beams, doors and windows, and carved pictures of bodhisattva and heavenly gods. Upon the body are the 13-layer dense eaves, each eave is propped up by bracket sets in rows, and the top is the pinnacle. Everything on the pagoda, from the top, dense eaves, body to the terrace; from protruding eaves, bracket sets, doors, windows to the seat and carved pictures of bodhisattvas and heavenly gods are all built or made of bricks. Therefore, the brick pagoda is really a large-size Buddhist art piece made of bricks. Such octagonal, solid pagoda built entirely with bricks became the typical pattern of the dense eaves Buddhist pagodas of this period in the north. The White Pagoda of Liaoyang and the Twin Pagodas in Chongxing Temple of Beizhen, Liaoning Province belong to this type.

Both the dense eaves pagodas of the Tang and the octagonal, solid dense eaves pagodas of the Liao pay special attention to the overall image of the Buddhist pagodas, beside the attention being made on the detailed decorations. The body on the lower part of pagoda must be made regular and upright, while the dense eaves part which takes up the major portion of the pagoda, each eave is made smaller and less protruding than the one immediately below, but the decrease is irregular, so that the outside look of the pagoda is an elastic curve line, which ends at the top with an imposing spike. Besides, the two corners of every eave are slightly cocked up, and in the case of the Qianxun Pagoda of Chongsheng Temple, Dali, Yunnan Province, the ends of every eave are made into a continuous curve. After making such treatment, the sturdy northern brick pagodas do not seem clumsy, yet strong while the slender southern brick pagodas do not seem pointed, yet high and upright. Taking into consideration that Buddhist pagodas are just the symbols of Buddhism, it was not necessary for the ancient artisans to make such minute treatment on their outside appearances, but they did so meticulously, because they regarded the Buddhist pagodas as pieces of art, on which they tried their utmost in creating the whole as well as the detailed part of pagodas. In doing so, they displayed their pious feeling towards Buddhism on the one hand, and on the other, enabled these Buddhist pagodas to be more impressive and more appealing to the public.

Tianning Temple Pagoda, Beijing

Part of Tianning Temple Pagoda

Dense eaves curve-line formation, Qianxun Pagoda

## Lama Pagodas

This is the kind of pagoda prevalent in the Tibetan Buddhism area. Since Tibetan Buddhism is also called Lamaism, so the pagoda is also called dagoba. Its lower part is the Sumeru Throne (high base with decorated moldings), on which sits the body which is round in plan, on top of which are several layers of wheels, and the highest part is the pagoda top. Such pagodas are introduced directly from India, because they have not yet been influenced by the Han nationality culture, so they have basically retained the form of "stupas".

The rulers of the Yuan Dynasty paid much attention to Lamaism, so the lama pagodas can be spread to the interior. The White Dagoba of Miaoying Temple, Beijing was built right in this period. Master architect Anigo from Nepal presided over the planning and construction of the pagoda in the 16th year (1279) of Zhiyuan reign which maintained the typical image of a lama pagoda. On the lower part is the Sumeru dais which is in square form, on the round body are 13 layers of wheels, and on the top are the treasure crown and a little pagoda like tip. It is 50.86-meter high, entirely built with bricks. Apart from the bronze treasure crown and the overall shaping of the image, there are almost no detailed decorations. The dagoba is all in white, and the general formation gives one a feeling of sturdy and imposing. In Wutai

0 1 2 3 4 5 6m

Curve-line formation. Songyue Temple Pagoda, Heibei Province

White Pagoda of Miaoying Temple, Beijing

Lama pagoda, Wutai Mountain, Shanxi Province

Mountain, one of the four great Buddhist mountains, there is such a lama pagoda in Taihuai Township, 50 meters high. The white and sturdy dagoba stands aloft in the center of buildings, and with the green mountains in the background, it becomes the landmark of the area of temples in the Wutai Mountains.

The dagoba are often built beside temples as tombs of lamas, which are not big, either singularly, or in a group. They maintain the basic form of three parts, terrace, body and top, but there are no set rules to each part: the terrace may be a single piece, or divided into two floors, it may be a square one or a round one; the body is always round, but it can be higher or lower; the forms of the top are more varied. In a word, they observe a set rule with small variations.

## Vajra Throne Pagoda

This form of Buddhist pagodas also come from India. In Tujiaya, India where Sakyamuni became Buddha, a memorial pagoda was built. Its base is a big throne on which five small pagodas were built for enshrining the sarira of five Buddhas of the Esoteric sect of Vajras, hence the name, Vajra Throne Pagoda. The earliest such pagoda discovered in China is in Dazhengjue Temple

Elevation. Vajra-throne stupa Big Dazhengjue Temple, Beijing

which was built in the 9th year (1473) of the Chenghua reign of the Ming Dynasty. The throne under the pagoda is in square form, 18.6 meters from south to north, 15.7 meters wide, and 7.7 meters high. The four walls of which are divided into six layers, on the bottom is Sumeru Throne, carved with Buddhist-theme pictures, the above five layers are all carved with row upon row of Buddhist niches. The throne is made of bricks, wrapped with stone material on the outside. The five stone dense eaves pagodas stand on the throne, the middle one is about 8 meters high with 13 stories of eaves, the other four standing at the corners are shorter, about 7 meters, also with 13 layers of eaves. All the stupas are covered with Buddhist-theme carvings.

There are two more famous Vajra throne pagodas in Beijing. One in Azure Cloud (Biyun) Temple built in the 13th year (1748) of Qianlong reign. Its throne is in the shape of a big character品, and it is divided into two parts, upon the rear part are five dense eave style stone pagodas, one big, four small; upon the front part which also protrudes out, there are a small Vajra throne pagoda and two small stone lama pagodas, thus a combination style of pagoda upon pagoda. The four walls of the throne as well as every small pagoda are carved with Buddhist-theme decorations, and the throne is also surrounded by balustrades, so it is magnificent and beautiful from the whole shape to the details.The Azure Cloud (Biyun) Temple is located on the Fragrant Hill of the western suburbs of

163

Biyun Temple pagoda, Beijing

Vajra throne pagodas, Xihuang Temple, Beijing

Beijing, and the buildings of the temple are arranged according to the terrain of the hill, this Vajra throne pagoda is situated on the highest point of the temple, which is very prominent in the background of the green hills on the sides. The other one is the Qing Jinghuacheng Pagoda in Xihuang Temple. In the 45th year (1780) of Qianlong reign, when the 6th Panchan Erdni

Throne of Biyun Temple pagoda

Little pagodas on the throne

Carved decorations, Vajra throne pagodas, Xihuang Temple

Cideng Temple Pagodas, Hohhot, Inner Mongolia

Throne of Cideng Temple Pagodas

came to Beijing to congratulate on the Emperor's birthday and stayed temporarily in Xihuang Temple, later died of illness in Beijing. The Qing court built in the temple a stone pagoda for keeping the effects of the 6th Panchan to commemorate him. Its throne is three meters high, upon it the main pagoda in the center is a lama pagoda, and the four small pagodas on the corners are in the shape of Dhanari column. The stone carvings which are very well done are concentrated on the central lama pagoda and its base. There is a stone archway each on the south and north of the throne which joins the pagodas into a group of architecture, adding a sense of importance to the Buddhist pagodas.

There is another Vajra throne pagoda in Cideng Temple of Hohhot, Inner Mongolia Autonomous Region, built in the 5th year (1727) of Yongzheng reign of the Qing Dynasty. There are storied pavilion type pagodas standing on the high throne, all made of bricks, carvings covering all four walls of the throne and pagoda, in addition, glazed tiles in yellow and green colors are used on every layer of the eaves and the pagoda top, which beautify the pagoda to a great extent.

This basic form of throne plus small pagodas varies in style and pattern, thanks to the creative work of the ancient artisans. There is the difference of time and style between Dazhengjue Temple Pagoda and Biyun Temple Pagoda of Beijing, the former is generally sturdy and simple, the latter is complex and beautiful. The Xihuang Temple Pagoda is a contemporary with Biyun Temple Pagoda, but also different in style. The Xihuang Temple Pagoda looks more concise in overall shaping and decoration of the details, while the Cideng Temple Pagoda is of distinctive nationality style of the region.

## Myanmar Style Pagodas

The pagodas in Hinayana Buddhist temples are entirely different in forms with the Han Bud-

Up: (left) Manfeilong Pagoda, Jinghong of Yunnan Province
(right) Terrace base of Manfeilong Pagoda
Down: Manting Buddhist Temple Pagoda, Jinghong

Yunyan Pagodas, Dehong of Yunnan Province

dhist temple pagodas. Since they are introduced directly from Myanmar and Thailand, hence the name: Myanmar style pagodas. The most famous one of such pagodas is the Manfeilong Pagoda in Jinghong Prefecture of Yunnan, which was built in1204. On an octagonal terrace stands a pagoda, surrounded by eight smaller ones. The bodies of the pagodas are all in round form, and divided into several sections from top to bottom in different sizes, resembling a slender gourd. On the top is the cone shaped pinnacle. The pagodas are all in white. The pinnacles are covered with gold sheet, and several layer of lids on the top, made of bronze. The main pagoda in the middle is 16.3 meters high, and the eight smaller one, eight meters, forming a group. Its overall shape is upright and beautiful.

There is another such pagoda also in Jinghong: Manting Temple Pagodas. On a square Sumeru Throne, there stands a big pagoda in the center, surrounded by four smaller pagodas

Pinnacle of Yunyan Pagodas

167

Pagoda tomb of Tang Dynasty, Foguang Temple, Wulai of Shanxi Province

in the four corners. All the bodies of the five pagodas are shaped octagonal in plan, piled up in different sizes one on the other, just like two layers of Sumeru thrones piling up. On the top is the cone-shaped pinnacle. Their shapes are similar, only the sizes are different. The main pagoda in the center is sturdy, and the four smaller ones slender, all white in color, those cone-like sharp spikes point upward to the blue sky, all these make the overall shapes sturdy, but not without beauty. In Dehong, Yunnan Province, there is a Yunyan Pagoda. On the Sumeru throne which is made of several layers, there is a main pagoda surrounded by 40 small pagodas. All the pagoda bodies are round, big at the bottom and small on top, resembling bronze bells. On top of them are several layers of wheels shrinking into cone-shaped pagoda top with a treasure lid as top. The throne and the body are all white, between the throne and the body, and the

wheels are decorated with lotus flowers. The pinnacle made of metal is full of hollowed-out flower patterns, hung on all sides with bronze bells. The white pagoda bodies and the silver-colored spikes seem pure and beautiful under the blue sky. The bells ringing in the wind intensifies the atmosphere of Buddhism. We may give a comparison between the Tibetan lama temples and the Hinayana Buddhist temples, both are directly introduced from India, Nepal, and Myanmar and Thailand, both retain basically the original type of Buddhist stupas, because they were not influenced by the traditional culture of the Han nationality. They are all built with bricks, and all white. But, their images are quite different: lama pagodas, sturdy and stable; Hinayana pagodas, slender and graceful. This is due to the difference in regions and nationalities.

## Single Story Pagoda, Flower Pagoda and Others

There are single story pagodas in temples across the country, among which several are left over by the Tang Dynasty, mainly tomb pagodas of monks. They are usually built with bricks, although there are also stone ones. In plan, most of them are in square form, with a few in hexagons, octagon and round ones. The Minghui Master Pagoda of Pingshun of Shanxi Province is a stone

Sectional drawing. Master Minghui Pagoda,
Pingshun of Shanxi Province

Square. Small stupa, Yunju Temple, Fangshan, Beijing

Octagonal, Stupa of Shousheng Temple,
Yuncheng, Shanxi

Round, Stupa of Dhyana master Fanzhou,
Yuncheng, Shanxi

Hexagonal, Stupa of Patriarchal master,
Foguang Temple, Wutai, Shanxi

Different types of one storey pagodas of Tang Dynasty

tomb pagoda, built in 877A.D.. It is in square form. Its terrace, body and spike are almost of the
same height, but the general proportion of it is balanced and dignified, thanks to the different
treatment on the outside shaping and decorations on details. No matter in the form of square,
hexagon, octagon or round, this kind of pagodas are generally consisted of the terrace, body and

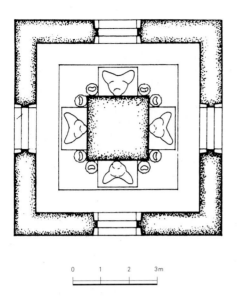

Plan. Four-gate Pagoda, Shentong Temple, Licheng of Shandong Province

spike, with the only difference in the height. Some terraces are lower and some are higher, with decorations mainly concentrated on the top part. There are also single story pagodas which are not tombs, e.g., the pagoda in Shentong Temple of Licheng of Shandong Province, built in 611A.D.. It is a square in plan, with every side measuring 7.4 meters and a total height of about 13 meters, built entirely with stone materials. There is a door to every side, and in the center of the pagoda stands a square column, with a Buddha statue backing each side of the column, which is just facing each door of the pagoda, so this is a pagoda built for the disciples to pay tribute to. Apart from a little decoration of stone carvings on pinnacle, the pagoda is built with all the straight and leveled stone material, so its image is plain and concise.

Flower Pagoda, Guanghui Temple, Zhengding of Hebei Province

Part of Flower Pagoda, Guanghui Temple

Lama pagoda group, Qingtongxia of Ningxia Hui Autonomous Region

There is another kind of pagodas in Hebei and some other areas which are built with bricks in the style of storied pavilion of dense eaves, but their upper parts are littered with brick carved little Buddhist pagodas, immortals, lions, elephants and lotus thrones, etc., closely related to Buddhism. Looking from a certain distance, these little images clustered together resemble flowers blooming on the pagodas, hence the name, flower pagodas. There is such a pagoda in Guanghui Temple of Zhengding, Hebei Province built in the Song, Jin periods. Between the third floor of the body and the pinnacle of this octagonal pagoda, there is a section all around the pagoda which is full of brick carvings resembling flowers looking from afar.

In Ningxia Hui Autonomous Region, there is a large group of lama dagobas on a mountain slope of Qingtongxia City, which is composed of 108 small lama dagobas, forming into an equilateral, with a single pagoda at the top, the following rows are arranged according to odd numbers of 3, 5, 7, until the final row, 19, with the exception of the number 3 and 5, each of which has two rows. The sizes of them are smaller on the bottom, but growing larger with the increase in elevation and distance, so that looking up from below, they seem to be of the same size due to the perspective difference of human eye.

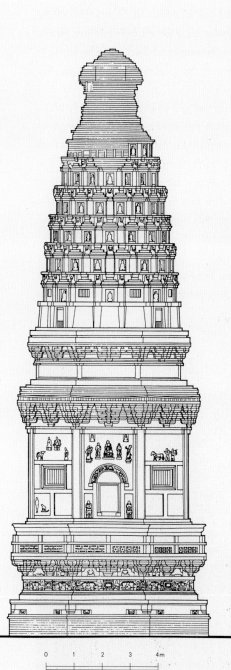

0  1  2  3  4m

Flower Pagoda, suburb of Beijing

## Pagoda as Land Mark

Ever since Buddhist statues entered the hall of temple, the Buddhist hall has replaced the Buddhist pagoda as the center of a temple. But, the pagoda after all is the symbolic architecture of Buddhism, which plays a big role in propagating Buddhism and attracting disciples. Therefore, in building pagodas in many places, efforts are made not only on the creation of their images, but also the selection of their locations.

In the 4th year (1001) of Xianping reign of the Song Dynasty, Buddhist sariras were taken back from Tianzhu, and were enshrined in a special pagoda in Kaiyuan Temple of Dingxian County (now Dingzhou) of Hebei Province, which was completed in 50 years. The pagoda is in the form of storied pavilion, built totally with bricks. It is 11 floors high, 84.2 meters, the highest existing brick pagoda of our country, inside which, a staircase made of bricks leading to the top. At that time, the Song and Liao in the north were at war with each other, and the Dingxian County was in the war zone. The Song army used this high pagoda as watch tower to supervise on the Liao army, so it is also called "Watch Enemy Pagoda", and so, the Buddhist pagoda also serves military purposes.

In 970 A.D., Six Harmony Pagoda was built in Kaiyuan Temple in Hangzhou. The temple is located on a hill by the Qiantang River; to build a pagoda here is for enshrining the sariras, but at the same time, to serve the symbolic purpose of suppressing the floods of the river. The Six Harmony Pagoda had nine floors originally, built with bricks in the interior, and timber-frame as the outside eaves. When it was destroyed and rebuilt in 1153, A.D., it became seven-story pagoda. In the 26th year (1900) of Guangxu reign, the outside timber-frame structure was changed into the present 13 floors. Because it is as high as nearly 60 meters on a hill and facing water, so it is visible from a long distance, especially during the night when the lamp on it is lit, it serves as the beacon tower for those boats coming and going on the river.

In Beijing Imperial City, the Qionghua Island of Beihai became the imperial garden since the Yuan Dynasty, and during the Ming and the Qing, some palaces were gradually built on the island. In the 8th year (1651) of Shunzhi reign of the Qing, Yong'an Buddhist Temple

Six Harmony Pagoda, Hangzhou of Zhejiang Province

White Pagoda, Beihai of Beijing

was built there and on top of the hill, a white lama dagoba was built, called Beihai "White Dagoba". The dagoba itself is 39.5 meters high, plus the height of the hill on Qionghua Island, 32.8 meters, a total of more than 70 meters abruptly rose from the ground. The lofty white dagoba setting off by the blue sky in the back, stands towering over clusters of green trees in the surroundings. It is not only the center of the Beihai scenic area, but also jointly form a skyline of the ancient capital together with the nearby five pavilions on the ridge of the Jingshan Hill. It becomes a prominent scene with the large patch of golden palaces and grey quadrangles in the background, which makes the ancient capital more enchanting.

Xiangyan Buddhist Temple of Jingmingyuan is located on Yuquan (Jade Fountain) Mountain, imperial garden in the northwest suburb of Beijing, in which the Buddhist pagoda is built on the top of the main peak of the mountain, hence the name "Yufeng (Jade Peak) Pagoda". It is a brick pagoda, seven stories high in octagonal shape, storied pavilion style. A staircase inside leads the way from the bottom to the top. Standing on the top and looking around, one enjoys a birds-eye-view of the beautiful scenery below, especially the Fragrant Hill to the west and the Summer Palace and Yuanmingyuan to the east. The Yufeng Pagoda becomes not only the highest point of the Yuquan Mountain and the scenic center of the whole garden, but also the "borrowed scene" of the nearby

Jade Peak Pagoda in the distance

imperial gardens because of its prominent position. This Buddhist pagoda is visible no matter whether it is from Jingyiyuan, top of the Fragrant Hill, or from the mountain ridges and lakeside of the Summer Palace, thus it becomes the famous scene: "Pagoda on Jade Peak".

In Zhenjiang City of Jiangsu Province, there is the Jinshan (Gold Hill) on the southern bank of the Yangtze River. A Buddhist temple is built on the hill by the name Jiangtian Temple, popularly called Jinshan Temple. The halls of the temple are scattered at the foot and half way up the hill, linked by covered corridors and stone steps, only the pagoda is built on the top, named Cishou Pagoda. It is seven stories high in the shape of an octagon, with bricks inside and timber-frame eaves on the outside. There is a balcony protruding out on each floor, and a staircase inside leads to each floor. Looking out from the balcony, one sees everything from the nearby street scene

Gold Hill Temple Pagoda, Zhenjiang of
Jiangsu Province

Brick pagoda body of Leifeng Pagoda, Hangzhou
of Zhejiang Province

New Leifeng Pagoda in the distance, Hangzhou

Buddhist pagoda, Guilin of Guangxi Zhuang Autonomous Region

to the sails of boats on the river in the distance. The pagoda is in slender shape, plus the up-raised eave corner and cone-shaped spike; it is even more lofty and imposing. It stands on the summit of the Gold Hill, facing the river, a landmark of Zhenjiang City.

The famous Leifeng Pagoda in Hangzhou, Zhejiang Province is built on top of Nanping Hill by the West Lake. Originally, it was a multi-story pavilion style pagoda with brick heart and timber-frame eaves, both the shape and location of which should be very beautiful, judging from the descriptions concerning it in the poems and articles by the ancient people. But, during the reign (1522-1566) of Jiajing, the Japanese pirates invaded Hangzhou and burned the temple where the pagoda belonged to, and the outside tim-ber-frame structure of the pagoda was also burned, with only the brick part of the pagoda standing by the lakeside. But, people still liked it, enjoyed it, especially when the setting sun gives this ragged pagoda a layer of golden light, hence the "Setting Sun on Leifeng Pagoda", one of the ten major scenic spots of the West Lake. In the twenties of the last century, the brick part of the pagoda totally collapsed, and the famous scene also disappeared from the West Lake. But in the beginning of the 21st century, the modern Hangzhou people built a new Leifeng Pagoda on the remnants of the original one. Although this is not the old pagoda, people can now enjoy the scene of the "Setting Sun on Leifeng Pagoda" again.

In the beginning of Buddhist pagoda construction, the role it could play was unknown other than the Buddhist belief. They stand by rivers and lakes, on top of high hills, going through thick and thin for thousands of years, until gradually, people discover and realize their values. Buddhist pagodas become the best scenic spots for sightseeing; they beautify the landscape, forming all kinds of special scenes with mountain and water; and they can also serve observation and navigation purposes. The Buddhist pagoda contains more and richer content and value a Buddhism.

# Extension of Buddhist Pagodas

Now that the Buddhist pagoda is of more values, its role is certain to be extended.

The Big Wild Goose Pagoda of Xi'an, Shaanxi Province is not only a famous Buddhist pagoda left over from the Tang Dynasty, but also a favorite place for the people to climb up for a birds-eye-view in ancient times. The Tang Dynasty practiced the policy of selecting officials through examinations. Scholars from all the provinces gathered in Chang'an to take part in the examination, the palace examination by the Emperor. Those who won the title of advanced scholars were bound to climb up the pagoda to write down their names on the pagoda to express their happy feelings. "To inscribe name on Goose Pagoda" became a matter of pleasure for officials and men of letters, and many of them from different parts of the country came here to express their feelings, therefore, quite a few valuable poems and articles were created. A Buddhist pagoda has become the place for men of letters to express themselves, thus, a lot of cultural connotation is attached to it.

Since Buddhist pagoda can bring added luster to the environment, there emerged some scenic pagoda, *fengshui* pagoda and memorial pagodas concerning somebody or some matters. In the long period of Chinese feudal society, where agricultural economy was the mainstay, if those people living in the vast rural villages wished to leave the countryside to embark on the road of officials, there was no way out but to study very hard under the circumstance of almost no commodity economy, to become an official after passing examinations one after another. Therefore, it was highly expected that there were more men of letters emerging from the villages, and according to the *fengshui* theory, if only a writing brush is built on the hill at the entrance of the village, or a high pagoda is built on the ground to resemble a writing brush, then the villagers could realize their wishes. There is such a pagoda at the entrance of Xinye Village in Jiande of Zhejiang Province. It is seven-story pavilion style, in the shape of hexagon, about 30 meters high. It is not a Buddhist pagoda, but a *fengshui* pagoda, which plays the symbolic role of promoting cultural luck for the village together with the nearby Wenchang Pavilion.

Guodong Village of Wuyi, Zhejiang Province is located in a gully between two hills, and there are two peaks in front of its entrance, through which runs the road to the village. The ancients took the two peaks as a lion and an elephant which are ferocious and powerful, capable of guaranteeing the auspiciousness and safety of the village. In order to strengthen this symbolic metaphor, the villagers built an additional three-story little pagoda on the western peak to emphasize the situation that the entrance of the village is like a pass. No matter what role the cultural pagoda or this little pagoda is going to play the cultural luck and auspiciousness for the village is only symbolic, and they can only give people certain psychological comfort. But, these pagodas, along with the corresponding mountain peaks and temples can form a scene which, through development in history, becomes a landmark for the village, a scenic spot with cultural connotations.

*Fengshui* pagoda, Xinye Village, Jiande of Zhejiang Province

Little pagoda, Guodong Village, Wuyi of Zhejiang Province

# Chapter 7
# Imperial Gardens

What is a garden? A garden is a beautiful environment created on a certain area through transforming the terrain, planting trees, flowers and grass, building architecture, paving reads, etc., by using technological and artistic means, where people can get a rest and enjoyment both physically and mentally.

# Classification of Gardens and Their Special Features

There were many such gardens in ancient China, both landscape gardens taking the natural mountains, rivers and lakes as the major part, and also artificially built imperial, private and temple gardens.

In ancient China, it was one of the important nature worships to worship mountain gods. Through selection by history, five mountains among all in the east, south, west, north and the middle became the concentrated places for worshipping mountain gods by the feudal emperors of all dynasties. After a long time of management, not only mountain god temples were built in all the five mountains, but the natural scenery had been developed and completed, making the five mountains famous scenic areas with unique features of mountain beauty. Beside the five mountains, the Yellow Mountain of Anhui and the Lushan Mountain of Jiangxi are all beautiful mountains, and through human development, they also become famous landscape garden areas.

In southern China, there are many gardens famous for the water scenery of rivers and lakes, such as the West Lake of Hangzhou, Zhejiang Province, and the

Taishan Mountain, Shandong Province

Emei Mountain, Sichuan Province

181

Nanxi River landscape, Zhejiang Province

Left: Slender West Lake, Yangzhou, Jiangsu Province
Right: (up) West Lake, Hangzhou, Zhejiang Province
      (down) Lijiang River landscape, Guilin, Guangxi Zhuang Autonomous Region

Slender West Lake of Yangzhou, Jiangsu Province, both located inside the cities; the Lijiang of Guilin, Guangxi Zhuang Autonomous region and Nanxi River of Yongjia, Zhejiang Province, located outside of the cities. These rivers and lakes are naturally beautiful in themselves, some of them enjoying the contrast of green mountains and some of them the grace of twists and turns. Furthermore, through human development, e.g., building a village by the river, lake and at the foot of a mountain, or a temple in the mountain with bridges and roads, they become gardens with the water scenery as the major attraction.

Since Qinshihuang unified China, it experienced the feudal society for two thousand years and the replacement of many dynasties. The beginning of all the dynasties, manifested in the field of architecture, is first of all, to build emperor's palaces and the corresponding ritual architectures of altars and temples, secondly, emperor's tomb, and thirdly, imperial gardens for the pleasure of the imperial family. Thus, among all the artificial gardens, the imperial gardens are the largest and most elaborate. At the same time, many royal family members, big officials of the court and powerful big landlords began to build gardens in their own residences by piling up a hill, diverting water, raising plants, birds and animals to create the beauty of nature and these are private gardens. During the periods of the Wei, Jin and Southern and Northern Dynasties, the cultural

Imperial garden: Summer Palace, Beijing

Private garden: Master of Nets Garden (Wangshiyuan), Suzhou

people began to be able to build their own residences and gardens, and when it came to the period of the Tang and Song dynasties, such private gardens became very flourishing. In the areas south of the lower reaches of the Yangtze River where economy was quite developed since ancient times and talented people gathered, plus convenient environment and abundant vegetation, the private gardens are more developed. There are many private gardens belonging to the Ming and Qing periods nowadays in Suzhou, Yangzhou. Wuxi of Jiangsu Province and Hangzhou of Zhejiang province.

Temple garden: Putuo Mountain, Zhejiang Province

Temple garden: Apak Hoja Tomb, Kashi, Xinjiang Uygur Autonomous Region

Temple gardens are those built in Buddhist, Taoist temples, and Islamic mosques. Buddhism emphasizes a quiet state of mind, free from care and desire; Taoism adores nature, and is for concentrating the mind for cultivation; Islamism is for clean and quite. The Buddhist and Taoist temples are usually built in places far away from busy cities, and inside the mosques, everyone must be clean and quite. So, the monks and Taoists like to plant a lot of trees inside and outside

Temple garden: Qingcheng Mountain, Sichuan Province

Temple garden: Qiqushan Mountain Temple, Zitong, Sichuan Province

the temples, bringing spring water into temples and built stone walks, so that the environment is like gardens, and the disciples, when paying respects to Buddhas and fairies, can also enjoy the beautiful scenery, so as to purify themselves both mentally and physically. Since the ancient times, temples were less affected by the changing of dynasties, and the temple economy had a stable guarantee for development, plus the religious culture as connotation, so, the temple gardens can be managed and developed for a long time. As a result, the four great Buddhist Mountains of Putuo, Wutai, Jiuhua and Emei, as well as Qingcheng, Wudang and other mountains with the concentrated Taoist architectures not only become famous religious mountains, but also famous scenic areas which are imbued with the beauty of both mountain gardens and temple gardens. In Id Kah Mosque and Mazar Mosque of Kashi, Xinjiang Uygur Autonomous Region, the halls of prayers are surrounded by green tree gardens with fresh flowers blooming by the road side. These mosques are also as beautiful as gardens.

In summing up those different kinds of gardens mentioned above, what common features do they have? Their special feature is that they are all in the shape of natural landscape. The mountain, river and lake gardens are composed of natural mountain and water; while in those artificially built gardens, an environment of natural mountain, water landscape is created by piling up rocks, digging ponds and planting trees and grass, and with regard to the buildings here, attention is paid to harmoning with gardens, so that they can merge into the landscape without harming the whole environment. This feature of Chinese gardens is especially prominent when compared with the regular shape of the western ancient gardens. We may enjoy an interesting phenomenon: Chinese ancient cities are regular in shape, while the gardens are irregular; it is the vice-versa in the West: cities are irregular, but the gardens are in squares. Naturally, this interesting phenomenon is by no means accidental.

In ancient times, cities in the West gradually came into being from small to big. The cities in Western Europe during the Medieval Age were originally based on the castles of feudal rulers, or military fortresses, and gradually expanded in all directions into cities, and the streets are in the form of radiation or rings. Those cities mainly for commerce and transportation are even freer in shape, taking a pass, a ferry or a thoroughfare as center, without observing any form. But contrary to the cities, the Western ancient gardens are very regular in form. Taking the representative French ancient gardens for an example: the palaces and residences are regular classical architecture, surrounding them are gardens where there are large pieces of lawns, row after row of meticulously trimmed trees, flower-beds either in squares or in long stripes, water pool, fountain and statues. And all the buildings, plants, statues and water pools are arranged in an open big space, and in good order. This is because, from the ancient Greece to the Renaissance, the classicism holds that beauty is a kind of order, of harmonious proportion, e.g., a building is designed and built according to a ratio from the whole building to the different parts of a single column. The demonstration of this aesthetic conception in building gardens is to plan the tree and grass planting, and the construction of pavilions, altars, corridors, pools and statues according to man's will and the harmonious ratio, so the layout is regular, flower-beds, pools and lawns are in geometric

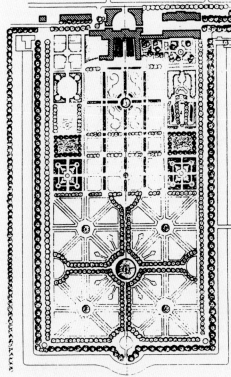

Plan. Herren Hausen Gardens, Germany

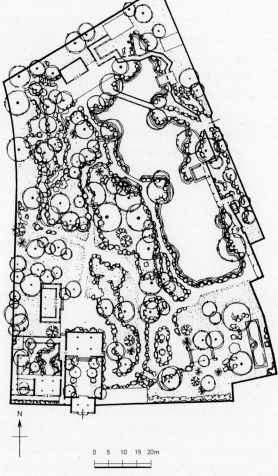

N

0  5  10  15  20m

Plan. Jichangyuan Garden, Wuxi, Jiangsu Province

Imperial garden, Munich, Germany

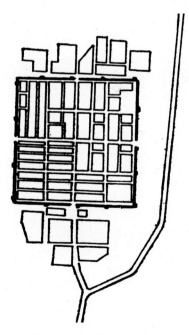

Plan. Shenmu, Shaanxi Province

Plan. Florence, Italy

figures. They hold that the simple reproduction of nature is not beauty; only through artificial treatment and refinement can the natural objects reach the realm of beauty.

In ancient China, feudal society lasted for a long time, when the country's politics and ideology were ruled by the ritual system, the feudalistic centralism was exercised all through the period, and the commodity economy was all along contained. The expression of this situation on architecture is the prominent ritual ideas of "the middle is lofty", and "the front is superior", so the palaces are regular; tombs, temples; even the residences in the city are also regular and upright; the layout is always in symmetrical balance; the important halls and buildings are located on the central position, in order to embody the centralized power of the emperor and the will of order from the upper to lower levels. A group of architectures is like that and a city is like that. In building a city, from the county seat on the lower level to the capital on the highest level, it is a must, first of all, to plan it into a square and regular one. The county office, the imperial city and the palace city are always situated in the center; city gates are placed correspondingly on the four sides of the city walls; the roads in the city are arranged in straight lines and symmetrically balanced way; everything from the city to architectures are arranged according to a clear order and hierarchy. But, people were not yet satisfied with such living environment. In as early as the 11th century, B.C., there appeared an enclosure outside the capital specially for the emperor to hunt and have leisure time, which is to enclose a certain size of the natural piece of land, including mountain and water, where there were plants, birds and animals for the emperor to hunt, rest and sightseeing, such is the earliest garden of China. Such environment of natural landscape and growth was of great attraction to people, so they were introduced from the suburbs to the city. Emperors of the following dynasties began to create such environment in their imperial palaces by piling up rocks into a hill, digging a pool and planting vegetation, so that they created a garden area with the interesting aspects of the natural landscape. The emperors found great pleasure playing in the gardens, and when it came to the Qing Dynasty, the emperors were reluctant to return to the Forbidden City, but dealt with state affairs in the gardens. Such gardens spread from the imperial palaces to the residences of officials and men of letters, becoming China's imperial gardens and private gardens. The regular and straight palaces, tombs, temples and the gardens with the flavor of nature jointly become the treasures of Chinese ancient architecture, which is unique in the long run of historical development of world architecture.

# Imperial Gardens of Qing Dynasty

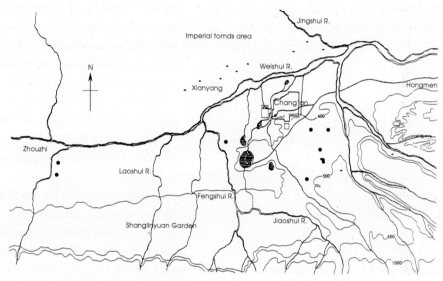

Sketch. Imperial Garden, Chang'an, Western Han Dynasty

Chinese ancient imperial gardens appeared very early. The enclosures used for hunting by the emperors can be regarded as their earliest form. The Qin and Han dynasties became the feudal empire ruling a unified China, they all built large-size imperial gardens in their capitals Xianyang and Chang'an successively. The Shanglinyuan Garden built by the Western Han Dynasty (206B.C.-25A.D.) to the south of Chang'an city had eight natural rivers going through south-north, and a water area as large as 150 hectares were artificially made, and the wall surrounding the garden was 130 kilometers long. There were 12 palace architectures and 36 small gardens inside. All kinds of visual and fruit trees were planted, many rare birds and animals raised. So Shanglinyuan became a large-size, all-inclusive imperial garden of palaces and gardens with animals and plants. During the Tang and Song dynasties, imperial gardens were built both inside and outside the imperial palaces in the capitals of Chang'an and Bianliang. Although their scales were not as gigantic as those in the Qin and Han periods, the technological level in building them had developed considerably. The imperial garden by the name of Genyue, built under the personal supervision of Emperor Huizong of the Northern Song Dynasty was located on the outside of the inner palace city of Bianliang. Although it was not big, there were hills and rivers in it, and the

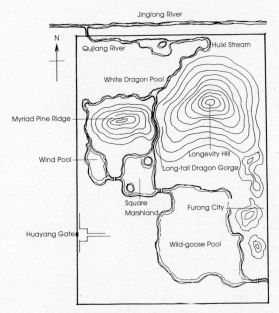

Imaginary plan. Genyue, imperial garden in Bianliang, Song Dynasty

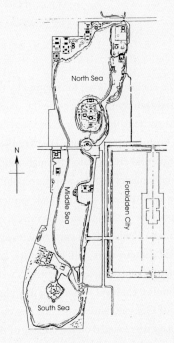

Plan. Western Garden of Qing Dynasty, Beijing

hills were divided into major and minor ones, the rivers were also different in sizes. The hills were built by following the pattern of the Phoenix Hill of Hangzhou, with hill path snaking through them. The vegetation in the garden was varied in species; there were both northern trees as well as southern flowers, planted for the purpose of taming them; there were also many pine trees, forming into a small hill, and large area of bamboo forest. This garden showed that the garden building in China had reached a high level.

The Ming Dynasty paid much attention to the development of gardens when building its capital of Beijing. It expanded the Qionghua Island Garden of the Dadu Capital of the Yuan Dynasty into the Western Garden, which became the largest imperial garden composed of three water surfaces in the imperial city of Beijing. Besides, there was the Imperial Garden built inside the Forbidden City.

When the Qing rulers entered the Shanhaiguan Pass from the northeast, they inherited the whole Imperial City and the Forbidden City of the Ming Dynasty as well as the big and small imperial gardens. After the Qing court secured the political control of the whole China, the economy restored and began to develop and the country's strength became stronger, it began to build gardens in a big way. Buddhist temple and pagoda were built on Qionghua Island in Western Garden, halls built around the lakes, smaller garden built inside the big garden, which resulted in a fuller Western Garden. But, they were not satisfied with gardens inside the capital, in addition, gardens in the suburbs were begun to be built.

Jingxinzhai of Beihai, Western Garden, Beijing

In the northwestern suburb of Beijing, backed by the Western Hills to the north, there is a large piece of flatland with rich resource of underground water which is just one meter below the surface. When the Yuan Dynasty established its capital in Beijing, they found water source in the northwestern suburb and built special channels to supply the capital with water. Therefore, this is a good place for building gardens. This area began to be developed during the two dynasties of the Yuan and Ming; temples were built in Fragrant Hill and Jade Fountain Hill in the west, and Jar (*Weng*) Hill and Jar Hill Lake in the middle, which became the place for sightseeing by the residents in the city. Especially in the Ming Dynasty, many officials and rich merchants built their gardens here, so this area became the place for private gardens. Starting from Emperor Kangxi of the Qing Dynasty, imperial gardens began to be built here.

Located in the west part of the northwestern suburb, the Fragrant Hill is a small hill of the Western Hills, where trees are in abundance, and green peaks piling up one after another. Because of the superb natural environment, temples were built in the hills as early as the Liao and Jin period. Further development was made during the Yuan and Ming dynasties, and a few more temples were built here. During the reign (1662-1722) of Kangxi of the Qing Dynasty, a traveling palace was built for the emperor for his temporary sightseeing and rest, and the Fragrant Hill was renamed as Jingyiyuan (Jingyi Garden) during the reign of Qianlong. The Jade Fountain Hill is to the east of Fragrant Hill, which is a small rocky hill abruptly propping up from ground with spring water gushes out all the year round in the hill, so it is an even better choice for building gardens than the Fragrant Hill. Temple and traveling palace were built here as early as in the Jin Dynasty (265-420). In the 19th year (1680) of Kangxi, an imperial garden was built here, and the Jade

Fragrant Hill, Beijing

Jingyiyuan Garden, Fragrant Hill

Fountain Hill was renamed as Jingmingyuan (Jingming Garden).

Emperor Kangxi made several inspection tours of the Jiangnan Area (the area largely south of the lower reaches of the Yangtze River). After enjoying the beautiful scenery and gardens there to his heart's content, he was no longer satisfied with the two gardens of Jingyi and Jingming, and began to look for a new site in the northwestern suburb for building a new garden. The place he chose was a private garden belonging to Li Wei, an imperial relative of the Ming Dynasty. It was located to the east of Jade Fountain Hill, a totally man-made garden by digging into the ground to make a lake, and piling up the clay to make a hill. On the basis of this private garden, a new garden was built and named Everlasting Spring Garden

Jingmingyuan Garden of Jade Fountain Hill in distance

"Jiuzhouqingyan" scenic zone, Yuanmingyuan (Old Summer Palace)

(Changchunyuan). Since then, he stayed in the garden for the greater part of a year every year, dealing with state affairs, playing and resting. Thus, Changchun Garden became a palace away from palace. There was another private garden left over by the Ming Dynasty to the north of Everlasting Spring (Changchun) Garden, which was nationalized by the Qing Court and bestowed on the fourth prince, i.e. the later Emperor Yongzheng, and was named Yuanmingyuan (Yuanming Garden). After he ascended the throne, Emperor Yongzheng expanded it into an imperial garden, and stayed in the

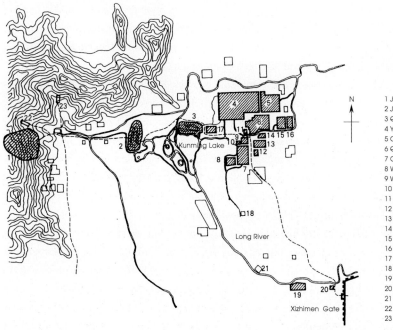

1 Jingyiyuan
2 Jingmingyuan
3 Qingyiyuan
4 Yuanmingyuan
5 Changchunyuan
6 Qichunyuan
7 Changchunyuan
8 Western Garden
9 Weixiuyuan
10 Chengzeyuan
11 Hanlinyuan
12 Jixian Courtyard
13 Shuchunyuan
14 Langrunyuan
15 Jinchunyuan
16 Xichunyuan
17 Zideyuan
18 Quanzong Temple
19 Leshanyuan
20 Yihongyuan
21 Wanshou (Longevity) Temple
22 Azure Cloud Temple
23 Sleeping Buddha Temple

Location of gardens in Beijing's northwestern suburb during Qianlong period of Qing Dynasty

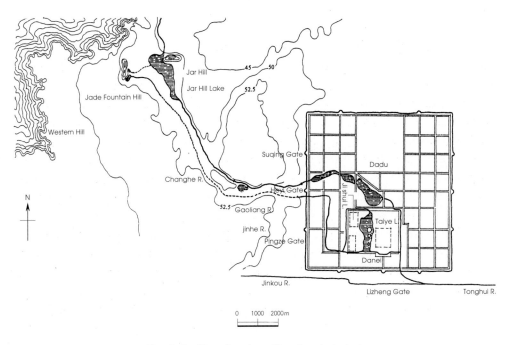

Plan. Dadu of Yuan Dynasty and its northwestern suburb

garden all the year round. But, he was in the reign only for 13 years and he was always busy with state affairs, so he did not unfold large scale construction in the garden. After he ascended the throne in 1735, Emperor Qianlong also stayed in Yuanmingyuan and began to build it in a big way. Emperor Qianlong loved gardens very much, and during his six inspection tours of the Jiangnan Area, he toured almost all the gardens and became very knowledgeable about gardens. He copied many famous scenic spots of southern China and had them copied in Yuanmingyuan, thus, greatly enriched the content of northern imperial gardens. He completed the 40 scenic spots in Yuanmingyuan and later, two additional gardens of Changchunyuan and Qichunyuan were built to the east and southeast of this garden, thus completed the construction of the three gardens of Yuanmingyuan. To commemorate this, Emperor Qianlong even wrote an article himself called The Postscript of Yuanmingyuan, in which, he described the magnificence and beauty of this garden, and he warned his posterity never to abandon it and waste manpower and wealth to build new gardens. But, in his heart, he was not satisfied with this garden and the other imperial gardens at all. He held that the Jingyiyuan of Fragrant Hill was a garden on a hill, water was not there; the Jingmingyuan of Jade Fountain Hill had water scenery, but not big enough; the three gardens of Yuanmingyuan were built on flatland, hill was not there. In a word, they were all not without flaws. He located a place with both hill and water, i.e. Jar (Weng) Hill and Jar Hill (Wengshan) Lake between the Jade Fountain Hill and Yuanmingyuan. As early as Yuan Dynasty, the Weng Hill Lake was made as the place for accumulating water from the northwestern suburb, and after the water was elevated to a certain level, it could be diverted into the city, so the lake was like a reservoir. During the two dynasties of the Yuan and the Ming, temples were built here, and the place was gradually made famous. In order not to go back to his warning made in his article, he found two reasons for building a new garden: first, to cerebrate the 60th birthday of his mother, the empress dowager; second, to dredge the Weng Hill Lake which had been left there unattended for many years and the water flow to the city was not adequate. Naturally, this is a sound reason. In the 15th year (1750) of Qianlong reign, the construction of a new garden began under his personal guidance. After 14 years, the work was completed in 1764. It was named Qingyiyuan (Qingyi Garden), the Jar (*Weng*) Hill in the garden was changed into Wanshou shan(Longevity Hill), and Jar Hill (*Wengshan*) Lake into Kunming Lake. By then, the construction of gardens lasted for almost one hundred years, through the three reigns of Kangxi, Yongzheng and Qianlong, as a result, five imperial gardens were built in the northwestern suburb of Beijing: Jingyiyuan of Fragrant Hill, Jingmingyuan of Jade Fountain Hill, Qingyiyuan of Longevity Hill, Changchunyuan and Yuanmingyuan, which were generally called "three hills and five gardens". At the same time, some smaller gardens were built, which were bestowed to princes and imperial relatives, for example, Xichunyuan, Shaoyuan and Langrunyuan, etc. near Yuanmingyuan. Thus, the largest area of imperial gardens in the world emerged from the northwestern suburb of Beijing. They demonstrate the highest achievement of the art in garden building in ancient China.

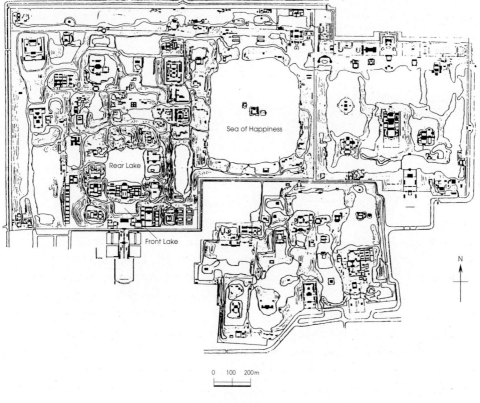

Plan. Yuanmingyuan

# Examples of Imperial Gardens

The construction of imperial gardens in the Qing Dynasty is the last high peak of the ancient garden construction in China, of which, the Mountain Resort in Chengde and the Summer Palace in Beijing are the two best preserved gardens. Although Yuanmingyuan was burned by the Anglo-French allied forces, we can still witness the achievements made in this garden from its remains

Painting showing the scenic zone of "Natural Painting", Yuanmingyuan

Fuhai Lake (Sea of Happiness) of Yuanmingyuan

## Yuanmingyuan

Yuanmingyuan began to be built during the reign of Kangxi, and expanded during the reigns of Yongzheng and Qianlong into three gardens, which was the largest imperial garden in the north-western suburb. It occupies an area of 350 hectares with the construction floor space of 160 thousand square meters which is tantamount to that of all the palaces of the Forbidden City. If we compare it with Jingyiyuan, Jingmingyuan and Qingyiyuan, the prominent feature of Yuanmingyuan is that it is a water scenery garden artificially built out of a flat piece of land.

"Fanghushengjing" scenic zone, Yuanmingyuan

Waterway of Yuanmingyuan

Yuanmingyuan is located on flat land with neither hill nor water. The only strong point of it is the rich resource of underground water which is just three *chi* (one meter) below the ground level, and in some places, there are spring water oozing to the ground. In view of such natural conditions, nearly half of the 350 hectares of land were dug into water areas, and the clay extracted from the land was piled up into a mound nearby. The major part of the water areas are lakes, the largest of which is called Fuhai (Sea of Happiness), 600 meters from south to north, with an area of 30 hectare; there are several lakes of medium size which are between 200 to 300 meters long and

Painting. Western building "Haiyantang", Yuanmingyuan

wide; besides, there are numerous small lakes. Linking all these water areas are the winding and twisting streams which like floating ribbons are linking all the big and small lakes to form a complete water system. The clay mounds are not big, but they are dotted here and there among the lakes and streams, though large in numbers, they do not hinder water scenery which is the major scenery of the garden.

The whole garden is divided into many land spaces, big or small, by the clay mounds and water areas, big or small, on which halls and houses are built, trees and flowers are planted, forming many scenic spots. If identified by the roles they play, there are: palace architectural groups of "Open and Above Board" and "Tranquility Under Heaven", which are for the emperors dealing with state affairs; ritual building Anyou (Peace and Blessing) Palace for worshipping ancestors; Shewei City for worshipping Buddha; Wenyuan (Literary Glory) Pavilion for keeping books; business street. But the most numerous are for sightseeing and enjoyment: pavilions, terraces, storied buildings and storied pavilions. Some scenic spots are mainly buildings, subsidized with water, hill and vegetation; the others are mainly waters, hills and vegetation, with pavilions, storied buildings, terraces and waterside pavilions dotted within; so the scenic spots are varied in their special features.

The architectures in Yuanmingyuan are not only varied in shape, but also in structures. There are different types of architectures: halls for state affairs, temples for worshipping ancestors and Buddhas, residences, houses for books, stores and places for enjoyment, and they are very different in shape. There is the traditional square and rectangular shape in plan, also shapes imitating Chinese characters of 工, 中, 田, 卍and the angler-ruler and the fan. Taking pavilions for example, there are square, hexagon, octagon, round, cross shaped ones, and special water flowing pavilions. For galleries, there are straight, zigzag, climbing ones and the one on different altitudes. Among the 100 and odd bridges, there are flat, zigzag, arch ones, etc. In architectural composition, the traditional quadrangle of symmetrical balance is not strictly observed. The buildings are varied according to the situation of nearby hills or water; they could be surrounded on three sides, or open without enclosure, or dotted here and there with ease.

During his tours down south, Emperor Qianlong ordered his painters accompanying him to take down his favorite scenic spots and gardens to bring back to Beijing for imitation. So, in Yuanmingyuan, there are famous scenes and scenic spots from the West Lake of Hangzhou: Viewing Fish at Flower Harbor (Huagang Guanyu), Three Pools Mirroring the Moon (Santan Yinyue), Lotus in the Breeze at Crooked Courtyard (Quyuan Fenghe), Autumn Moon on Calm Lake (Pinghu Qiuyue), as well as the Slender West Lake of Yangzhou and the Forest of Lions in Suzhou of Jiangsu Province, and the Business Street on a River. Although these are only the miniatures or make-believes of the originals, the Emperor's wish to embrace all the beautiful scenery in the country has attained. Besides, there is a scene of "Western Building" completely formed by western architectures in the garden. There were some western missionaries serving the Qing Court at that time who introduced to the Emperor western architectures which roused his interest, as a result the emperor decided to build a group of western style architectures in Changchunyuan, Baroque style, which was prevailing in Europe at that time. It was built entirely with stone materials with stone carving decorations all over the surface. Even the trees and flowers and grass were arranged according to geometric figures. This was the first time western architecture appeared in Chinese gardens.

The 350-hectare Yuanmingyuan is composed of more than 100 smaller gardens which are independent yet related to each other, and each bearing its own special feature. The Foreigners refer to it as "The Garden Composed of Numerous Gardens".

## Mountain Resort in Chengde

During the reign (1662-1722) of Kangxi of the Qing Dynasty, imperial gardens were built in the northwestern suburb of Beijing on a large scale, and another one, even larger was built in Chengde, Hebei

*Hunting Scene in Mulan Enclosure,* painting of Qing Dynasty

Province, the Mountain Resort.

The Qing rulers were of Manchu nationality, who maintained the habit of their ancestors of loving nature, of galloping on horseback in an open and wild area and shooting games with bow and arrow. After they entered the Pass and became the rulers of the entire China, the Emperor

1 Myriad Tree Garden
2 Horse-drilling Causeway
3 Rehe Hot Spring
4 Serene Water Lake
5 Upper Lake
6 Lower Lake
7 Mirror Lake
8 As-you-wish Lake
9 Silver Lake
10 Lengthened Lake

0    300m

Plan. Mountain Resort in Chengde, Hebei Province

would lead a large number of people every autumn to go to the areas outside of the Pass to hunt within an enclosure. When emperor Kangxi held such an activity, he would specially invite the chiefs of Mongol tribes to take part in the hunting to show his consolation, in order to strengthen harmony and unity among nationalities. The scale of such hunting with political purposes was very large, involving the officials, civilian and military, and an army of around ten thousand people accompanying the emperor; and the content is also rich: hunting, fighting competitions, call in meetings, award granting, army drilling, etc. Therefore the place for enclosure hunting was selected on the Inner Mongolian grassland which was a traditional pasture land with an area of 15,000 square kilometers. This place enjoyed mild climate, abundant grass and woods, and numerous wild animals. But the enclosure was 350 kilometers away from Beijing, for such a distance and so many people, there ought to be several touring palaces on the way for resting and supplying of necessities. There were simple as well as complete touring palaces, and along with the enlargement of the scale and the increase of importance of the enclosure hunting, the touring palaces became more and more complex, finally, a place of the then Rehe Province was selected for building a permanent touring palace which was where the Mountain Resort located.

This piece of land boards the Wulie River on the east and the Lion Ditch on the north, within which, there are large areas of mountain forests in the west and north, grassland in the northeast, lowland in the east and south, rich in spring water, at the same time, the water from the Wulie River in the east can be diverted here to form lakes. Thus, the Resort is composed of the three areas, occupying 564 hectares, and the largest imperial garden of all in the Qing Dynasty. In this place, forests and woods are here and there, water channels and lakes crisscross the land area, and the weather is cool in summer, so, it is an ideal place to stay in summer, thus, called "Summer Resort". The construction of it lasted through the reigns of Kangxi and Qianlong, and finally, a palace-type imperial garden was completed, which was composed of four areas of palaces, lakes, plain and mountains.

Major hall of the main palace, palace area of the Mountain Resort

**Palace Area**  Located on the southern end of the mountains, this area is composed of three groups of palaces standing abreast from left to right, among which the major palace is on the west. It has nine courtyards from the front to the rear, of which the front five ones are halls dealing with state affairs, the four in the back are living quarters. When the mountain resort was completed, the successive emperors all came here to escape the summer heat. In 1860, when the Anglo-French allied forces invaded Beijing, Emperor Xianfeng escaped here and signed the humiliating "Beijing Treaty". He died here the following year, and since then, the Qing Court experienced a special period of the two Empress dowagers dealing with state affairs behind a screen. And the Empress Dowager Ci Xi also performed one court struggle farce after another here, making the calm mountain resort become an important political arena. In the middle is a group of palaces called Pine and Crane Palace, the living quarters for the Queen and concubines. In the east is a group of palaces especially for the emperor to watch operas and to spend leisure time where housed a big theater.

**Lake Area**  Located on the southeast, this area occupies 43 hectares which is less than one tenth of the whole resort. But this area is leveled and low, and abundant in water resource. Through artificial planning and management, eight lakes and eight islands big or small are built here which are linked to one another by dykes and bridges. Attention has been made to mix the different sizes of them, so that there is no sense of repetition, but every sense of interesting nature. More than half of the architectures are concentrated in this area, scattering on the continents and islands,

Islets in lake area of the Mountain Resort

Earth Dyke in lake area

Piled up rockeries and pavilions, lake area

some are regular quadrangles, and some are pavilions or waterside pavilions surrounded by piled-up rocks, trees and forests, forming different scenes. Beside some individual architecture of the Smoke and Rain Tower and the Golden Hill Pavilion, the others are all one story houses which can not harm the wide view of the lake area. With regard to plants, apart from some constant green trees like the pine and cypress, willows are always planted along the river dykes, mixed with sunflowers, cassia and magnolia trees, and in water, lotus and water chestnut plants are widely grown. Owing to the high temperature of the spring water in Rehe, lotus flowers can last until the early autumn. The lakes close by reflecting the surrounding hills and mountains far and near boasts a beautiful landscape very similar to gardens of southern China.

　　**Mountain Area**　Located in the northwestern part of the resort, it occupies two thirds of the total. The shape of the mountain shows continuous ups and downs with clusters of green hillocks linking up one after another, looking full and sturdy. Since it faces southeast, it enjoys full scale sunshine, which makes the forest luxuriant which is a fine scene of the resort. There are four prominent peaks in the mountain, and on top of each peak, a pavilion is built, they are: Snow-capped South Mountain, Two-peak North Pillow, Cloudy Mountains All-around and Hammer Peak in Setting Sun. These names indicate the locations they hold and the different scenes one can enjoy. In winter, the snow on top of the south mountain and the two peaks in the north can be seen from the Lake Area, and the two pavilions pinpoint the two scenes. In the Cloudy Mountains All-around and the Hammer Peak in Setting sun Pavilion, one can enjoy the mountains under the changing clouds all around and the beautiful scene of the Hammer Peak under setting sun. There are four gullies at the foot of the peaks, and on both sides of the roads in the gullies are patches of pine, pear and hazel trees, forming different scenes of Pine and Cloud Gully, Pear Tree Gully and Hazel Gully. The pine-trees forming an evergreen corridor snake along the gullies. In spring, there is a special scene of "pear flowers accompanying the moon". Besides, there are many small gardens in the mountains, in which, halls, pavilions and covered corridors are built according to the mountain situation. There are small paths linking them with the roads in the gullies. Thus, scenes are richer in the gigantic mountain area, with more cultural connotation added to it.

Mountain area of the Mountain Resort

Snow-capped Pavilion of south mountain, mountain area

Pines and Clouds Gully

**Plain Area**  Located in the north of the east, it borders the boundary wall to the east, the mountain area to the west, and the lake area to the south, in the shape of a triangle, and about the same size as the lake area. This is a piece of flat land with little architecture. Its east is a forest of several thousand elm trees in which raised deer run about, seemingly wild animals. Its west part is grassland, maintaining the original look of a grassland north of the Great Wall, a perfect place for Mongolian yurts. In the summer of the 19th year (1754) of Qianlong, the Court held a grand gala party, Mongolian yurts were put up here, the Emperor enjoyed a feast of wild games together with the Mongol dukes, watched wrestling match, riding match, colorful lanterns, and acrobatics, and in the evenings, fireworks. This went on for five days and five nights amid bright lights and cheerful music, achieving evident good results both in politics and entertainment.

**Outer Eight Temples**  There are 12 temples built on the hilly terrain, east of the Wulie River and north of the Lion Ditch, among which, eight larger ones are managed by the monks directly sent by the Qing Court. They are called Outer Eight Temples, because they are located outside of the capital. These temples encircle the Mountain Resort from the east and the north, and all of them were built because of the political need of the Qing Court. Almost all the people in Tibet, Mongolia and Qinghai of the north and west of China believe in lamaism, and the religious

*Banquet bestowed by Emperor at Wanshuyuan, painting of Qing Dynasty*

Yurts in plain area

leaders in those places are at the same time wielding political and economic power, so the rule combines politics with religion. While the Qing Court conquers them with armed forces, at the same time, it also pays attention to uniting the upper levels of the Mongolian and Tibetan people by means of religion, to ensure the political unification of the whole country. In the 52nd year (1713) of Kangxi, the Mongol dukes came to Chengde to congratulate on the 60th birthday of Kangxi, two temples were specially built for that purpose. Since then, several temples were built on the occasions of receiving nobles at the upper level of the Mongols and Tibetan, welcoming the immigrants from border areas, quelling the rebellions on the border, etc. Furthermore, these temples usually adopt the form of Lama Temples, or that of the mixed Tibetan and Han temples in order to better display the role of unity and harmony, thus they are Buddhist architectural groups with prominent special features. Together with the Summer Resort, they became very important places for political activities by the Qing Court.

A view of Putuo Zongcheng Temple from the Mountain Resort

A complete view of Puning Temple

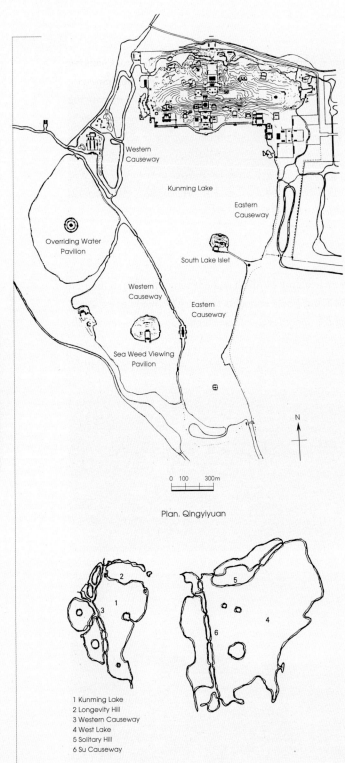

Western
Causeway

Kunming Lake

Eastern
Causeway

Overriding Water
Pavilion

South Lake Islet

Western
Causeway

Eastern
Causeway

Sea Weed Viewing
Pavilion

N

0   100   300m

Plan. Qingyiyuan

1 Kunming Lake
2 Longevity Hill
3 Western Causeway
4 West Lake
5 Solitary Hill
6 Su Causeway

A comparison of Qingyiyuan and West Lake of Hangzhou

The Summer Resort is not only large in size, but also numerous in scenic spots; it has both the interesting scenery of a water country of the Jiangnan Area and the magnificence of the mountain gardens of northern China, and even more, the vast expanses of the scenery north of the Great Wall. It is both a garden and a political center; therefore, it holds a special position among all the imperial gardens. Nowadays, the Mountain Resort, together with the Outer Eight Temples has been listed on the "World Cultural Heritage" by the UNESCO.

## Qingyiyuan

The work on Qingyiyuan (Garden of Clear Ripples) began in the 15th year (1750) of Qianlong, and completed after 14 years, in the 29th year (1764) of Qinglong. The name was changed into the Summer Palace (Yiheyuan) in the 24th year (1898) of Guangxu. Since the reasons for building Qingyiyuan were to commemorate the Empress Dowager's birthday and to dredge the water way, the Jar Hill Lake must be deepened to make a big reservoir, named Kunming Lake, at the same time; the earth from the lake was used to pile on the Jar Hill to make it higher, named Longevity Hill. And the whole garden was built into three scenic areas of palaces, the front hill and front lake and the rear hill and rear lake.

**Palace Area**  This area is located on the eastern part of the garden, because Emperor Qianlong often lived in Yuanmingyuan, and Yuanmingyuan was to the east of Qingyiyuan. For the Emperor's convenience, the palace area was naturally put in the eastern part which is closely linked with the lake and hill area behind it. The palace area is composed of four architectural groups of Benevolence and Longevity Hall (Renshoudian) which is for dealing with state affairs, and Jade Ripples Hall (Yulantang), Yiyunguan Hall and Happiness and Longevity Hall (Leshoutang) which are living quarters. The Renshoudian Hall is seven bays wide, with covered corridors surrounding it, and an imperial throne is installed inside, so it shows the menace of a palace hall. But after all, this is a palace court in a garden, so there is no high terrace under the hall, and glazed tiles are

A bird's-eye view of Summer Palace

Hall of Benevolence and Longevity

Inside view of Happiness and Longevity Hall

Up: three islands in Kunming Lake     Down: West Dyke of Kunming Lake

Left: Binfeng Bridge on West Dyke
Right: (up) Jade Belt Bridge on West Dyke
     (down) front mountain and front lake area, Summer Palace

not used on the roof. In the yard before the hall, a Taihu Rock is built, pines, cypresses and begonias are planted, showing the elegant atmosphere of a garden environment.

    Front Hill and Front Lake Area  It is the largest and principal scenic area of Qingyiyuan. In expanding the Jar Hill (Wengshan) Lake into Kunming Lake, the West Lake of Hangzhou was imitated. The West Lake is located in the south, and in the north, there is solitary Gushan Hill. Here, Longevity Hill is located in the north, and Kunming Lake is in front of it; on the West Lake, there is a Su Dyke, on which, six bridges are built, here, a west dyke is built, which is similar to the Su Dyke both in position and in shape, and also six bridges are built on it. In digging the Kunming Lake, three islands were shaped, which symbolize three fairy mountains in the East Sea: Penglai, Yingzhou and Fangzhang, observing the traditional garden arrangement of "one pool with three hills". On the three big islands are built groups of temples or buildings and pavilions, which are scenic spots in the lake, and at the same time, good places from which to enjoy the lake and hill scenery. The six bridges on the dyke are either bridges with pavilions, or large-size stone arch bridges, and the pavilions are in square shape, or hexagon shape, with double eaves and roofs, and painted beams, forming beautiful scenery on the lake.

After piling-up and building, the originally small Jar Hill became Longevity Hill which is 60 meters above ground, and 1,000 meters from east to west. The architectures on the hill are arranged according to the system of symmetrical balance. The group in the middle is composed of Paiyunmen (Cloud Dispelling Gate), Paiyundian (Cloud Dispelling Hall), Foxiangge (Pavilion of

Wisdom Sea and Zhongxiangjie Archway

Architectural group of Baoyunge Pavilion

Long Corridor

Huazhongyou Pavilion

Up: architectural group of Zhuanlunzang Temple    Down: architectural group of Paiyundian Hall and Foxiangge Pavilion on Longevity Hill

Buddhist Incense), Glazed Tile Archway, Wisdom Sea, auxiliary halls on the left and right, and covered corridors. The former is the hall for birthday celebration, and the latter, Buddhist temple. There are two groups of Buddhist temples on their two sides, called Baoyunge and Zhuanlunzang. These architectures are built along the slope of the hill from the foot to the top, forming a gigantic group of buildings, sitting on the center of the Longevity Hill, facing south, which is the major body of Qingyiyuan. Especially the Pavilion of Buddhist Incense, the height itself is 40 meters, a four-story building in octagon shape, stand on the halfway up hill slope, with a large stone terrace below and glazed tiles on top, the image of which is very prominent, becoming the center of the front hill and front lake area, and also the landmark of Qingyiyuan. On the east and west sides of this group of major architectures, there are also Jingfuge, Huazhongyou and other groups of buildings and pavilions, etc., symmetrically arranged on the front slope of the Longevity Hill, they are either in groups or in individuals, vividly standing among the surrounding pines and cypresses, becoming important scenic spots on the slope. If one climbs up Jingfuge or the pavilion of Huazhongyou, he may enjoy a birds-eye-view of the hill and lake, so they are also good places for enjoying the landscape. Along the south foot of the Longevity Hill, there is a long corridor from east to west, which is as long as 728 meters. Walking in the corridor, one enjoys the beautiful scenery of the Kunming Lake on the outer side, and the group after group of buildings along the hill slope on the inner side, the corridor seems to link these buildings into a scroll of paintings; inside the corridor, there are colored paintings on all the beams and lintels, showing traditional legendary tales, famous scenes from operas, plants and landscape. A long corridor for escaping from the rain and sun becomes one for sightseeing and virtually an art gallery which is unique in all the imperial gardens.

**Rear Hill and Rear Lake Area** Originally, there was no lake in rear hill, and the distance between the feet of the hill to the north wall is only several dozen meters. But, within this long strip of land, a man made stream is dug, and the earth dug out is piled up on the north side of the stream to make an earth hill. The water from the Kunming Lake was diverted into the stream from the west end of the Longevity Hill to make a stream with many twists and turns between two hills. The stream is not wide, but purposefully, it is made wide here and narrow there, the wide part becoming a lake, the narrow part, a strait. When sightseeing by boat, sometimes, one feels the stream is deep in the valley, gripped by two hills, sometimes, the boat comes to an open area. Little bridges and wharfs are dotted here and there. When coming to the middle part of the stream, one sees stores line on both shores, selling cloth and silk, shoes and hats, pastries and tea leaves, and many kinds of snacks, one store linked with another. In front of each store, a sign is flying, and some stores even have archways built to create an atmosphere of a busy street. Emperor Qianlong liked those business streets on rivers in Suzhou and Nanjing area when he toured the south, and now, he made it a point to build a similar street on the river in Qingyiyuan, so it was called "Rear Hill Suzhou Street". Of course, this Suzhou Street was just for demonstration. When the Emperor was arriving, the eunuchs and palace girls would serve as temporary buyers and sellers coming and going through the stores and along the street. The Emperor, coming along the

Xumilingjing architectural group, rear hill

stream in his dragon boat would be drunk with joy in such boisterous atmosphere. After the Emperor finished his tour, the demonstration was over, the stores closed, and the street became quiet on a quiet stream. At the middle of the rear hill slope, a group of Lama Temples is built in the form of Tibetan Lamasery to show the respect by the Court towards the Tibetan nationality, for the purpose of strengthening the unity between nationalities. There are many Buddhist temples, arranged according to the hill situation on the upper or lower part of the slope, which are the major part of the architectures on the rear hill. Besides, there are several small gardens scattered in the forests of the rear hill, not easily visible. So, in the rear hill, with a stream snaking by the foot of the hill, earth hill on both sides, there is a hill path half way up the hill, trees on both sides, forming the scenic area of rear hill and rear lake. If a comparison is made between the two, the front hill area is open and wide, while the rear hill area is deep and quiet, constituting a sharp contrast. This demonstrates the super technological level of the builders, enabling Qingyiyuan to become a representative piece of the Chinese traditional garden at a time when the building technology has reached its zenith.

Rear lake, Summer Palace

Suzhou River street, Jiangsu Province

Suzhou Street, rear lake, Summer Palace

Mountain paths in rear hill

# Famous Gardens Looted

In the 6th year (1856) of Xianfeng, England and France launched aggressive war against China. In 1860, the Anglo-French allied forces occupied Beijing, and first of all, the northwestern suburb. They found in front of them, a large area of rich, beautiful and brilliant palaces and gardens, especially, Yuanmingyuan where several emperors of the Qing Dynasty had been staying for a long time, so large quantities of peals and treasures were kept in those palaces. The commander-in-chief of the Anglo-French allied forces even issued an order that soldiers were allowed to loot the palaces at will. More than 10,000 invaders rushed in Yuanmingyuan to engage in a frenzied looting of treasures, and then set fire on the buildings. The fire lasted for two days and two nights which burned to ashes nearly all the halls, pavilions and other buildings amounting to 160 thousand square meters except some stone buildings in the area of western buildings. After Yuanmingyuan, the invaders continued to loot and burn Qingyiyuan, Jingyiyuan of the Fragrant Hill and Jingmingyuan of the Jade Fountain Hill. After the disaster, Qingyiyuan was almost burned

Remnants of Xieqiqu, Yuanmingyuan

Xieqiqu, western buildings, Yuanmingyuan

Yuanyingguan, western buildings, Yuanmingyuan

Yuanyingguan distroyed

to ashes, except some brick and stone architecture. The imposing Foxiangge was gone, only the stone terrace was left there; the business street on the stream was gone, only the stone bases for pillars were left there. The largest imperial gardens area, constructed in a period of 100 years, the essence of Chinese garden art was wantonly and completely destroyed by invaders in a matter of days. It is the greatest insult to China in Chinese history.

In the middle of the 19th century, the Qing Court entered the period of Tongzhi and Guangxu reigns, in which the Empress Dowager Ci Xi dealt with state affairs behind a screen. First of all, Emperor Tongzhi dreamed to restore Yuanmingyuan, but he did not succeed due to repeated wars and insufficient government financial ability. In the 14th year (1888) of Guangxu, the work on restoring Qingyiyuan began. But owing to the limitation of financial sources, only the front hill and front lake area and the palaces were restored which took ten years, and the name was changed to "Yiheyuan" (Summer Palace), meaning, a peaceful and happy remaining life for Empress Dowager Ci Xi. In 1900, the eight allied forces occupied Beijing, and the invaders from Britain, Russia, Italy and others stationed in Yiheyuan for over a year. The treasures in the garden were looted again, and architectural decorations sabotaged. In 1902, Empress Dowager Ci xi repaired Yiheyuan again, in order to celebrate her 70th birthday in the garden. This was the last time the feudal dynasty made use of this imperial garden.

After New China was established, these imperial gardens received good protection. The totally destructed Yuanmingyuan became "Ruined Garden", from which, farmers, factories, schools and government organs were moved out, the topography and water system in those areas were gradu-

Jianbi Pavilion rebuilt, Yuanmingyuan

Stone terrace under Foxiangge Pavilion after the burning of Qingyiyuan

Bridge remnants, Yuanmingyuan

God of Silk Worm Temple rebuilt, Yuanmingyuan

ally restored, and a few key scenic spots were also reconstructed. The Kunming Lake of Summer Palace has been dredged several times, and water is now full and cleaner; the old channel linking the lake with the city has been dredged and reopened, becoming a new route for sightseeing; the architectures in the front hill area have been repaired many times; the business street and a few small gardens have been reconstructed; in the lake area, the then scenic spots of the Picture of Ploughing and Weaving and the Temple of the God of Silk Worm have all been restored. In 1998, the Summer Palace was ratified by the UNESCO to the list of "World Cultural Heritage".

Renovated waterway of Yuanmingyuan

Qinzheng Hall rebuilt in Jingyiyuan, Fragrant Hill

# Chapter 8
# Private Gardens

In Chinese ancient gardens, private garden is an important type on the par with imperial gardens. It has been mentioned in the previous chapter that as early as the two Hans period, princes, big officials and rich landlords began to build gardens in their residences, opening the history of private garden building. But it was during the period of Wei, Jin and the Southern and Northern Dynasties that private gardens were accepted by the people. Owing to repeated wars and social instability, many men of letters and officials left political arena and cities into the countryside, indulging themselves in nature. They enjoyed watching and studying landscape and plants, and for a time, landscape poems and paintings flourished, through which, they tried to express their own personal feelings. Apart from touring the natural mountains and rivers, these people also created the scenes of mountains and water in their own residences in the hope of seeking the interesting aspects of the natural landscape, thus, private gardens gained big development. According to historical records, there were many private gardens in Luoyang city during the Northern Wei period.

The Tang Dynasty was at the zenith of Chinese feudal society, with a stable political life and developing economy. At that time, apart from several imperial gardens in the capital, there were private gardens in most of the lanes in Chang'an. The famous poet, Bai Juyi had his garden built meticulously in his own residence in Luoyang, and wrote an article to describe his garden. The residence of the poet occupied the land of only a little over ten mu, in which, buildings only took up one third, water pool, one fifth, bamboo forest, one ninth, the rest were for little island, bridge, roads and plants. The area was not large, yet containing many things, in which, the poet led a life of reading and writing poems while drinking wine, enjoying songs and dances, did everything he liked leisurely, and did not wish to leave there until the end of his life. One can imagine to what extent was the poet attached to the garden residence.

The private gardens of the Ming and Qing dynasties inherited the tradition of garden building of the Tang and Song dynasties, and further developed on that basis in many places, especially, the northern private gardens taking Beijing as the center, and the southern ones taking Suzhou, Yangzhou and Hangzhou as the center.

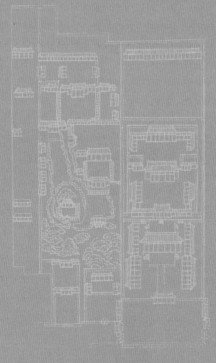

# Private Gardens, Beijing

Beijing was the capital of the Ming and Qing dynasties, where, there were large numbers of imperial relatives and big officials who had both money and power. When they built a residence, there must be a garden attached, and that was the garden residence of Beijing. In the Qing Dynasty, all the princes were concentrated in Beijing, who was given high positions with a handsome salary, but no real power. In order to keep these princes, a number of special residences were built, called prince residence. They were larger than ordinary quadrangles and more elaborate. Different grades of residences are given to princes and members of aristocracy according to hierarchy. Prince residences have gardens attached, either behind the houses, or on one side. Prince residence was a special kind of private garden in Beijing.

## Prince Gong Residence Garden

Prince Gong Residence is a very large residence. Located on the west side of Shichahai, its garden part occupies an area of 28 thousand square meters, the largest and well protected one among all the prince residence gardens. Behind the residence is the garden which is divided into three columns from left to right abreast. The middle column is the major part, composed of the gate to the garden, a water pool, Anshantang Hall, a big man-made hill and two halls with two yards, all of which are on the central axis. The water pool and the halls are made in the shape of a bat which symbolizes "happiness", thus, they are called "Bat River" and "Bat Hall"; on the wall of a cave in the man-made hill, there carved a big Chinese character *Fu* (happiness) hand-written by Emperor Kangxi himself, indicating the master's loyalty to the Emperor. The eastern column is composed of a courtyard in front and a theater in the rear, a place for the master to enjoy operas. The west-

Song painting, *Buddhist temple in mountains*

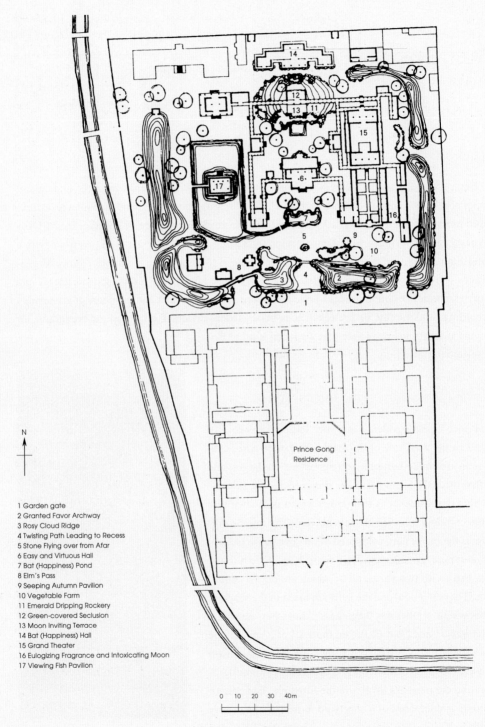

N

1 Garden gate
2 Granted Favor Archway
3 Rosy Cloud Ridge
4 Twisting Path Leading to Recess
5 Stone Flying over from Afar
6 Easy and Virtuous Hall
7 Bat (Happiness) Pond
8 Elm's Pass
9 Seeping Autumn Pavilion
10 Vegetable Farm
11 Emerald Dripping Rockery
12 Green-covered Seclusion
13 Moon Inviting Terrace
14 Bat (Happiness) Hall
15 Grand Theater
16 Eulogizing Fragrance and Intoxicating Moon
17 Viewing Fish Pavilion

Prince Gong
Residence

0  10  20  30  40m

Plan. Prince Gong Residence

Left: (up) Anshan Hall, Prince Gong Residence Garden
     (down) Eastern column of Prince Gong Residence
Right: (up) Bat Hall, Prince Gong Residence
     (down) Big Theatre, Prince Gong Residence

ern column is composed mainly of water and hill scenery, with a big pool built in the center, and a water-side pavilion in the middle of the pool, flanked by rocky hills. Prince Gong Residence Garden is located in downtown area, but it succeeded in creating a quiet garden environment, thanks to the adoption of man-made hills and the different spaces created by building different halls, winding corridors and rocky hills.

## Xichunyuan

While the Qing Court was building the imperial gardens in the northwestern suburb on a large scale, it also built some small residence gardens and bestowed them on princes and imperial relatives, called "bestow gardens" which were a special kind of private gardens. Xichunyuan was one of them. It is located to the east of Yuanmingyuan, inside the present Tsinghua University. It was built in the reign (1662-1722) of Kangxi, and bestowed to two princes to live during the reign (1821-1850) of Daoguang. Afterwards, it was divided into two parts; the eastern part was Qinghuayuan, and the western part, Jinchunyuan. The architectures in Jinchunyuan were dismantled during the reign of Tongzhi, but remnants are still there. Qinghuayuan has been kept intact for three hundred years,

Viewing Fish Pavilion, Prince Gong Residence

Jinchunyuan, Beijing

226

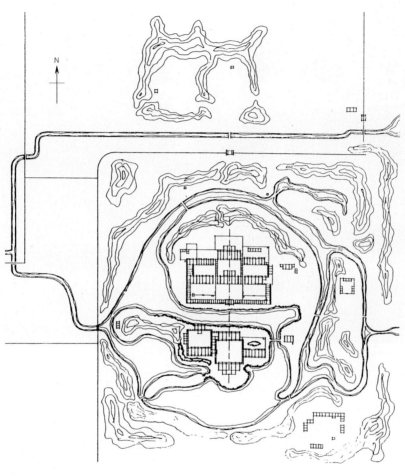

Plan. Xichunyuan, Beijing

Residence, Qinghuayuan

Square Pavilion, Qinghuayuan

Lake, Qinghuayuan

which is very rare among all the gardens built during the reign of Kangxi.

The two gardens are all built on plane ground by digging the ground to make a pool, and piling the earth from the pool up into a hill. In Jinchunyuan, the pool is in the shape of a ring, and in the center is the ground on which buildings are put up, surrounded by earth hills, thus, the garden is surrounded by water scenery from outside. The layout of Qinghuayuan is a formal quadrangle, with residences in front and garden in the rear. The residence is composed of two buildings, front and rear, and one column on each side, linked by winding corridors and accessible through round doors on the walls. In the yards, there are rocky hills, begonia and pear trees, truly a garden-like residence. Behind the residence is a big water pool, with irregular water surface, filled with lotus. On the northwestern corner is an earth hill, on which are planted pines and cypresses, and on water front, willows, forming a secluded yet pleasant garden environment.

# Private Gardens, Jiangnan Area

The building of mountain-water gardens are depended on natural, economic and cultural conditions. The Jiangnan Area of China is geographically rich in water resources with rivers and lakes crisscrossing the whole area. Its climate belongs to the temperate zone with ample rainfall and mild winter which is very suitable for the vegetation. Politically, when the center of China was suffering from repeated wars during the post Tang period of Five Dynasties and Ten States, the Wuyue State of this area maintained peaceful and stable situation which lasted about 80 years

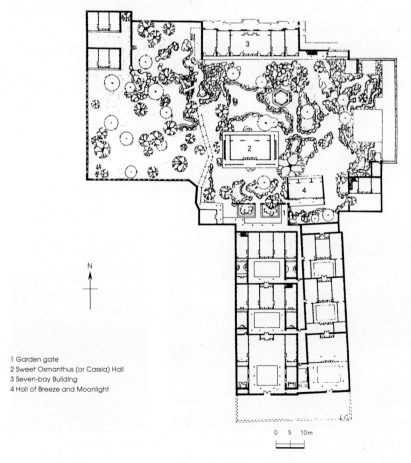

N

1 Garden gate
2 Sweet Osmanthus (or Cassia) Hall
3 Seven-bay Building
4 Hall of Breeze and Moonlight

0  5  10m

Plan. Geyuan, Yangzhou, Jiangsu Province

until the Northern Song period. The Southern Song moved its capital to Lin'an, which further promoted the development of political stability, economy and culture of this area. Since ancient times, this area has been rich and profound in the Han cultural tradition, bringing about a galaxy of talents. The Tang poet Bai Juyi and Song poet Su Shi both held the position of *zhifu* (mayor) of Hangzhou. They not only presided over the renovating of the West Lake, built the Bai Dyke and Su Dyke in the lake, but also left behind many poems in praise of the beautiful scenery of the lake, greatly enriched the local cultural connotation. After Southern Song Dynasty moved its capital to Lin'an, many officials and men of letters followed here. They wrote poems and painted pictures, greatly promoted the flourishing of landscape poems and pictures in this area. Superior natural environment, stable political situation, prosperous economy, and profound cultural traditional, all these have provided favorable conditions for garden building. Yangzhou of Jiangsu Province, situated at the juncture of the Yangtze River and the north-south Grand Canal was a port for foreign trade since the Tang Dynasty, with a highly developed commerce and a concentration of merchants, therefore, a prosperous city. Suzhou was at the center of southern Jiangsu, famous for its silk production since ancient times, with developed handicrafts and commerce. It was already a famous city in the Tang Dynasty. There was a system of streets as well as a system of rivers in the city. The business street by the river attracted the attention of Emperor Qianlong and was imitated in the imperial garden in Beijing. Many officials and rich merchants came to Suzhou to buy land, in order to build residences for spending their times after retirement. Thus, many private garden residences gathered in Yangzhou and Suzhou. As of today, there are still many private gardens left from the Ming and Qing period, which are the representatives of private gardens of the Jiangnan Area.

Bamboo grove in front of gate, Geyuan

Autumn Hill, Geyuan

Summer Hill, Geyuan

## Geyuan of Yangzhou

Located inside Yangzhou City, Geyuan was built in the 23rd year (1818) of Jiaqing, the private garden of a rich merchant of the locality, Huang Yingtai. The garden is behind the residence of the Huang family, a small one, occupying an area of about 0.55 hectare in square form. The garden gate is in the middle of the south side, bamboos on both sides of the gate, and bamboo sprouts made of stone are planted in them, meaning "spring bamboo grows wild after rain". Entering the gate, one confronts a hall, with many cassia trees planted in front of it, thus, it is called "Cassia Hall". Immediately behind the hall is a pool, and north of the pool is a two story building with two large-size rocky hills on its side. And the essence of Geyuan lies in the man-made rockeries hills.

Rocky hill number one, located on the northwest side of the pool, built totally with Taihu rocks. It is about four meters high and in big proportion, yet it does not seem clumsy because the shape of Taihu rocks is naturally and ingeniously formed with all kinds of holes on them. The hill is close by the pool and there are stone caves built in the hill, which are deep and twisted. Pool water is introduced into the cave, and above water, stone benches are constructed. It is especially cool in summer, so it is called "summer hill".

Rocky hill number two, located on the northeast side of the pool, built totally with yellow stones. It is about seven meters high and bigger in proportion than the summer hill. A square pavilion is built on top of the hill; the raised corners of the roof offset the sense of heaviness of the piling rocks. There is also a cave in the hill, in which there is a stone table and stone stools, and also stone steps winding up and down inside. The hill made by piling yellow stones look very strong, in dark yellow color, under the setting sun, the hill shows golden autumn color, so it is called "autumn hill".

To the east side of its south gate, there is a hall, in front of which and along the wall is a hill of Taihu rocks, all in white, as if there is snow on the rocks. And on the walls, there are row upon row of round holes, so that when there is wind, the sound resembles the north wind in winter. This hall is for enjoying snow scenery by the side of a heating stove, so this hall is called "winter hill". This hill, together with summer hill, autumn hill and the spring hill which is the stone bamboo shoot amid the bamboo plants by the side of the gate are all in one garden, a special feature of Geyuan of Yangzhou, and this garden is famous because of the hills of four seasons.

## Garden of the Master of Nets in Suzhou

Located inside of Suzhou City, the Garden of the Master of Nets (Wangshiyuan) was first built in the Southern Song Dynasty. During the reign (1875-1908) of Guangxu of the Qing Dynasty, it was renovated by the then master to its present status. It occupies only 0.4 hectare, a medium residence garden inside the city. The residence and the garden are closely connected, with the residence occupies the southeastern part, while the garden, northwest part. The residence part is composed of four yards: in the order of, the gate, sedan chair hall, big hall, main hall. Several high and bright halls and formal yards demonstrate an imposing manner of the residence. All the halls have black tiles, white walls and brown beams inside the halls. The wooden furniture in original color, together with ornaments and books and paintings, all shows an air of elegance. Above the gates of the front wall and rear wall are brick carving crowns, totally imitating timber-frame structures. There are several layers of beams at the bottom upon which is a layer of bracket-set which in turn supports the roof. On the roof are the ridge and roof corners, and all the members are made of bricks. Those raised roof corners, the bracket-sets, the cranes, lions, *lingzhi* (precious herbal fungus), lotus flowers carved on the beams, those carved pictures of figures of operas between the beams and lintels are very time and labor consuming when carved on timber, requiring high technique, but they were all carved on bricks which is even harder. This demonstrates super technological level of the artisans of Suzhou area.

The garden is located to the west of the residence, which takes the pool as the center, surrounded by pavilion, terrace and storied buildings, among which are pavilion and storied pavilion facing water, a studio for reading and writing poems and painting pictures. Between them are piles of stones and rocks with pines and cypresses planting on them, forming different kinds of scenery. The pool is almost a regular square; each side is only 20 meters, but the builders put more turns on the four corners, especially the southeast and northwest tips are shrunk into small streams flowing into the man-made hills, which makes one wonder about the origin of the water. A stone bridge on the pool divides the water into big and small areas, which reduces the feeling of a small and stiff water surface. The masters of Suzhou garden residences in the later Qing period were

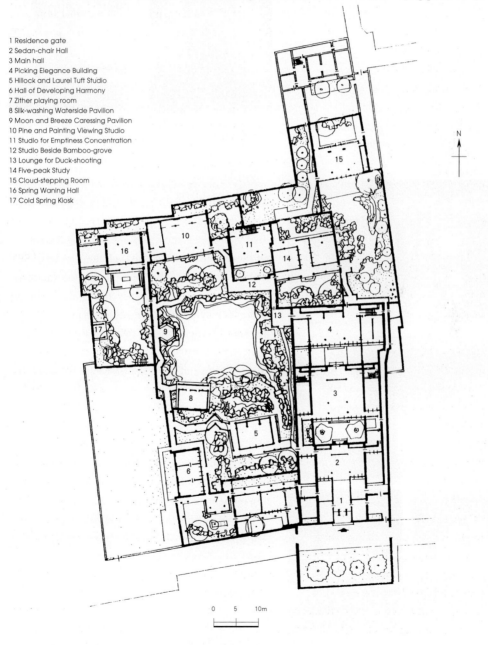

1 Residence gate
2 Sedan-chair Hall
3 Main hall
4 Picking Elegance Building
5 Hillock and Laurel Tuft Studio
6 Hall of Developing Harmony
7 Zither playing room
8 Silk-washing Waterside Pavilion
9 Moon and Breeze Caressing Pavilion
10 Pine and Painting Viewing Studio
11 Studio for Emptiness Concentration
12 Studio Beside Bamboo-grove
13 Lounge for Duck-shooting
14 Five-peak Study
15 Cloud-stepping Room
16 Spring Waning Hall
17 Cold Spring Kiosk

0   5   10m

Plan. Wangshiyuan, Suzhou, Jiangsu Province

Gate of Wangshiyuan Garden, "Zhusongchengmao"

Gate of Wangshiyuan Garden, "Zaoyaogaoxiang"

Up: Studio for Viewing Pines and
      Appreciating Paintings
Central: Zhuwaiyizhixuan Studio
      (Lone Bamboo outside the Grove)
Down: front hall, Wangshiyuan

mostly officials and rich merchants whose positions and interests were different from their predecessors since the Tang and Song period. They are not satisfied with the isolated, self-appreciating leisure life of those men of letters. Instead, they are busy with social activities, and require multi-functional architectures: guestroom, study, hall for dining guests, room for playing musical instruments plus many scenic spots. Wangshiyuan is just such a garden, the architectural density of which is 30 percent, and even more if the front and back yards are included, the pure garden part occupies only a little over half of the whole garden residence. It is very difficult to create an environment of natural landscape in such a garden, but the builders, through their designing, succeeded in building a garden of natural interest by combining closely the architectures and gardens, arranging meticulously pavilions, terraces, storied buildings and piling up rocks for hills. Therefore, Wangshiyuan became a masterpiece among Suzhou gardens. "Suzhou Gardens" have been listed as "World Cultural Heritage" by the UNESCO, and Wangshiyuan is one of them.

Moon and Breeze Caressing Pavilion

# Theory and Technology of Chinese Ancient Garden Building

The Chinese ancient gardens took shape during the Qin and Han, developed through the Wei, Jin, Southern and Northern dynasties, Tang and Song till maturity, reached the highest peak in the Ming and Qing dynasties. In the course of productive practice lasting for more than two thousand years, large numbers of capable and wise artisans were brought up, among whom, there were artisans for all kinds of work: piling up rocks to make a hill, digging the ground to create a water system, building architectures, growing plants, etc. Their technologies were passed on from generation to generation and through a long time inheritance and acumination, a group of masters emerged in all fields. It is due to their painstaking labor that many exquisite gardens were created, and on the basis of which, a group of theoretical books concerning garden building were published, among which, the most important one was *Yuan Ye* (*Garden Building*) by Mr. Ji Cheng.

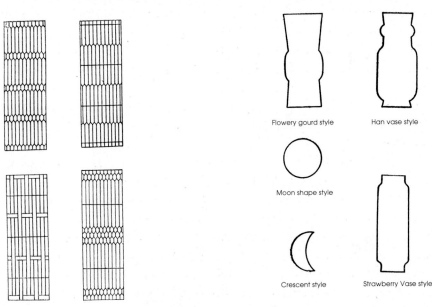

Flowery gourd style     Han vase style

Moon shape style

Crescent style     Strawberry Vase style

Different types of windows in *Yuan Ye* (*Garden Building*)     Different types of doors in *Yuan Ye*

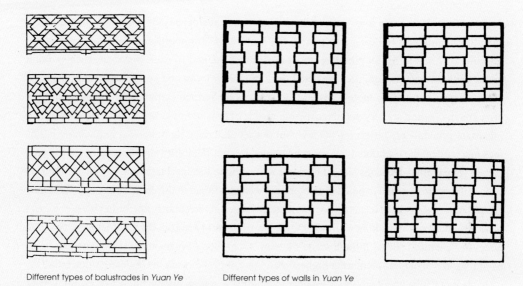

Different types of balustrades in *Yuan Ye*    Different types of walls in *Yuan Ye*

Mr. Ji Cheng was born in the 10th year (1582) of the Wanli reign of Ming Dynasty, a native of Wujiang, Jiangsu Province. He loved painting when he was young, and in his middle age, he traveled widely and toured many gardens and places of interest. After he returned to his homeland, he chose to live in Zhenjiang and began to practice garden building. At first, he built hills by piling up rocks for some people, which resembled genuine hills. Later, he gradually participated in the planning and designing of gardens. Because he was very good at learning and studying, and his technological level developed from better to the best, so the gardens he built won widespread praises from the public, which were found in Zhenjiang, Nanjing, Yangzhou and other places, thus, he became a well-known specialist of garden building. Since he enjoyed both solid cultural foundation and rich experiences in garden building, he finally published the book *Yuan Ye* at the age of 52. This is a book on garden building, and the most important theoretical writing on gardens in ancient China.

*Garden Building* gives an all-round description of the theory and practice concerning Chinese gardens from the planning, designing, building to the patterns of doors, windows, walls, the floor, and the hill making and the selection of stones. Roughly, it can be generalized into three categories. The first concerns the knowledge about gardens and the building technique. For example, in the section of architectural decorations, the book lists 62 kinds of windows and more than 100 kinds of balustrade patterns. And in the section of walls, the special features of all kinds of walls, the materials used, the method of building as well as the places suitable for the walls are described, with the drawing patterns of those walls attached. The second concerns the summery of garden building experiences. In the chapter of "ground examination", the author analyses the different environment of mountain forest, city, village, suburb and residence side, and suggests the corresponding features of building gardens. In the section of "stone hill arrangement" and "stone selection", 17 best forms for piling up stones are introduced, and 16 stone materials, such as Taihu rocks, yellow stones and granites are listed, including their looks and how to use them. The third concerns garden building theory. Mr. Ji Cheng gives theoretical summery of the planning, the principle in creating scenery and the concrete means of how to implement it. He puts forward an important principle of "observing the law, but not set patterns". He holds that in planning buildings in a garden, the traditional law must be abided by, but flexibility should be adopted towards certain set patterns; decisions should be made according to the special features of the building as well as the environment. He believes that principle can be found in different forms, and variations can reflect certain rules. He states that no matter whether in the countryside or in cities, one must observe natural law in making a hill, digging a pool and build a house, etc. in order to achieve the effect of "a natural scene, though made by man". A garden of man-made landscape can be as natural as in real nature; such is the highest realm one hopes to reach in Chinese garden building.

In ancient China, there are four elements in building a garden: mountain, water, buildings and plants. Now, I wish to state both from theory and practice.

## Piling up a Hill and Managing Water

Among the four elements, mountain and water occupy very important position. Without mountain and water, there is no Chinese garden.

**Piling up Hills** Apart from a few imperial gardens which include real mountains in them, man-made hills are needed in most of the gardens. In nature, there are earth mountains, rock mountains and mountains with both; it is the same in the garden. We can use earth, rock or a mixture of them in making a hill in a garden. The ancients hold: rock mountain has a weathered look, but no grass can grow on it; the earth mountain is not erect and imposing; the best choice is the mixture of earth and rock, with the earth inside and rock outside, which maintains the mountain shape as well

Earth and rock hill in a garden

Rock hill, Heyuan, Yangzhou

Large-size rock hill, Jingxinzhai (Tranquil Heart Studio), Beihai, Beijing

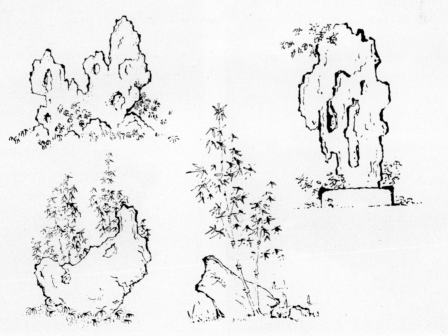

Different types of lone stones in gardens

as the vegetation. Since the garden to be built is a mountain water garden, it should be as natural as possible. But if a miniature mountain is put in a garden, it is bound to be like a big pot-scenery. So the ancients believe that the essence or the typical look of a mountain should be reproduced in the garden. Mr. Ji Cheng sums up the key points in making a hill in his book *Garden Building*: when two mountains are side by side, one should be higher, the other lower; one should be the main, the other subordinate, and they should not be the same in shape. A famous mountain can be viewed from a distance, but inside it, mountain stream, mountain gully, mountain cave and waterfall can all be scenic spots for people to enjoy. Therefore, for those bigger hills in the gardens, apart from the natural outlook which is important, it is better to arrange a stream, climbing steps and caves.

Apart from piling up rocks to make a hill, it is very common to see a single rock which forms a scene in Chinese gardens. Very often, a single piece of grotesque rock is an ancient picture worth appreciating. When Emperor Huizong built the imperial garden in Bianliang, he specially sent people to Suzhou to collect strange rocks. Those rocks were arranged on both sides of the road inside the garden gate to form a special scenic area. According to the ancient people, the beauty of a rock lies in its shape: it should be a slender instead of a sturdy one, to show its dexterousness; the surface should not be smooth, but full of wrinkles to show it is time-tested;

Water pool: water ends under the pavilion

Yellow stone shore of water pool

there should be holes on it to show it is hollow and easily changes its images. This kind of shapes is often found on the Taihu rocks of southern China, so the best shape of the Taihu rocks is generalized to be "hollow, transparent, slender and wrinkled".

Stone bridge in water pool, garden of northern China

Stone bridge in water pool, garden of southern China

Taihu rock shore of water pool

**Managing Water** Gardens can not be separated with mountain and water, with mountain, they seem to be old; with water, and they are intelligent. None of the natural lakes are formal; therefore the pool in the garden should never be formal, even though the outside shape is formal, the four shores should be made with turns. When the surface is wide enough, it is advisable to build a little dyke or bridge to partition it into different sizes of water area, or to pile up a small hill in water to achieve water scenery of multiple layers. When the surface is not wide enough, it is better to shrink the pool corner into a slender water mouth to divert the water beneath the pavilion or a pile of rocks, just like the pool in Wangshiyuan, which gives an impression of the water having a source but the origin is not to be found, so that a pool of still water becomes lively. Attention must be made concerning the treatment of the shores of the pool, since the pool should not be a square, likewise the shores can not be with square rocks. A natural river or lake must have an earthen shore; only a lake in the mountain may have irregular rock shore. The shore in a garden should be both natural and solid, so yellow stone and Taihu rocks are commonly used, or a mixture of earth and stone. To decorate the shore, it is not advisable to use square and leveled stones; there should be ups and downs, and a mixture of dense and sparse rocks. In a word, all should be natural, from the shape of the pool to the shores.

## Architecture Management

There must be architectures in gardens, the only difference lies in the number of buildings. The first special feature of garden architecture is that there are many types of them. In the imperial garden, Yiheyuan, there are halls of palace architecture, temples of religious architecture, and many types of garden architecture: pavilion, terrace, storied building, storied pavilion, studio, waterside pavilion, covered corridor, bridge, as well as stores, wall gates, archway, wharf, boat house, farm house etc., almost all the types of architectures are included. In Wangshiyuan which is not large, there are more than ten types, such as hall, storied building, house, studio, waterside kiosk, pavilion, covered corridor, etc.

Beside the different types, there are many forms. The main hall in the palace area of the Summer Resort in Chengde is also an important place for dealing with state affairs, but the glazed tiles are not used here, only the ordinary pottery tiles, and there are no colored paintings as decoration on the doors, windows, beams and lintels, only the precious nanmu is used. In building pavilions and waterside arbors, the ancient builders are opposed to certain definite form; they are for deciding the form according to the concrete situation in the garden. That is why both in southern and northern gardens, we can see different forms of pavilions: square, rectangular, hexagon, octagon, plum flower pattern, cross, round, two round pavilions interlocking, two square pavilions interlocking, etc. The gallery is very common in gardens, which can be used as a shelter from rain

Different types of garden pavilions: rectangular pavilion (Zhuozhengyuan, Suzhou)

Different types of garden pavilions: octagonal pavilion (Beihai, Beijing)

Different types of garden pavilions: pavilions on water (West Lake, Hangzhou)

Different types of garden pavilions: pavilion with zigzag roof corners (Mountain Resort, Chengde)

Different types of garden pavilions: two round pavilions interlocking (Temple of Heaven, Beijing)

Left: (up) different types of garden pavilions: two square
        pavilion interlocking (Temple of Heaven, Beijing)
      (central) different types of garden galleries: bridge
        gallery (Suzhou garden)
      (down) different types of garden galleries: wall gallery
        (Beihai, Beijing)
Right: (up) different types of garden galleries: straight gallery
        (Summer Palace, Beijing)
      (central) different types of garden galleries: zigzag
        gallery (Suzhou garden)
      (down) different types of garden galleries: water gallery
        (Zhuozhengyuan, Suzhou)

Different types of doors in Suzhou gardens: house door

Different types of doors in Suzhou gardens: round door

Different types of doors in Suzhou gardens: round door

Different types of doors in Suzhou gardens: pavilion door

Different types of windows in Suzhou gardens: latticed windows on garden wall

Different types of windows in Suzhou gardens:
window opening without screens

Different types of windows in Suzhou gardens:
window opening without screens

Windows opening without screens in Liuyuan, Suzhou

Up: (left) different types of windows in Suzhou gardens: house window
    (right) different types of windows in Suzhou gardens: window with flowery decorations
Down: (left) garden floor in Suzhou gardens
     (right) garden floor in Suzhou gardens

and sunshine, and also as a partition. Beside the commonly seen straight and zigzag galleries, there are wave-like galleries, double galleries, water galleries, galleries attached to a wall, climbing galleries and dropping galleries, etc.

In a residence, doors can be divided into the gate, door of a yard, door of a room, which can be opened or closed with a few exceptions of the yard doors. But it is different in gardens. For the pavilion, waterside pavilion, studio and room, the doors can also be used as objects for sightseeing, beside their function of being used as entrance and exit. Therefore, the studios and rooms usually have no wall on one side or several sides, instead, screen doors are used, which can all be opened if necessary. For some pavilions and studios, there are no screen doors, instead, round, or multi side gate holes are assembled, so that they are at the same time objects for sightseeing as well as for passage.

The function of a window is for getting light and ventilation, which can be opened and closed. But in a garden, windows can form a scene and be used for sightseeing. In some studios, waterside pavilions and houses, the windows on the walls are just window openings without window screen, from which, one can look out at the pavilions and buildings in a distance, or a pile of rocks, bamboo and banana leaves nearby, and in this case, the window is used as a frame within which one sees a picture, called "window picture". In many private gardens of the Jiangnan Area, in order to create a changing space in a small area, the wall is often used to partition the garden. To avoid the feeling of seclusion and tightness, window openings are often used on the wall to achieve the effect of separation, yet interrelated. Some window openings are decorated with hollow flower patterns, called flower windows or leakage windows, some have no decorations at all. Such window openings have very rich forms, which is a unique scene of the gardens in the Jiangnan Area.

Raising your head, you see architectures, lowering your head, you see the road. So, the pavement in a garden also needs designing. To imitate nature, a formal road of stone slabs is rarely used. Normally, pebbles, crushed stones, bricks and tiles are used to form different patterns as pavement and garden floor. They are simple and natural, especially after a spring rain, tiny green grass would grow out of the stone crack which adds life to the garden.

## Planting Design

No matter whether in Chinese or western gardens, trees and flowers are indispensable, only the designing is different. In Chinese gardens, planting design is even more important in order to

Plants by balustrade, garden of southern China

Begonia trees, courtyard, Summer Palace, Beijing

Lotus, Summer Palace

Willow trees by the pool, Summer Palace

Water-lily, Summer Palace

251

Old pines, Summer Palace

Bamboo grove, Suzhou gardens

create an environment of natural mountain landscape or a plain wildness.

To pile up some hills, dig a pool and build some houses in a garden can be completed in a year or so, but it takes years for the plants to grow, especially for the ever green pines, cypresses and other precious trees. Therefore, it has been a set rule in building gardens to preserve the existing plants on the site of a garden. The Tang poet Bai Juyi built a residence for himself in Lushan Mountain of Jiangxi Province, named Thatched Cottage. On the original site, there were several dozen pines, about a thousand bamboos, and under the pines were abundant bushes, which were all preserved by the poet. Those tree branches and leaves shielded the poet in hot summer, with a little breeze; it was as cool as in autumn. All the plants in the mountain area of the Summer Resort in Chengde were preserved, furthermore, a scenic area "pine and cloud strait" was created by using the original large area of pines. But it is very rare for the private gardens in the cities to have such favorable conditions. The plants would have to rely on the artisans to grow and nurture meticulously in order to achieve expected results. The garden builders have summed up a lot of experiences through long-time building activities. For examples: in front of a hall or terrace and beside the balustrade, it is better to have an old pine tree; near the stone steps of a house, some grass flowers would add vitality to the environment; water plants should not be planted full in the pool, even the most beautiful lotus should be controlled in the pool; on a large water surface, it is better to grow the lotus in a farther away area, while the sleeping lily can be planted nearby, because, lotus grows to form a big area with big flowers and leaves which can be enjoyed from a distance, while the flower of sleeping lily is small and delicate which is suitable for viewing in close range; peach and apricot trees are not suitable to plant in a yard, because they are good to look from afar; beans and vegetables are for the farmland, not for a courtyard, but they are suitable on an open land in the garden; etc. These are incisive viewpoints summed up from practice.

## Scenic Spots and Scenic View

   To see a garden is to see the garden environment and the scenic spots in the garden. The scenic spot is for viewing, so it can also called scenic view. The garden builder is to create many scenic spots and organize them well for the tourists to view. The mountain, water, architectures and plants are the basic elements of the garden; naturally, they are also the basic elements of the scenic spots or scenic view. Each of them can be a scene independently, or combine with the others to be a scene.

   Mountains form a scene naturally by itself. The mountains in Summer Resort with many peaks and deep forests become the major scenery of the resort. In private gardens, the hills are usually

Left: (up) Guanyunfeng Stone, Liuyuan Garden, Suzhou
      (down) stone scenery by a wall
Right: (up) stone scenery in heaven well of Liuyuan
      (down) stone scenery in water

253

Smoke-rain Building, Mountain Resort, Chengde

Gold Hill Temple, Mountain Resort

piled up with rocks. In Geyuan of Yangzhou, different stones and different methods are used to form the scenery of the spring, summer, autumn and winter. Not only this, a single rock can also become a scene. In Liuyuan (Lingering Garden) of Suzhou, a gigantic rock is erected in the middle of a courtyard, which can be enjoyed from all sides, named "Cloud Hat Peak", a famous scene of the garden. Such single rock scene or the stone scenery composed of several rocks, small in proportion and varied in forms, can stand in front of a hall, by a wall, or in the middle of a pool, they are widely adopted both in imperial gardens or private gardens.

To create scenery with architectures is a means commonly used in gardens; it can be as big as a group of halls, or as small as a single pavilion. The numerous architectures in the lake area of the Summer Resort scattered on those islands, among which the Gold Hill Pavilion standing alone on the hill top, its imposing storied pavilion becomes very prominent. Another one is the Smoke-rain Building, its two-story hall standing by the lake, with a pavilion and a waterside pavilion accompanying it by the side. They form a group which is more prominent than all the nearby buildings. The Gold Hill Pavilion and the Rain-Smoke Building are important scenic spots in the lake area.

Plants can be as big as the pine or cypress, or as small as a bunch of banana or bushes, they can all be a scene if only the posture is good and the place they occupy is appropriate. In the front and back of the private gardens in Suzhou, a kind of cassia trees and loquat trees are often planted, which form a special view of "cassia studio" and "loquat garden". There is an old and decayed wood in a small yard not far from the entrance of the Lingering Garden, its old yet strong branches form a special view, "ancient bare tree branches". Two banana plants by the wall, or a thicket of green bamboo standing near the wall, their green leaves contrasted by the white wall can also be a pleasant scenic view.

The above-mentioned mountain, water, architectures and plants can all be a scene independent, but in most cases, they are combined with each other to form good views. For example, the temple and white pagoda on Jade Flower (Qionghua) Island in Beihai and the Cloud-dispelling Hall and Pavilion of Buddhist Incense on Longevity Hill are all the combinations of mountain and architecture. The two hills are more charming because of these architectures; and the architectures are more imposing because they are standing on these hills. The hills were originally very ordinary, but now, together with the architectures, they become prominent scenic spots bearing cultural connotation. In private gardens, such combination scenery can be seen everywhere. The Sheya Pavilion facing water in the Master of Net Garden in Suzhou, is a one-bay pavilion, with an old pine standing by, the raised roof corners and the branches and leaves of the tree seem both flying up in the air; the rocks piling up stretch to the tree with the white wall as background, the reflection of which in water is a beautiful picture. This is a combination of architecture, plant and rocks. A lonely rock stand by the wall in front of a hall, accompanied by some grass and a few flowers can also be a good view. Even the courtyard floor paved with smashed stones, with a few grass and flowers planted all around it can show a pleasant look of the small slender leaves and flowers contrasting with smashed stones.

Sheya Pavilion, Wangshiyuan, Suzhou

Banana leaves by a wall

Bamboo grove beside a gallery

Rocks and plants

Rocks and plants

White Dagoba in Beihai, Beijing

## Organization of Scenic Spots

The numerous scenic spots in a garden must be organized so that there are major scenes and accompanying ones corresponding to each other which would make the interest of tourists last from the beginning to the end. Only such a garden can be called a successful garden.

To be a scenic spot, its image must be beautiful and peculiar, occupying a suitable place, which can be an object of enjoyment, then it is called "a scene established". When two scenes are in opposition to each other, they must be able to respond to each other, that is, when you enjoy this scene, you can at the same time see the other, then it is called "corresponding scenes". The Pavilion of Buddhist Incense on Longevity Hill is opposite to the Hanxutang on Nanhu Island in Kunming Lake, so they form corresponding scenes. The beautiful scenery outside of the garden can also be organized into the garden, called "borrowed scenes". Mr. Ji Cheng said in his book *Yuan Ye*: looking out from your garden to all directions, all those good scenes can be included into your garden; all those bad scenes should be kept away from your garden. So to borrow scenes, you can borrow from afar, borrow from your neighbor, borrow from a higher place or lower place, and borrow for a certain time. The Jade Fountain Hill is a few kilometers away from the Summer Palace, yet, the pagoda on top of the hill can be borrowed into the Summer Palace, and one can enjoy watching the pagoda both from the Longevity Hill and the Kunming Lake, and this is called "to borrow from afar". For two neighboring courtyards, the storied pavilion in the other yard, and

A view of Jade Peak Pagoda in the distance from Summer Palace

A view of Baoen Temple Pagoda from Liuyuan

Corresponding scene of Buddha Incense Pavilion, Summer Palace

Round door frame scenery from Windy Terrace of Slender West Lake, Yangzhou, Jiangsu Province

even a few red apricot flowers over the wall, can be borrowed into your garden, and this is called to borrow from a neighbor. Looking out from your garden to a high hill, there could be a dense forest, or full of strange rocks and this is called to borrow from a higher place. Looking down from the Jade Flower (Qionghua) Island in Beihai to the Zhongnanhai half hiding in the morning haze is like looking at a picture, and this is called to borrow from a lower place.

In organizing the scenery, the "frame" is often used, that is to use a door, window or pillars as a frame to show the scenes within it. In the Slender West Lake of Yangzhou, there is a pavilion in the Windy Terrace, through the gate of which one can see the pavilion bridge and the white pagoda, and this is called frame scenery. When the scenery is organized by this way, you can get a more concentrated picture, and the sightseeing effect is especially strong. Those well-designed gardens are good at arranging many scenes on a touring route, and by following this route one enjoys one scenic spot after another, among which there are major one and accompanying ones, rich in scenery and no repetition, so that from the beginning to the end, one enjoys a changing scenery after every step.

Looking down at Zhongnanhai from Qionghua Island, Beihai

# Artistic Conception of Chinese Gardens

In artistic creation work, certain ideas conveyed by the creator through images are called artistic conception. Take paintings for example, those things painted on the picture are not only the objects of the existing world, but through the objective images, the painter wishes to express some of his ideas and feelings. The landscape painters travel widely while drawing the natural mountains and water. Through observing and drawing, the painters not only acquire deeper understanding of them, but also acquire his personal feelings towards them. By this time, the landscape painting created by the painter is no longer the particular mountain or water, but his understanding of the mountain and water images in his mind. Many ancient men of letters loved to draw bamboo. They went to the bamboo grove to observe them, imitating the bamboo sticks and leaves with their brushes. They were able to draw on paper only after they have mastered the details of how they grow and what their images are like. But at this time, the bamboo he paints is no longer any particular bamboo grove, but the bamboo with his personal feeling on them. He may express his personal moral integrity by painting the bamboo sticks very straight with strong knots, and the leaves very simple and clear. Thus, the bamboo he paints needs not to be life-like, but should be able to show his feelings. Because of this, the "black ink bamboo" which is peculiar to Chinese painting has been created. Black ink bamboo has replaced green bamboo, what the painter is after is not the form, but the spirit, spiritually-like is far better than life-like, such is the artistic conception in painting.

Likewise, the components of a garden: mountains, water, architectures and plants are not just substance, but imbued with spirit. Because in building the garden, the master projects his thoughts and feelings into the material environment, and when the sightseer is enjoying the scenery, he may strike a responsive chord in his mind, and this is the artistic conception of a garden, an environment which is able to give rise to thoughts and feelings. Whether there is artistic conception or not, or whether it is lofty or not, became an important criteria in evaluating gardens in ancient China.

What methods can be used to create the artistic conception in Chinese gardens?

The methods most commonly used are symbolism and metaphor. Emperor Qinshihuang, instigated by a wizard, sent his envoy together with several thousand boys and girls to the East Sea in the hope of getting longevity fruit on the fairy islands, so that he can live forever and be an eternal emperor, naturally, nothing came out of it. Nevertheless, he diverted the water from Weishui

Old pine trees in Fragrant Hill, Beijing

*Orchids and Bamboo*, painting by Zheng Xie, Qing Dynasty

River into his capital, Xianyang to build a water pool, in which the fairy islands were constructed in order to pray for happiness. This practice of building make-believe fairy islands lasted for a long time. In the imperial palaces of the Han and Tang dynasties, there were pools for the fairy islands. In Taiye Pool of the imperial city of the Yuan Dynasty, there were the three islands. Finally, in the Qing Dynasty, they were in Fuhai of Yuanmingyuan, and in Kunming Lake of the Summer Palace, there are three islands symbolizing the three fairy islands of Penglai, Yingzhou and Fangzhang.

Since the Wei, Jin, Southern and Northern dynasties, many Chinese men of letters and officials loved to indulge in nature to strengthen their moral integrity. They often observed and studied natural objects. They discovered that those pines in the mountains were strong and healthy, green bamboos, upright and knotty, they bent, but not easily break, plum flowers alone bloomed in bitter cold. Their nature and posture remind one of the moral virtues of persistence, pure and simplicity; so, the pine, bamboo and plum are looked upon as the "three friends in winter" which also symbolize the lofty integrity of human beings. Therefore, pine, bamboo and plum become the constant theme of landscape poems and paintings, and they are often planted in gardens. It can be said that there is no garden without pines in north China, and in south China, no garden without bamboos. They have not only created the scenery with their shapes and colors, but also added artistic conception with their special symbolic significance.

Li Shizhen, the famous pharmacist of the Ming Dynasty, gave a detailed account of the lotus, which grows in mud, but it is not affected by the mud in the least, and the lotus flower is pure and beautiful; the lotus root is very crisp, but it can grow in sticky mud without breaking. These special features also contain human life philosophy, meaning, when people are in difficulties, we should still persevere in our endeavors, and in filthy social environment, we should not be affected, but should maintain our lofty virtue. Therefore, painters often paint lotus to encourage friends or for self encouragement. And lotuses are often found both in imperial gardens and in private gardens.

Lake full with lotus, Yuanmingyuan, Beijing

Listening to the Rain Pavilion,
Zhuozhengyuan, Suzhou

There was a scenic spot in Yuanmingyuan around which was a water pool full of lotuses, for which Emperor Qianlong especially wrote an inscription: "all around me are gentlemen". There is a small pavilion built on the clay hill of Zhuozhengyuan (Humble Administrator's Garden), and below the hill is a pool planted with lotuses. In autumn when the flowers have all withered with only lotus leaves left in the pool, then there comes autumn rain and the leaves give a kind of sound. For the learned men, this is called, "the remaining lotus leaves are left there for the purpose of listening to the rain". The remaining leaves have no beauty to speak of, but the sound they give in the autumn rain can produce some imagination of learned men, and then, the little pavilion is named "listening to the rain pavilion" which adds artistic conception to it.

Garden builders also like to reproduce famous mountains, temples and scenic spots in their gardens in order to create and add artistic conception. As representatives of Chinese mountains, *Wuyue* (five famous mountains) were worshipped by emperors of all dynasties, thus, bearing rich cultural connotations. Usually, five big rocks are erected against the wall in front of the hall to symbolize the five mountains in a garden, or even select little interesting rocks to form pot sceneries and place them on the long table in the hall, thus, the five mountains are moved into the building. These "five mountains" are definitely not the real five mountains, but, they can remind people of the cultural connotation of the real five mountains. In the rear hill of the Summer Palace, there is a small buddhist temple—Huachengge, with several little halls and a pagoda made of glazed bricks, which is a three story pagoda in octagonal shape. There are bells hung under every eave, and when wind blows, the bells ring, and ringing sound lingers in the mountain forests which makes one feel that he has got rid of the secular world. In Xiequyuan (Garden of Harmonious Delights) of the Summer Palace, there is a little path flanked by rockeries and surrounded by trees which enjoys very quiet environment. It is said that when people tour this little path, they may have the urge of writing poems. Emperor Qianlong made an inscription for the path as "seeking poems path", which became a scenic spot with much artistic conception.

Seeking Poems Path, Summer Palace

Stone scenery of *Wuyue* (five famous mountains), Suzhou garden

Huacheng Pavilion, Summer Palace, Beijing

Artistic conception has become the soul of the ancient Chinese gardens. It gives rise to people's thoughts and feelings through concrete scenic views and the garden environment. Apart from those scenic spots with definite symbolic significance, a lot of thoughts and feelings emerge upon sightseeing may be different with different people. In the face of the same environment and same scenic spot, different people may have different feelings and understanding, and even the same person may feel differently when his age, experience and mood is different. Such is the widespread effect a garden can exercise.

# Chapter 9
# Residences

The residence which provides the living space for people is the most numerous among all types of architectures. China has a vast expanse of territory. The geographical environment of different areas inhabited by different nationalities is different, and furthermore, the life habit of people is also different. As a result, the lodgings suitable for their living vary greatly in forms.

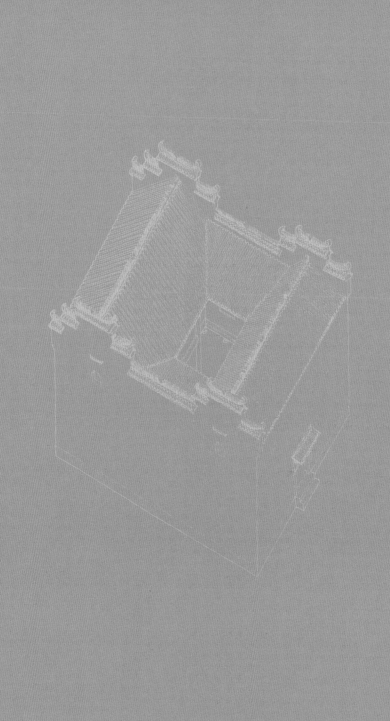

# Quadrangular Residences

It has been discussed in the first part that quadrangle type residence was rather complete in form in the Han dynasty. A picture of residences on tomb bricks shows to us the image of quadrangular residence two thousand years ago. The residences represented by Beijing quadrangles are widely accepted by people, because they can create a quiet and private living environment, and they also meet with the requirement of Chinese traditional ritual system and family ethics. But the quadrangles in Shanxi, Yunnan as well as the Jiangnan area are somewhat different, each with its different features.

## Quadrangles in Shanxi

Since ancient times, Shanxi has been a place rich in coal resources. With coal and the inexhaustible yellow clay, brick, tile and colored glaze production became the traditional handicraft of Shanxi. Since the Ming Dynasty, commercial industry gained a big development, and many merchants were from Shanxi. They traveled all around the country, and were very good at doing business, becoming known as the powerful "Shanxi Merchants". After returning to their hometowns, those rich merchants busied themselves in buying land, building shops and residences, thus, they left many elaborate shops and residences in the cities and countryside as of today. Pingyao City of Shanxi is a commercially developed city since ancient times in which there are houses one after the other along the street. These houses are shops as well as

Quadrangle, Pingyao of Shanxi Province

Grand Quadrangle of the Wang Family, Lingshi of Shanxi Province

Residence, Dingcun Village, Xiangfen of Shanxi province

residences, with shops in front and residences in the rear. These special residences all adopt the form of quadrangles, the shop facing the street and the main house in the rear are arranged on the axis, and there are wing rooms on both sides. Since there should be as many shops as possible on the street, so each shop should not occupy a big space. As a result, the quadrangle is long and narrow, and the wing rooms on the sides are also narrow, while the roof is made into a slant towards the yard. So the narrow courtyard and one slope roof becomes the special feature of the quadrangles in Shanxi.

But it is different in the countryside, because there is a lot of space. The quadrangles are only for the residences, so the courtyard is larger, some of the main houses and wing rooms around it are built into two story ones, and on both sides of the rooms, there are small ear-rooms, so the quadrangle is composed of four big houses and eight small rooms, called "four

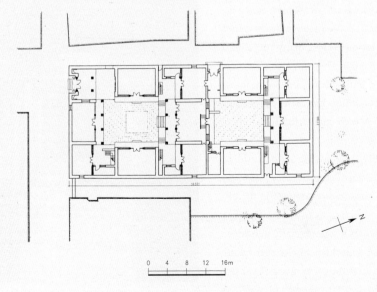

Plan. "Four-big-eight-small" quadrangle, Shanxi Province

Up: brick carving, "Carp fish jumping over dragon gate", residence of Shanxi merchants
Down: (left) stone carving decoration, residence of Shanxi merchants:
　　　　"Monkey with peach", symbolizing longevity and promotion
　　　　(right) "Carp fish jumping over dragon gate", symbolizing human being becoming an immortal through self cultivation

Quadrangle residence, Dali of Yunnan Province

Screen Wall of a quadrangle

big and eight small", which is another special feature of quadrangles in Shanxi. This kind of quadrangles can be seen in the Grand Courtyard of the Wang Family and the Grand Courtyard of the Qiao Family of rich merchants, and big buildings in the country-side belonging to rich merchants and landlords. To show the financial strength and personal interest, these buildings in the cities and country-side are decorated with many brick, stone and wood carvings using the animal images of dragon, lion, deer, monkey, bat and bo-tanical images of the peony, lotus, as well as the patterns of "as you wish", myriads, longevity, etc. to ex-press their wishes for making money, becoming official, and for happiness and auspiciousness.

## Quadrangles in Dali, Yunnan Province

Dali is located in the western part of Yunnan, inhabited by Bai nationality. The city is backed by Cangshan Mountain in the west, facing Erhai Lake in the east. There is wind blowing in all four seasons, which is very strong at times, so the houses here are all facing east, and the roof is in the style of flush gable, some houses even have the back eave sealed with bricks and mud, so that the roof would not be ripped off by big wind. The Bai people also live in quadrangles which are composed of houses on three sides and a screen wall. The main house is usually facing the east, one or two stories, with a wide corridor in front which is for family chore work and resting. On both sides of the main house are wing-rooms. In front of the main house is a screen wall, an independent wall made of bricks, whitewashed with lime and decorated with colorful designs on all sides. It is just opposite of the main house, similar to the height of wing-rooms, serving as a scenic spot of the yard, and the reflection of the white wall makes the yard brighter. The gate is on the corner of the quadrangle, on the same side with the screen wall. In the locality, a house is called a *fang*, so this kind of quadrangle is called "three *fangs* and one screen wall".

If the screen is changed into a house, then we have a quadrangle of houses on all sides. The houses on all sides plus the ear-rooms on the sides of each house constitute a big heaven well in the middle and four small heaven wells in the four corners, so it is called "five heaven wells in a quadrangle", which is also commonly seen in Dali. The walls, apart from

Costume decoration of Bai nationality girls, Dali

those facing the courtyard, are built with bricks and white washed with lime, decorated only along the edges with colorful patterns, so the effect is like a colorful ribbon. The decorations are concentrated on the gate, on which there are wood carved bracket sets and other designs, very beautiful both in form and in color. One after another quadrangles cherished by the Bai people get together into villages by the foot of the Cangshan Mountain and near the shore of the Erhai Lake. Their grey roofs and snow white walls with glistering colorful gate head and wall ribbons seem very fresh and beautiful contrasted by the green mountain. At the same time if one takes a look at the clothing of the Bai girls, one sees them in white coats and trousers, with only a little decoration on the edges of clothes and sleeves, but the head is wrapped with a white cloth full of colorful flower decorations, so they are lightly decorated yet richly beautiful. The decoration of clothing shares the same style with house decoration; such is the tradition of the Bai people, the art of the Bai people.

Gate of a quadrangle,Dali,Yunnan Province

## Heaven Well Courtyard of Southern China

The Jiangnan Area of Jiangsu, Zhejiang, Anhui, and Jiangxi belong to the warm temperate to sub-tropical climate where there are four distinctive seasons and it is rainy in spring, hot in summer, cold in winter. This area is not large, but the population is big, with scarce arable land, therefore the land use is very tight. Under such conditions, the quadrangle residences are usually houses on four sides closely linked to one another, and in the middle, an enclosure called heaven well. To make full use of the land, the houses are usually two storey buildings. With two storey buildings all around, plus protruding eaves on the roof, the heaven well in the middle seems even smaller as a well, hence the name "heaven well quadrangle". No matter in the city or countryside, these heaven well quadrangles are all closely linked to each other, the houses on all sides only have windows and door open to inside, and there are very few windows on outer walls except the gate. Therefore, heaven well becomes the main means through which to get light and ventilation for the residence. Since the heaven well is rather small, the direct sunshine on the houses on all sides is much reduced, and it performs the role similar to a chimney which sucks out the dust and filthy air inside the residence, strengthening air ventilation and reducing the heat in summer. The houses all around the heaven well all have a roof slope slanting inside which makes the rain water flowing into the heaven well. The house owner can collect the water in a big jar for drinking water on the one side, and at the same time, the water can be discharged out of the yard through the ditches around the heaven well. In the countryside, water is precious both for agricultural production and

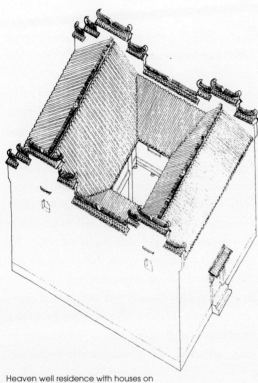

Heaven well residence with houses on
four sides, southern China

daily life and people look on water as
wealth, so they call the method of collecting water as "four waters join into one",
and "good water is not allowed to flow
away". They think this method can bring
luck to the family. Some well-to-do families would arrange stone platforms in the
heaven wells on which to put some pots
of flowers or pot sceneries in order to
beautify the heaven well.

Like the quadrangles in the north, the
houses around the heaven well are divided
into main house and wing-houses, and the
main house is called upper house, the
house opposite across the heaven well is
called lower house, the middle of which
is usually the gate of the residence. The
main house is mostly three bays wide, or,
five bays and seven bays wide in big
residences. The middle bay of the main
house is a hall which is for family
gathering, entertaining guests and worshipping gods and ancestors, thus, the
center of the residence. The hall faces the
heaven well, with no doors or windows
for lighting and ventilation. In the rear part
of the hall is usually a long table, in front

Looking up from a heaven well

Main house of a quadrangle

of which a square table and two chairs. On both sides against the wall, a tea table and two chairs are arranged. The long table is placed in the middle, on which are the tablets of ancestors and candles and incense burner for worshipping purposes, at the both ends of the table are usually flower vase and a mirror, which means safety and silence by using the pronunciation of the words of those objects. The long table is elaborately made, usually carved with flower patterns. Pictures and calligraphies are hung on the walls of three sides, and the pictures of the god of happiness and god of longevity or pines and cypresses are on the middle wall. Such arrangement of the hall is almost a set form in the wealthy families of the Jiangnan Area of China. In times of festivities or the New Year, the square table is moved on to the middle of the hall, on which are placed all kinds of food and sacrificial articles and the whole family would pay respects to the ancestor tablets by means of kowtowing, or face the heaven well to worship heaven and earth. The hall is also used to celebrate the elders' birthdays and the marriages of the sons and grandsons of the family for holding ceremonies and banquets. Whenever the elder is dead, the coffin is stationed in the hall for a few days for sacrificial ceremony before being moved out and buried. On both sides of the hall are the bedrooms of the owner, but the doors do not directly connect with the hall and heaven well, they can only open in the back. Women and children can not meet with outsiders by passing through the hall. The wing-houses on both sides of heaven well can be used as bedrooms or for other purposes. The second floor is lower than the ground floor, so it is hot in summer and cold in

Decoration of the Hall

winter, usually for the storage of grains and utensils. The kitchen is usually not in the heaven well, because under the self-suffcent petit-agricultural economy, the function of the kitchen, apart from preparing for three meals a day, also to husk rice, make preserved vegetables, grand soybeans to make bean curd, feed pigs, store firewood and when the New Year's Day approaches, to make new year cake and brew rice wine. So, we can say it is a family workshop for preparing food and drinks and also the dining room and rest room for hired laborers where there are stoves, dining table, tools, as well as a pig-sty. Such a kitchen is not convenient and sanitary to be put in the heaven well. Usually, a small piece of land next to the residence is used to build the kitchen.

A quadrangle with one heaven well is only a basic unit of residence. A big family with many people and rich financial means often build several heaven well quadrangles and link them with doors from the front to the rear or stand abreast from left to right, forming a big quadrangular residence. No matter whether big or small, their appearance is always white high walls with a gate and a few windows. Such residences are all timber-frame structures with brick walls enclosed from outside, easily subject to fire. To avoid the fire being spread to the immediate neighbors, the wall between the families are built higher than the roof, and along the two-slope roof the wall is made into the ladder type. The wall is called "sealing fire wall", because it can keep the fire inside. The sealing fire wall has a ridge with both ends raised up high which resembles a raised up horse head, thus it is also called "horse head wall". In the countryside of Huizhou of Anhui Province,

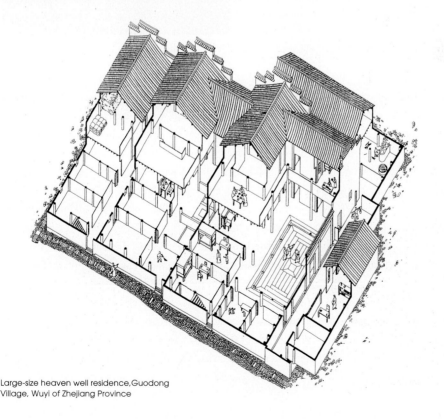

Large-size heaven well residence, Guodong
Village, Wuyi of Zhejiang Province

Sketch. Lane between heaven well residences

Lane of Huizhou residences

there are more people but little land, so there have been many merchants since ancient time going out to deal with business matters and quite a few are good at it and become rich. These are the famous Anhui merchants in Jiangnan area. Like the Shanxi merchants in the north, the Anhui merchants return to their native places with money to build family temples and residences and leave behind a few elaborate heaven well quadrangular residences. Just like the Shanxi merchants who try their best to decorate their residences with carvings to show off their wealth, the Anhui merchants also emphasize the decoration of their residences. The gate of a residence shows the fame and position of the owner, so the ancients also refer the fame of a person to "gate fame", so the gate naturally becomes the place to be decorated the most. Above the gate, there is usually a gate head, made of carved bricks, showing beams and lintels, bracket sets and roof, and on these members are carved symbolic animals and plants. With such kind of make-up, a simple gate becomes elaborate. Even those ordinary people who can not afford a brick carved gate head, they feel like drawing one on the gate instead. Inside the heaven well, one can see wood carving on the beams and lintels of the hall, and the windows of the main house and wing-houses are littered with flowery frames and patterns, especially on the windows of two bedrooms on both sides of the hall, because women inside should not be seen by guests, and some windows even have two layers, which almost become wood carving decorations on both sides of the heaven well instead of windows with the function of getting light and ventilation.

In the countryside of Huizhou area, we can see the heaven well quadrangles in patches; they are closely linked to one another, lining up both sides of a lane. To make full use of the land, these lanes are very narrow, only three to four meters the widest, some are even as narrow as two meters. So the typical look of this residential area is high walls and narrow lanes, in which there are typical Huizhou residences with white walls, grey bricks, black tiles, one gate head after another emerge out of narrow lanes and horse head walls galloping on high walls. This is also the representative type of the heaven well quadrangular residences in Jiangnan Area.

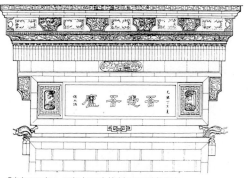

Brick carving, gate head, Huizhou residence, Anhui Province

Fire re-preventive outer walls of Heaven Well residences

Windows, Huizhou residence

Windows, Huizhou residence

277

After serving as officials, group after group of Jiangnan talents returned to their native places with fame and honor, and after earning a lot of money, many Anhui merchants returned to their native places with glory. They invariably built one elaborate residence after another with grey bricks and white walls outside and carved and painted pillars and beams inside. This type of heaven well quadrangle which resembles a pillbox is exactly what they want: they have their family wealth to protect, and wives to confine. The merchants usually went out alone to do business, enjoying their lives at will, leaving their wives alone at home. If the husband died outside, the wife could only remain a single all her life, taking care of the old and the young, then after her death, she might get the title of a chaste woman, and some of them can be remembered with a chastity archway built in her name. If one takes a look at so many such stone chastity archways in Jiangnan countryside, or reads so many stories recorded in the family and clan history, one will understand the fate of the women confined by the high walls and deep yards. Therefore, the high heaven well quadrangles covering a large area in Jiangnan are not only the products of the local geography and economy, but also reflect the traditional ritual system and family virtues of Chinese feudal society.

## Fujian's Earth Buildings

In ancient Chinese countryside, farmers of the same clan used to live together, they built their residences by circling their clan temple, and in this way, they could rely on one another in time of difficulty. These residences formed into groups, and gradually into a village. In Fujian area, there

Earth buildings, Nanjing County, Fujian Province

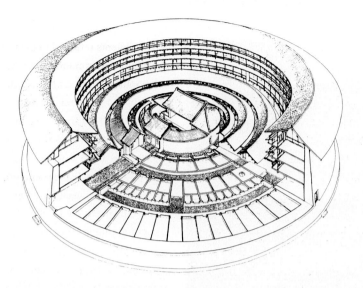

Elevation. Chengqi Building, Yongding County, Fujian Province

were repeated wars and numerous bandits in ancient times, and strives among different clans were rather common, so the need for living together as a clan was urgent, then a large size building which can get the scattered residences together came into being. In the area of Yongding, Longyan and Zhangzhou in the southern part of Fujian where it was rich in natural resources of forests, rocks and clay, the local artisans succeeded in creating a large-size residence. They combined several dozen residences together, forming a square or round quadrangle. In order to be able to resist attacks from outside, they built a thick and pressed outer wall with the yellow earth, hence the name: "earth building". The earth building could be square or round, a yard in the center surrounded by residences, thus, it is a kind of quadrangular residence.

In the countryside of Yongding County, Fujian Province, there is a Chengqi Building which is large and typical. It is a round one, built in the 48th year (1709) of Kangxi, and completed in three years. The diameter of the round building is 62.6 meters, divided into four rings from inside out. The innermost ring is the clan temple for worshipping ancestors. There are 20 rooms on the second ring, 34 the third and 60 the outermost ring plus four room for staircases. A big gate facing south is directly opposite the clan temple, and there is a side door of the east and west. The inner three rings are all one story buildings, while the outer ring has four floors, the first floor, kitchen, second floor, grain storage, third and fourth floor, bedrooms. Every family occupies one room, but all four floors, so there are no main rooms and wing-rooms, no front yard or back yard, and every family has the same amount of floor space which does not show the status of the owner. All of them are facing the central clan temple, because it is the same ancestors that bring them together. After completion of the construction, more than 80 households moved in, with a population of over 400.

Since the earth building is built for safety, it has very strong defending ability. The outer ring of Chengqi Building is 14 meters high, in which the houses are built with timber-frame structure,

Earth building in square form

Ancestral temple in the center of earth building

Inside view of round earth building

but the outer wall is built with rammed earth, 1.9 meters thick at most, the foundation is made of big pebbles and big pieces of rock, from underground to the point higher than the flood could reach, for fear the flood water would crush the earth wall. From the third floors up, there are loopholes and small windows on the wall, the former can be used for shooting at the attacking enemy, the latter for throwing rocks and pouring boiling water at them. There are ring passages on all the floors facing the yard for moving people and materials in defense. Within the round building, there are water well, granary and places for keeping domestic animals, so that in time of the enemy siege, the people inside can maintain several months without the fear of shortage of food and water. Because the gates are vulnerable to attacks, so the frame is made of stone, the doors are made of thick wood planks wrapped with iron and supported by a wood pole. Besides, to guard against fire attack, a water channel is installed above the gates which can form a water curtain if necessary.

Most earth buildings are not as big as Chengqi Building, mostly, they are just one ring with several floors, centering on the clan temple, but they all have very good protective equipments. Several dozen families of the same clan live together, taking care of one another. Such earth buildings scattered on Fujian ground are like "flying saucers falling from the sky", or "mushrooms growing out of the ground" to the eye of the foreigners. They display the structure and thinking of the blood related clans in the feudal society both in form and in content.

# Caves

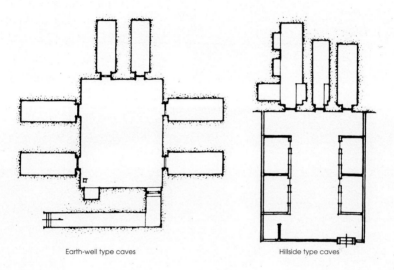

Earth-well type caves                    Hillside type caves

Plan. Cave residences

In Shaanxi Province, the eastern part of Gansu Province, central and southern part of Shanxi Province and the western part of Henan Province where the weather is dry, the economy is less developed, the people are poor in the countryside, and the earth is solid, the people there build their residences by digging caves which are economic and convenient for them. This is called cave dwellings. In some areas of Shaanxi, caves take up almost 80 per cent of the countryside dwellings.

The common method of building a cave is to dig into an earth hill or an earth gully, the cave is in rectangular, and the cave top is an arch which is about three meters high. A farmer can build a cave by himself by using a spade. First to dig a hole, then, to make a kang bed and stove with yellow earth, and finally, hang a straw certain at the entrance, thus, a cave is completed in which one can live and cook food. When the economic conditions have improved, he can build more caves, make doors and windows with timber, white wash the inside walls with lime, use some bricks to build the entrance walls. In a self-sufficient agricultural society, the farmers must rely on themselves to produce and process grains, grow vegetables, raise pigs, cows and sheep, so they enclose a yard in front of the caves for these purposes, then their dwellings also have a yard attached to it.

Elevation. Caves, countryside of Shanxi Province

Doors and windows, caves, Shanxi Province

Because the cave is wrapped by a thick layer of yellow earth, it is cool in summer and warm in winter, but it is damp inside and the ventilation is not good. Even though it is warm spring outside with flowers blooming, the elder people in the cave should still sleep on a fire-baked *kang* (a heatable brick earthen bed).

In the yellow earth area where there is no earth hill or gully, there is another method of building a cave by digging downward from ground level. First, to dig a square pit on the ground, 15 meters on the side, 7 to 8 meters deep, then, dig inside on each of the four sides, thus, an under-

Sketch. Cave residence, Shilipu Village, Changwu County, Shaanxi Province

ground quadrangle with living quarters on all four sides comes into being, which is called pit style or earth well style caves. From one corner, earth steps can be built leading to the yard. In such a quadrangle, the three bay residences become three caves in abreast, with doors linking them together. In order to get sunshine in winter, the caves facing south are usually used as living quarters, while the caves on both sides are for raising domestic animals, storing grains, utensils and water well, etc. On the four sides of the pit, dredging ditches and seeping wells are built for draining rain water. On the floor, there are also passes paved with bricks or stone slabs like on-ground quadrangles, trees, flowers and grass planted, windows and doors decorated with flowery patterns, red paper cuttings sticking to white window papers, all these would please the residents. Although the quadrangle is underground, it is still pleasant to live, with elderly people resting and children playing in the yard. But, after all, the living environment is not as good as on the ground, so the underground quadrangles are less and less, with the economic conditions improving, more and more people would like to live in the houses on the ground.

Earth well type cave, Shilipu Village

# Houses on Stilts

The southeastern part of Guizhou Province is inhabited by minority nationalities of the Miao and Dong people. The characteristics of its geography and climate are expressed in the following lines, "there is not a leveled piece of land larger than three square *chi* (one third of a meter), and fine weather never exceeds three days in a row." There are always higher and lower mountains from which the farmers can not escape both in production and daily life, sometimes, terraced fields are extended from the mountain foot to the top. The weather is hot and humid, especially in summer, you can never tell whether it is going to be fine or rain, it may be fine when you are at the foot of the mountain, but when you climb to the top, there is a downpour. The local people have created the houses suitable for them under such conditions. The house is built with the local cypresses; its timber-frame structure of two floors is standing on the uneven hill slope through

Stilt-houses, Dragon-spine Village, Longsheng, Guangxi Zhuang Autonomous Region

House on stilts, Miao nationality village, Guizhou Province

pillars. The upper floor is for human beings, and the ground floor is for raising domestic animals and storing farm tools and miscellanies, which has no outer walls. The upper floor is petitioned into a hall and bedrooms with wood planks, and a corridor is protruded out from all four sides where the owners can work and rest. The protruded corridor is rested on the protruding beams, so the pillars of the corridor are hung in the air, which provides convenience for people and animals under the corridor, and thus, the local people call this "hanging feet building". Such buildings can also be found in large numbers in the mountainous areas of Sichuan, Hubei and Yunnan provinces where the weather is humid, the merits of which are: good ventilation and keeping away from wild animals attacks, because people live on the upper floor.

Such hanging feet buildings may be slightly different with different nationalities, because of different life habits. In the villages where people of the Dong ethnic group live in compact communities, every family has a fireplace built in the hall which is the center of family gatherings. Besides, there is a center in the village for all the people to get together, the drum building. The form of the drum building resembles a Buddhist pagoda dense eaves style, it could be in square, or hexagon, octagon shape with a spacious ground floor, above which is hollow, without any more floors, but on the outside is several layers of dense eaves, which becomes evidently smaller from the lower to the upper floor, until finally, a pyramid top. The drum building is linked with a

Dong nationality village, Guizhou Province

Drum Tower, Dong nationality village

Villagers gathering in front of Drum Tower

Decoration of Drum Tower, eaves and the top

spacious yard which is the center for the villagers to gather. A drum is hung in the building; hence the drum building, to beat the drum is the signal to gather all the people in the village. People gather to dance on inside and outside of the building during festival days and in other times, they can come here to chat and rest. Thus, the drum building is the cultural center of the village. On eaves of every floor, there are painted pictures, and sometimes, there are statues on top of the building, and the house corners are raise up high. So, the drum building has become the landmark of the Dong people village.

# Ganlan Houses

In the classification of residential architectures, those residences with the ground floor only serving as a prop are called as the Ganlan houses. The above-mentioned hanging feet building is a kind of Ganlan houses, but the bamboo building of the Dai ethnic village in Xishuangbanna of Jinghong area, Yunnan Province is the standard form of Ganlan houses. Jinghong area varies greatly in altitudes and climate, ranging from temperate zone, subtropical to tropical zone, with no snow, but ample rainfall, and there are only two seasons, rainy season and dry season, the mean temperature being 21 degree Celsius. The Dai people have created the Ganlan residences under such conditions. They choose the flatland in the mountains to build residences and villages, using local bamboo as the main materials; the big and thick ones are used to form the frame of the house, weaved bamboo as walls, and weaved bamboo or wood planks as house floor and rice stalks for the roof, hence the name, bamboo house. It is divided into two floors; the ground floor is for raising domestic animals and for storing farm tools and miscellanies. The upper floor is for

Dai nationality village, Xishuangbanna of Yunnan Province

Bamboo houses on stilts, Dai nationality village

Hall, Ganlan houses

Ganlan houses with wood plank wall and tiled roof

the people, divided into the hall and bedrooms, and there is also a fireplace in the hall, for cooking, making tea, and for all the people to gather. In front of the hall is a spacious front corridor and balcony, the former for the owners to work, rest and entertain guests, the latter for washing, drying clothes and farm products. Because such bamboo houses are on stilts, and the bamboo walls on all sides are good for ventilation, so they have several merits: first, to avoid dampness and ensure ventilation; second, keep wild animals off the house; third, allow flood caused by heavy rain to pass under the house. Thus, the bamboo houses have been widely accepted by the local people, because they have evident merits, the building materials are easy to get, and the construction is simple and fast.

In ancient times, the Dai people all believed in Buddhism, and there were Buddhist temples almost in all villages. In order to maintain the dignity of Buddhism, there were regulations set by the local authorities that no residences were allowed opposite to Buddhist temples, and the height of residences must be lower than the terrace of Buddhist statues. Within a village, there were also many regulations regarding the residences between the ordinary villagers and the chief of the village and head of clan, e.g., no tiles should be used by the villagers, their corridors should not be larger than three bays, six screen doors were not allowed in the hall, the pillars on both the ground and first floors must not be the long and single ones, no pillar bases made of stone should be used and no carvings allowed as decoration, etc. Owing to the restrictions of economic conditions and those regulations, the building technologies of the villagers are not able to improve and develop, and most of the bamboo buildings can not last long. Nowadays, the Ganlan buildings have mostly changed into timber-frame structures, with wood plank walls and tiled roof, but they still maintain the form and merits of bamboo buildings.

# Yurts

In Inner Mongolia Autonomous Region and Xinjiang Uygur Autonomous Region, the local Mongols and Kazaks have maintained a nomadic life for a long time. They herd large herds of cattle, sheep and horses on grassland and always move from one pasture land to another according to the change of the grass situation, thus, a kind of dwelling suitable for the nomadic life comes into being. This dwelling is round in plan, with a frame made of wood strips which can assemble and dismantle, and wrapped with felt from outside. It is called yurt, and since the Mongols use them the most, so they are also called "Mongolian yurts". The most striking feature of the yurts is that they are easily dismantled when the pasture land is exhausted, and then the family would put the frame and felt as well as all the belongings on horsebacks, and the family members herd the cattle and sheep to a new pasture land and assemble the yurt again.

Mongolian yurts on Inner Mongolian grassland

The yurts are all in round shape, two meters high, with a diameter of four to six meters. The door is opened on one side, and there is a window on top for light and ventilation, and also for discharging the smoke from cooking and burning horse manure for heating in winter. The outside of yurts are plain and simple, but inside the yurt, if only economic condition is provided, there are carpets on the ground, colored tapestries on the walls and all kinds of decorations, which shows the aspiration of the grassland herdsmen for a happy life.

Yurts at the foot of Tianshan Mountain, Xinjiang Uygur Autonomous Region

Inside view of yurts

# Stone Pillbox Residences

Stone pillbox residence of Tibetan nationality, Kangding, Sichuan Province

Inside stone pillbox residence

China's Tibet, Qinghai, and the western part of Sichuan are inhabited by Tibetan people in compact communities. These areas are mountainous; therefore, stone is the major material for building residences. A typical residence has walls made of stone, two or three stories high with a flat roof, and the upper part of the outer walls are a bit smaller than the lower part, resembling a pillbox, hence the name "stone pillbox residence". The ground floor is for reception rooms and bedrooms; on the second floor, beside the bedrooms, there is a specially arranged Buddhist scripture hall, where the whole family chant scriptures and pay respects to Buddha. This hall is the center of the residence, because almost all of the Tibetan people believe in Buddhism.

The outside look of the stone pillbox residence is very special: the four sides are solid walls, the lower part of which is built with big rough rocks in dark color, and the upper part is usually whitewashed, so that there is a sharp contrast of color and substance between the two parts. There are rows of windows on the outer walls, and every window is surrounded by a ladder-shaped frame, which is a special architectural form of the Tibetans. This form is also found on palace and temple architectures. The windows are also decorated with colorful eaves, which bring beauty to the formal look of the stone pillbox residences, displaying the rough, heavy yet beautiful style of the Tibetan architectures.

In summing up, there are so many forms of residences on the vast land of China, and these are not all. The residences in Xinjiang, the stone houses along the seaside of Shandong and other places, and among the quadrangles, the big courtyards in the northeast areas and the "single seal" in Yunnan all have their special features which can not be introduced one by one. But, from the above-mentioned residences we know that they all have their striking features in structures and shapes which are by no means accidental.

China has a vast land area, with many nationalities, thus, many residences are needed. Especially in the countryside, people always try their best to use local materials, adopt the local traditional technologies to build residences suitable for the local people according to the local geographical conditions. In Shanxi, there is coal and yellow earth which can produce great quantities of bricks and tiles, so there are brick and tile residences; the mountainous Guizhou is rich in cypresses, so there are hanging feet houses built on the hill slopes using cypress wood; in hot and humid Xishuangbanna of Yunnan, there are bamboo houses on stilts using the local bamboo materials; Shaanxi is located on the loess plateau, so there are cave dwellings. It is precisely because of this that those residences are bound to be bearing with the special features of the locality and the nationality. Different geographical environment and different life habits of different nationalities produce different residences with their own special features from the structures to the outside looks.

For a very long period, China was a feudal society with undeveloped commodity economy and backward transportation means. It not only adopted a self-seclusion policy towards the outside world, but also lacked in exchanges internally between different areas in the fields of economy, culture, technologies, etc. This resulted in the very slow development or little changes in the architectural technologies and shapes of a certain area or minority nationality area. The Nanxi River basin of Yongjia, Zhejiang Province has been a scenic area since ancient times and rich in agricultural products, where dozens of villages and many of the residences, temples and pavilions were built in the Ming and Qing periods. These architectures follow the traditional means of making timber-frame structures, in which many members are produced according to the rules published by the Song court. This shows that in the secluded mountainous area, the ancient, traditional technologies have always been adhered to, while outside the area, several dynasties have passed, and the timber-frame structures have developed or changed. This phenomenon shows that in a relatively secluded area, the architectural technologies and forms with a special feature can very easily become a relatively set tradition which can last a long time.

Under the prolonged centralized feudal system of China, in order to maintain the ritual dignity, many restrictions and rules were formulated in architectures. Starting from the imperial palaces, architectures of different grades must observe distinctive rules in the width of buildings, height of terraces; form of roofs, and even in the material and color of tiles. It is the same with decorations. Dragon and phoenix symbolizes the emperor and empress respectively, especially the dragon which was forbidden to be used on the other architectures than the palaces. The little animals on the ridges and the studs on the doors are numbered nine and nine rows at most on palace architectures which can not be surpassed on the other buildings. These prohibitions and rules can be observed in the capital, but in the localities, especially in the countryside, many of these are neglected, and the court was unable to deal with so many breaches. In various places, residences are decorated with dragon and phoenix patterns. Those rich and powerful officials and merchants build their residences so wide, the stone terraces so high and the decorations so beautiful that they far exceed those of prince residences in Beijing. Once the rules and regulations of the court are breached, the forms of architectures become varied. This is the social and historical causes for the rich architectural forms of residences in many places.

# Chapter 10
# Petty Architectures

It has been stated before that apart from the timber-frame system used in the building structure, the structural group is also the main feature of Chinese ancient architectures. All architectures, whether they are palaces, tombs, altars and temples or gardens, residences and religious ones, are structural groups of single buildings which may be exactly the same or different. In the imperial architectures of palaces, tombs, altars and temples, there are more halls; in garden architectures, more pavilions, terraces, corridors and water pavilions; in residences, more main houses, wing rooms, halls and the like. But beside these buildings, there are some petty and sporadic buildings, e.g. archways and screen walls in front of a group of architectures, lions on both sides of a gate, stone steles by tombs and temples, and also the ornamental pillars in front of Tiananmen Gate, the bronze tortoise, bronze

Stone archway, Azure Cloud (Biyun) Temple, Beijing

Stone animals, Xiaoling Tomb of Ming Dynasty, Nanjing, Jiangsu Province

Stone tablets of a temple

Ornamental pillar in front of Tian'anmen Gate, Beijing

crane, the measures and the sundial in front of the great hall, Dharani column in front of a Buddhist hall, stone figures, animals and pillars on both sides of the spirit way in front of tombs, etc. these architectures are all small, so they are called "petty architectures". Although small, they all have different shapes and their respective functions among the group of architectures, and they play important roles in the environmental art of architectures. Now, we are going to introduce some of the major ones to you.

296

Stone column, Western Tombs of Qing Dynasty,
Yixian County of Hebei Province

Brick screen wall, residence of northern China

Five Offerings, Western Tombs of Qing Dynastry

# Archways

Archways are often situated in front of important architectural groups, or on both ends of a street and a crossroad. There is a gigantic stone archway at the foremost of the Ming Tombs area. In front of the main entrance, East Palace Gate and the main halls and Buddhist buildings inside the Summer Palace, there are archways, big or small. Archways can play the role of a mark for the architectures, so they are regarded as petty symbolic architectures which can not only partition and control the environmental space, but also add artistic expression to the architectural group.

How did archways come into being? Archways were often positioned in front of buildings or on both ends of a street, which were equal to the position of the gate or entrance, so their birth were inseparable to the gates of the buildings. The gate of early Chinese architectural group is called "Hengmen", i.e. to erect two pillars on the yard wall, and then, place a beam on top of

Wood archway, East Palace Gate, Summer Palace

pillars and fix doors between the pillars, thus, a gate was built. Later, a roof was added to the beam to prevent erosion by rain and snow. Such Hengmen can be seen in the Song painting *Riverside Scene at Pure Brightness Festival*. The book *Building Standards* published by the Song Court in the 12th century recorded the "bird head gate" which was also composed of two vertical pillars plus one beam and doors in between, but more elaborate than the early Hengmen, because there are decorations on top of pillars. Both the Hengmen and bird head gate are the microcosms of archway.

How many types of archways are there?

If we classify them by the materials used, there are wood archway, stone archway, brick archway and glazed archway.

**Wood Archway** Since the Chinese architectures adopt timber-frame structure, wood archway is the

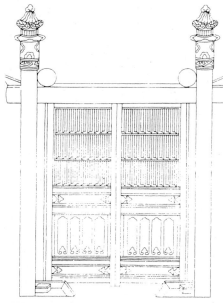

Elevation. Bird head gate as in *Building Standards* of Song Dynasty

basic form. Just like ordinary houses, an archway is made by several pillars linked by beams and lintels topped with a roof. However, archways usually only have one row of pillars, there is no "bay" formed by four pillars. Below the pillars are stone bases, and for those high pillars, there are props in the front and back. The width of an archway is measured by the "bay" between two pillars, so there are two pillars of one bay, four pillars of three bay and six pillars of five bay, etc. The roofs can also be more or less, for an archway of two pillars of one bay, its roof can be one, or three, even five. Therefore, with more bays and more roofs, the proportion of the archway would

Elevation. Ancient Hengmen gates

One-bay wood archway on Chengxian Street, Beijing

Four-pillar-three-bay wood archway

Four-pillar-three-bay wood archway with seven roofs, Yonghegong, Beijing

Wood-stone archway, ancestral temple, Foshan, Guangdong Province

also be larger with more decorations. The decorations of wood archways are like buildings; the good ones would paint the pillars red and decorate the beams and lintels with green and blue paintings. And the archways of imperial architectures are also decorated with gold dragons and phoenixes.

Stone Archway  Wood archways easily decay due to sunshine and rain, so stone archways gradually came into being. At the beginning, they were bound to adopt the form of wood archways, pillars plus beams, with roofs on top, all the members of timber-frame are there, but made of stone. Their decorations also imitate those of wood archways, carving the beams and lintels into the patterns of colored paintings; some are decorated with stone carved images of animals, plants and human figures.

Brick and Glazed Archways  It is impossible to produce timber-frame beams and lintels out of a brick archway, so the only way is to make a vault out of the brick archway to form a gate which makes the archway seem sturdy and heavy. If the surface is glazed, then we have a glazed archway. Furthermore, we can make pillars and beams with glazed bricks, and brackets and roofs, and then use different colors to patch colored paintings similar to those on timber-frames, making the archway wood-like. Since glaze is even better than bricks in resisting sunshine and rain, and shines in different colors, so such an archway is beautiful in shape and lasts long.

301

Elevation. Stone archway, Summer Palace, Beijing

Glazed archway, imperial college, Beijing

Brick archway, Azure Cloud (Biyun) Temple, Beijing

Stone carving decoration of stone archway, Western Tombs of Qing Dynasty, Yixian County, Hebei Province

If we classify them by their functions, then we have the following:

Landmark Archway  Standing before a group of architectures, or on both ends of the main street of a city, or on crossroads, such archways play the role of the landmarks. For example, on Qianmen avenue and east and west Chang'an Avenues of the old Beijing, there were such wood archways; in front of the architectural group of the Dispelling Clouds Hall on the front side of the Longevity Hill and by the shore of the Kunming Lake, Summer Palace, there is one wood archway; on the square in front of Sumeru Lingjing Buddhist Temple in the rear side of the hill, there are three archways facing three roads of the left, front and right; these archways are landmarks.

Gate Archway  Although the landmark archways are situated at the entrances of architectural groups, they are by no means the gates. These archways stand alone in the middle of roads, which have gate passages, but no doors, so they can not open or close like real gates, and people can pass by them without hindrance. The gate archway is the real gate of an architectural group, with doors between pillars or in the gate passage, which can open or close, and are linked with the surrounding walls, and there is no other way to enter or exit except through the archway. For example, the Lingxingmen Gate of the Confucius Temple in Qufu, Shandong and the Renshoumen Gate of the Summer Palace all belong to such archways.

Archway in front of temples, the rear hill, Summer Palace

Gate of Confucius Temple, Qufu

Renshoumen Gate, Summer Palace

**Memorial Archways** In ancient times, in order to commemorate or praise one person or one event, an archway was usually built on the spot with the name and the story carved on it, such being the memorial archway. In the feudal society of China, to be loyal to the country, filial to parents, righteous to brothers and friends, and wife being loyal to husband are the main contents of the traditional virtue. To commemorate a person or an event by building an archway is the best way to propagate such virtues. If a person had won honor as an official for the court, an archway would be built on order of the emperor or by himself in his hometown, which, on the one hand, propagates the idea of being loyal to the country, on the other hand, makes his own clan prominent. The Wenxing Village of Qinshui, Shanxi is the native place of Liu Zongyuan, famous poet in the

Stone archway, Wenxing Village, Qinshui, Shanxi Province

A closer look of the seven archways, Tangyue Village, Shexian County, Anhui Province

Tang Dynasty where the Liu clan lived in compact community. There were two persons from this clan who served as officials in Shanxi, Shaanxi and other places. In order to commemorate them, the court built two stone archways in the village, which are already more than 450 years old, and they are the landmark architectures of this village. In Tangyue village of Shexian County, Anhui Province, there is a group of archways composed of seven standing along the road leading to the village, one of which is to praise an official, three of which for people staying at homes to show filial to parents, two of which for women faithful to husbands, the final one for good deeds for the villagers. These archways give people education in the traditional virtues of loyalty, piety, benevolence and righteousness, and also reflect the glorious history of the village.

Ornamental Archways  In the business street of old Beijing, there were stores after stores on both sides. Some stores built archways before them in order to show off. Such archways stuck to the stores, the pillars of which were much higher than the store roofs. A closer look would find them beautifully decorated; looking from afar, the high pillar heads make the stores very prominent. There are also archway decorated gates in some temples, family temples and elaborate residences.

305

Store archway, the rear lake, Summer Palace

Gate archway of ancestral hall, Houwu Village, Yongkang, Zhejiang Province

Seven archways, Tangyue Village, Shexian County, Anhui Province

Gate archway of Baidi Temple, Fengjie, Sichuan Province

Such archways also have pillars, beams, roofs, and decorations on beams, but they are different with the store archways. They are not independent archways but a layer of archway decoration stuck to the walls surrounding the gate, mostly made with bricks, some are made with lime pasted on the wall which is also prominent on the white wall. All those mentioned above are ornamental archways.

There used to be many archways in old Beijing. On main avenues, in front of important temples of Sleeping Buddha Temple, Azure Cloud Temple and White Cloud Temple there were wood archways as landmarks; on the business streets of the eastern city and western city, there were many ornamental archways in front of stores; in Summer Palace, there were wood, stone or glazed archways in front of the gate, halls and temples, and on both ends of the bridge, totaling nearly 20 big and small archways. In the fifties of the last century, those archways standing in the middle of roads of Beijing were dismantled one by one because they were obstructing the traffic; those ornamental archways on old business streets disappeared along with the renovation of the old stores into new shops. But in recent years, along with economic development and social progress, archways begin to appear in big streets and small lanes again one after another. There used to be a three bay wood archway on the street outside of Qianmen. When it was dismantled 50 years ago, almost nobody would expect that a new archway be built on the same spot. Archways are also built in front of new shops. The famous Quanjude old roast duck restaurant on Wangfujin Street has put up a new building wrapped with mirror glass, and right on the gate, a three bay archway has been built closely sticking to the glittering glass wall. The comparison between and combination of the two architectural cultures of the new and old, Chinese and western demonstrate the state of mind of this old traditional restaurant when it provides services worldwide. Moreover, archways have been constructed outside of the country. They are often used as the symbols of entrance at the Chinese cultural and economic exhibitions held outside of China; they can be seen at the entrances of Chinatowns of foreign countries; to commemorate the friendship cities relationship between Beijing and Washington, D.C., Beijing built a big archway at the entrance of Chinatown of Washington, D.C. as a gift, thus, the ancient archway has added a new symbolic function. It is probably because that the archways demonstrate the typical image of Chinese timber-frame architectures: vertical pillars, horizontal beams, bracket sets, roofs, beautiful colored paintings and glazed tiles, and at the same time, they are as simple as gates without depth, thus, suitable to be used widely, therefore, they have become a symbol which can represent Chinese traditional culture and taken up their new historical tasks.

Left: (up) archway on cross roads, old Beijing
    (central) archway on Qianmenwai Street, old Beijing
    (down) new archway on Qianmenwai Street, Beijing
Right: (up) gate archway of Quanjude Roast Duck Restaurant, Wangfujing, Beijing
    (down) archway, Chinatown, Washington, D.C., USA

# Lions

Among Chinese ancient petty architectures, lions are the most commonly seen. There are four stone carved lions in front of Tian'anmen (the Gate of Heavenly Peace), Beijing. In the Forbidden City, we can see bronze lions guarding the gates of the Supreme Harmony, the Heavenly Purity, the Ningshou Palace and the Hall of Mental Cultivation; in front of some prince palaces, there are stone carved lions; even on both sides of quadrangular gates belonging to ordinary people, a pair of lions' heads are carved on stones as gate keepers. It is an interesting question why the lions, which are wild beasts, should act as sacred animals guarding the gates.

## Where Did Lions Come from

Like the tiger, lion is a ferocious animal, popularly called the king of animals. But the tiger is native to China, which is familiar to people and regarded as sacred animal and its image was already found on tomb stones of the Han Dynasty. While the lion was imported, which was native to Africa and some Asian countries of Iran and India, where it was regarded as treasured animal. In ancient Persia, it was fashionable to revere lions and the throne of the king was a gilded lion. Therefore, in the Eastern Han period of China more than 1,900 years ago, the king of the State of Anxi (present Iran) sent lions as gifts to the emperor of the Eastern Han. The Chinese were not familiar with lions which were regarded as ferocious animals and kept them in cages

Buddhism also regards the lion as the king of animals. As the legend has it that when the Buddha was born, 500 lions came out from the snow-covered land and lined in front of the gate to welcome the birth of the Buddha. When the Buddha preached, he was sitting on a lion seat, so the lion became the sacred animal guarding Buddhism. When Buddhism was introduced into China, together with it came the lion, but it was not the real lion presented by the king of Anxi State, it was the deified and artistic image of lions. From then on, the lions began to walk out of cages into people's life and the realm of art.

## Lions and Architectures

There was such a phenomenon in ancient China, when people came to know and get accustomed to a certain thing in the objective world, they would reproduce it on their utensils as deco-

Lions in front of Paiyunmen Gate, Summer Palace, male in front

Lions in front of a palace, Forbidden City, female in front

ration and feel glad about it. Man can not live without water, and there are fish and frogs in water which became the food for the early ancients. Therefore, on the pottery bowls and jars used by the ancients, we can find water patterns in waves and swirls, fish and frogs as decorations. These images are not only on the utensils, but also on architectures. On the pictured bricks and stones of the Han Dynasty, we find the images of tigers, horses, and the pictures showing how people grow and harvest crops, hunt and spend leisure time, etc. It was the same with lions. Since people have come to know it, accept it and regard it as a sacred animal, they definitely show its images on architectures. Owing to the fact that lions are ferocious, and regarded as sacred animal guarding Buddhism, naturally they are placed outside the gate as the sacred animals guarding the architecture. It has almost become a set formula that a pair of lions is put on both side of the gate, the mother lion on the right, with one foot resting on a baby lion, the father lion on the left, stepping on an

Small beams with two lions playing with a ball

Wood-carved lion on an corbel

Stone lion on terrace of archway

Stone lion as pillar base

embroidered ball. Besides the gate, lions are also put on the beams. By the little pillar on the beam there is a pair of lions keeping the pillar stable from the left and right; sometimes, the short beam is carved into two lions facing each other playing with an embroidered ball in between; the corbel which props up the eave from below is carved into a lion upside down, etc. Besides the houses, lions of all kinds are also found on pillar bases of archways and pillar heads of balustrades of stone bridges. Lions have become very common on architectures.

## Images of the Lion

In various places and on all kinds of architectures, we see many types of stone, bronze and iron lions whose images are very different to the real wild lions. Why?

Let us first of all, observe how the images of the tiger changed. The tiger native to China was known to the people very early. The images of tiger appeared on the pictured bricks and stones of the Han Dynasty were rather true to life with the big mouth opening wide, the legs stretched, the teeth and claws very sharp, and they were very ferocious overall. The ancients took it as the protective sacred animal and the symbol of strength precisely because it was so ferocious. When a general was sent out on an expedition, the emperor would give a tiger-shaped tally made of jade to the general which meant the general was given the power to command the army. When a son or grandson is born in the family, the baby would have a quilt embroidered with tigers, a pillow in the shape of a tiger head, a hat in the shape of a tiger, a vest decorated with tigers, playing tiger-shaped toys, and on his birthday, tiger-shaped bread would be made to entertain friends and relatives. In a word, the tiger becomes the protective god of the baby, and the boy is often called "tiger boy", the girl, "tiger girl", and the children are often praised as "tiger-like", meaning very strong. The ferocious beast from the mountain forest has entered the home of people and become constant company. The people need the company of the ferocious tiger, but do not wish to see the fearful image beside them, so the image of the tiger gradually change through hundreds and thou-

Tiger, painting on stone, Han Dynasty

Tiger pattern on ancient eave end

Tiger pillow, countryside of Shaanxi Province

Tiger embroidered on child apron, countryside of
Shaanxi Province

sands pairs of hands into strange, sturdy and naughty tigers, in a word, the ferocious side gradually reduced and the amicable side increased, and finally, the tiger enters hundreds and thousands of homes and become the loved sacred animal of the people. The tiger culture has come into being on the vast land of China.

It is the same with the lion. Since it has entered the buildings and people's lives as the sacred animal, its original ferocious image is bound to be remolded, and all kinds of different images of the lion are created through the hands of artisans and artists, and these creations are bound to be stamped with the marks of different times and areas. Let us first examine the images of the lion through historical development. In the 6th century, the Southern Dynasties (420-589) established their capitals in Jiankang (present Nanjing) and left behind some stone animals placed in front of imperial tombs, among which, the stone *pixie* in front of the tomb of Liang Xiaojing is very representative. *Pixie* is a stone animal created out of the lion, which is placed in front of a tomb with the symbolic meaning of expelling the evil spirits. This stone animal is very big, almost three meters high, with the head raised and chest throwing forward; its mouth is open with half a tongue out, the four limbs are thick and strong; and the body lines showing mighty strength. Its image does not conform to a real lion, but shows very well the powerful spirit of the lion.

Several stone lions before Shunling Tomb of the Tang Dynasty in Xianyang, Shaanxi Province are closer to real lions in appearance than those of the Southern Dynasties, but the method of artistic exaggeration is used in making the legs and claws especially thick and strong. Their whole bodies are erect as if they are swaggering forward with claws tightly clutching and sinking deep into the ground, which frightens people at sight of them. These stone lions fully demonstrate the grand and mighty style of art of the Tang Dynasty. Those stone lions before the imperial tombs of the Northern Song Dynasty are even closer to real lions in appearance than the Tang lions in terms of expressions of the lion body, especially the lion head and the curled hair on it, but in overall spirit, they are far inferior to those of the Southern and Tang dynasties. Many lions of the Ming and Qing dynasties have survived until today. Take those lions on palace architectures for example; their appearances are created in an even more matter-of-fact way: detailed parts of the lion body are

Stone *pixie*, tomb of Liang Xiaojing, Nanjing of Jiangsu Province

Stone lion, Shunling Tomb of Tang
Dynasty, Xianyang of Shaanxi Province

Stone lion, Song Tombs, Gongxian
County , Henan Province

Laughing stone lion

Bronze lions in front of Gate of
Supreme Harmony, Forbidden City

Ferocious bronze lions in front of
Ningshoumen Gate, Forbidden City

Dog-like lion

meticulously expressed, with curled hair on head, a ring of bells on neck, mussels on the limbs showing ups and downs, but overall, the creation lacks spirit, and the menacing air of the lion is not there. This special feature conforms to the tendency of pursuing triviality and beauty in artistic expression in Qing, especially the late Qing period. The above is the different styles of lion images in different historical periods.

If we observe carefully the large number of stone lions left behind from the Ming and Qing periods, we may find that they all have their respective charms and their images are rich and varied. They are in different postures, squatting, standing, receiving a ball with a foot while carrying a baby lion on the back, regardless of male or female, and some even resemble dogs in outside look. Judging from their facial expressions, there are naughty and amicable ones, but also grotesque, laughable and merry ones, and even a totally rascally look. Naturally, all these phenomena are not accidental.

As the sacred animal, the lion entered China, houses and people's lives. During festival days and the New Year, the lion dance is the favorite of the people. The lions dance in big streets and small lanes, in cities and countryside, hopping around, rolling on the ground; under the guidance of a young man, they climb up the high ladder, tiptoe on the ball, jump through the fire ring, and when tired, they lie on ground, panting, sometimes, they even yawn, scratch their bodies with claws, making all kinds of merry movements. Are all these done by the real lions? No, these movements are performed by men in disguise of lions according to their imagination of what real lions can achieve which can make people happy and bring auspiciousness to them during festival days. This phenomenon can be called the humanization of lions. Once the lion is humanized, just like the tiger which is developed to be tiger hat, tiger pillow and all kinds of tiger-shaped toys, it evolves into many different kinds of images which are not restricted by the image of real lions. In Beijing, there is a bridge built in the Jin Dynasty (1115-1234), called Lugouqiao (Marco Polo Bridge), all the pillars on the stone balustrades on both sides are carved with lions. There are several hundred pillars, so at least there are several hundred lions, some of which have baby lions under their feet, others have baby lions on their backs, still others embrace babies on their bosoms and some infants are hidden under the armpits. The artisans at that time purposefully created countless lions, big and small, as a result, they not only left behind many graceful groups of lions, but also provided materials for creating a legend: it is impossible to count the stone lions on Lugou Bridge, if someone succeeds, all the lions on the bridge would run away.

Stone lion on Seventeen Arch Bridge, Summer Palace, Beijing

Stone lion on Seventeen Arch Bridge, Summer Palace, Beijing

Folk lion dance

Stone balustrade on Seventeen Arch Bridge, Summer Palace

If we make a comparison of the image of the lion in China with that in Africa and India, the difference is evident. For those lions placed before both sides of the gate of buildings, the Chinese ones are more spiritually than physically alike, while the foreign ones are more physically alike, i.e. their images are closer to real lions from the overall appearance to body and legs.

We have entered the 21st century. If we take a look of the lions on the land of China, there are lions left behind by our ancestors, which are still guarding the gates of palaces, temples and residences and beams of buildings, performing the role of the god of protection on the one hand; on the other hand, there are many new lions in the cities and countryside of entire China. Stones lions can be seen before the gates of universities, libraries, hotels, stores, restaurants, even small shops in the cities, and before clan temples, Buddhist temples, big gates and bridge heads in the countryside. In Hui'an County of Fujian Province of south China and Quyang County of Hebei Province of north China which have a tradition of producing stone materials and stone carvings, there are stone carving factories one after another on both sides of the street full of stone lions on display. As of today when the economic and cultural life of the people have been improved and developed, they still take the lion for the god of protection, and like the peace and happiness brought about by the lion. What is different from the past is that the vision of the people is wider today; quite a few foreign lions true to life have appeared in front of the gates of architectures. On the occasion of the centennial celebration of the famous Beijing University, the alumni presented a pair of green stone lions to be placed before the newly built library, with red silk ribbon decoration. There is a newly built commercial building in Beijing with a pair of stone lions standing in front of the gate, surrounding the male and female big lions and on the stone terraces are many small lions, totally 100 in all, with the name of "a hundred lions celebrate the peace", meaning "peace forever". On the Chinese land, there is the lion culture in addition to the tiger culture, which implies the wish of the people for joy and happy life.

Stone lion in front of gate of a building, Germany

Stone lion in front of Tian'anmen, Beijing

Up: (left) stone lion in front of a business building, Beijing
(right) stone lion in front of a business building, Beijing
Down: stone lion in front of a building, Nanshecun Village,
Dongguan, Guangdong Province

# Screen Walls

Screen wall is a wall either inside or outside of the gate of a quadrangle which faces the gate, so it can perform the role of a screen. In Chinese, it is called *yingbi* or *zhaobi*.

## Classification of Screen Walls

If we divide by the locations they stand, there are four kinds: outside the gate, inside the gate, on both sides of the gate and in other places within the yard. The one outside the gate means a wall facing the gate, standing on the road or across the square within a certain distance. It can tell the passers-by that there is a group of important architectures here which makes the architectures more important. Such screen wall is often found in front of a temple, a garden or a large-size residence building. Wenshu Temple of Chengdu, Sichuan Province and Foguang Temple of Wutai Mountain of Shanxi Province are famous ancient temples, each of which has a screen wall before the gate with the name of the temple inscribed on it. The Fuzi (Confucian) Temple of Nanjing, Jiangsu Province also has a screen wall. Because the temple uses the Qinhuai River in front as the water pool (which is a custom to have a pool in front of a temple), the screen wall is built on the other side of the river. The wall is very long, standing just opposite of the gate across the river, which also adds importance to the temple.

The screen wall inside the gate is used precisely for protection, preventing the passers-by and those who have just entered the gate to see the situation inside the yard

Screen wall, Forbidden City, Beijing

Screen wall outside gate of Grand Quadrangle of Wang Family, Lingshi of Shanxi Province

Screen wall outside gate of Foguang Temple, Wutai, Shanxi Province

Screen walls on both sides of Gate of Heavenly Purity, Forbidden City, Beijing

right away, which is why it is placed not far from the gate. In Forbidden City, those courtyards used for living quarters all have screen walls. In the courtyards of the ordinary people, the screen wall facing the gate is definitely the first scene people see after they enter the courtyard.

The screen wall also has the role of decoration aside from protection. So, there are screen walls on both sides of the gate and inside the courtyard. In Forbidden City, there are such screen walls on both sides of the Gate of Heavenly Purity, Ningshoumen Gate and the Gate of the Hall for Mental Cultivation. They either form in one line or in the form of the Chinese letter of eight on both sides of the gate, which become one with the gate, making the gate more glorious. In the countryside, some large-size quadrangles also have such screen wall on both sides of the gate,

Screen wall in heaven well courtyard, southern China

Screen wall inside gate of residence, countryside of Shaanxi Province

Screen wall in a residence, Dali, Yunnan Province

Screen wall inside a Palace courtyard, Forbidden City

which, like the gate, are also decorated on the top with carved bricks, making the gate more prominent. The screen wall standing in the yard is entirely a piece of decoration; there are quite a few of them in Forbidden City, which are decorated with glazed bricks in green and yellow, and patterns of animals and plants. They stand just opposite the living quarters, for the owners to appreciate. The quadrangles in Dali of Yunnan Province also have a screen wall opposite the main house; the white wall is decorated with colored patterns in the surroundings, which is a large piece of art for appreciation both in the yard and outside of it. In the heaven well residences in the south, some of the outer walls opposite the main hall are made into a screen wall with decorations which becomes a scene in the heaven well.

If we divide by the materials used, there are screen walls made of bricks, stone and timber, among which brick ones are the majority, because the screen wall is a wall and walls are usually built with bricks. In the palaces, glazed bricks and tiles are added to the surface of brick walls, so they become glazed screen walls. Stone screen walls are rare, only one is found in a courtyard of Forbidden City, which is built totally with stone materials. Its frame is made with stone slabs, and the wall is a large piece of marble, the natural lines of which is the only decoration. There are few screen walls made of timber, because they stand in the open air, and the timber is easily decayed under sunshine and rain. The stone screen wall in Forbidden City has a roof with protruding eave, and the wall itself is made into four doors, when they are closed, it is a screen wall, and when there are important guests, they can open into another gate of the courtyard.

If we divide by the outside look of the screen walls, there are also several patterns; the one

Wood screen wall, Forbidden City

Stone screen wall, Forbidden City

Long screen wall in Wenshu Temple, Chengdu, Sichuan Province

Screen wall in the shape of " 八 "

commonly seen is a simple dash (—), with a terrace in the lower part, the body of the wall in the middle and the roof on the top, the size of which is decided according to the size of the architectural group. If the screen wall is too long, it may be divided into three sections, with the middle section made larger and taller, and the two sections on the sides smaller and lower. The three sections can form in one line, or make the right and left sections turning inwardly to form the Chinese letter of 八(eight), embracing the gate.

## Decoration of Screen Wall

The locations of screen walls are prominent, no matter whether it is placed inside or outside the gate, on both sides of the gate or right in the courtyard, they are the focus of architectural decorations. For the commonly seen brick screen wall, there are two types of decorations: one is to paste lime on the brick wall, there can be a combination of different colors, or paint pictures on white lime; the other is to decorate directly with carved bricks. The first type is often seen on the screen walls of Buddhist temples in the south. Before Leifeng Pagoda of Hangzhou, there is a screen wall in the shape of eight, on which, the wall is yellow, roof tile is black and the terrace bricks are grey, and on the wall, there are four Chinese characters in red against white background, meaning, "setting sun on elegant pagoda"; before Lengxiangge Pavilion of Huqiu in Suzhou, there is a screen wall with white wall and black tile top, and three grey stone on the wall carved with the name Lengxiangge in three Chinese characters in blue. The decoration of these two screens is simple, but it has made the screen wall seem dignified and poised. The screen walls of the northern residences are mostly decorated with carved bricks, which are concentrated in the center of the wall and on four corners. The content of decorations varies with the type of buildings, dragons and phoenixes are used in imperial gardens, while plants and flowers are used in the residences of the ordinary people. In the method of carving, high relief is used on large screen walls, which makes the images very prominent; low relief on small screen walls which seems harmonious and delicate. Some screen walls are full of carvings, especially large-size pictures which demonstrate the owner's financial power and personal aspiration. There is a large-size screen wall before a

Screen wall before Leifeng Pagoda, Hangzhou, Zhejiang Province

Screen wall before Lengxiangge Pavilion, Suzhou of Jiangsu Province

Painting of screen wall of a residence, Zhangbi Village, Jiexiu of Shanxi Province

temple in Songjiang County of Shanghai which is decorated with paste and carved bricks. The long wall is divided into three sections, the middle section is decorated entirely with carved bricks, the left and right sections are pasted with white lime, and decorated only in the center and the four corners with grey bricks. The whole screen wall has only two colors: grey and white, but the gigantic screen wall appears dignified and poised looking from afar, and very delicate when watching closely, without the original feeling of clumsiness, because the creator has adopted an appropriate treatment of partition in overall shaping, and fully used the different feeling one has towards the different materials of the grey bricks and white lime and the contrast of their colors.

The most elaborate decoration is of course the glazed screen walls. Such screen walls are also decorated in the center and the four corners, apart from the decorative role of the color and the material feelings of the glaze itself. In the palace inhabited by the emperor and empress, there is a screen wall on which a pair of love-birds is swimming in the midst of lotus flowers and leaves, which symbolizes that the husband and wife will never separate from each other. On the four corners, there are always plant and flower patterns symbolizing wealth and auspiciousness. The most elaborately deco-

Decorations on brick screen wall

Brick screen wall full of decorations

Big Screen Wall, Songjiang, Shanghai

rated is the nine-dragon screen wall which is situated in front of the palace hall or imperial temple. Such screen walls are big in size and located at important places, so they are decorated with nine dragons, hence the name "nine-dragon screen wall". There is a nine-dragon screen wall in front of the gate of Huangjidian Hall in Forbidden City, built in the 36th year (1771) of Qianlong reign of the Qing Dynasty. It is 29.4 meters long, 3.5 meters high. Apart from the stone terrace, the whole body is covered with glazed bricks and tiles. On the body of the wall of more than 20 meters, there arranged nine big dragons below which are green water waves, and between the dragons are blue mountain rocks and blue clouds scattered all around. The nine dragons are flying and dancing above the waves and between the clouds and rocks, varying in postures. The left and right are not symmetrical; there are dragons flying with heads on top, and others surging forward, and the dragon in the middle is a yellow sitting dragon. All the dragons are curling with ease which demonstrate fully the beauty of living creatures, and at the same time, show appropriate density of the whole picture. The nine dragons take five respective colors of yellow, blue, white, purple and orange, in the order of the yellow sitting dragon in the middle, the other four on each side are arranged in the order of blue, white, purple and orange in symmetrical way, so that they are different from each other and colorful, yet they are following a certain rule which do not seem in a mess. Apart from the wall body, there are also nine dragons on the main ridge of the roof made of glaze, four each on the left and right, facing the central dragon, with a ball in front of each dragon head, forming a picture of dragons in pursuit of balls. All the dragons are green and all the balls are white with yellow clouds all around on top of the roof which is not high, thus, very attractive to the eye. The roof and body of the screen wall are made of many small glazed bricks and tiles patched together. The method is: first, make the wall body with clay upon which carve the images

Nine-dragon screen wall, Forbidden City

Decorations in center of glazed screen wall,
Forbidden City

Decorations in center of glazed screen wall,
Forbidden City

of the dragons and other decorative objects, then, divide the body into small pieces, on condition that the vertical seams of them must not be on the same line, and they should necessarily avoid to fall on the head of dragon in order to keep the head a whole piece; then, the small pieces are painted with colors and sent to the kiln to bake into glazed bricks; and then, patch them on to the wall body according to order, in doing so, every piece must be closely connected with the neighboring pieces all around it and the flower patterns and colors should confirm, only then a perfect nine dragon screen wall is completed. And this nine dragon screen wall in the Forbidden City must also embody the auspicious figure of nine, so, apart from the number of dragons on the wall body and the roof is nine, the number of those small glazed bricks on the wall body is 270, which

Nine-dragon screen wall, Datong, Shanxi Province

is 30 multiple by nine. Nowadays, after going through more than 200 years of wind and rain, this screen wall is not only still intact, but the nine dragons are as good as before, every piece is still in place, the colors of the dragon, water wave, clouds and rocks are still glittering, and even the glaze on the bricks are still there. From this, we know that in the Qing Dynasty, the designing, making and assembling of glazed art products had reached very advanced level.

There is a nine dragon screen wall in front of the Beihai Park in Beijing which is covered entirely with glazed bricks and tiles from the base to the top; therefore, its colors are even more attractive to the eye. Before the prince residence in Datong, Shanxi Province, there is a nine dragon screen wall which is 45.5 meters long, 8 meters high, and 2.02 meters thick in the body part, the biggest of all existing nine dragon screen walls in China. All nine gigantic dragons on the wall are yellow in color, against a purple blue background. Although the color is not as bright as the two nine dragon screen walls in Beijing, because the wall is bigger, the dragons seem to move and curve more freely and more forcefully, thus the wall seems full of power and grandeur. The Beihai Temple and the prince residence are no longer in existence, so the two nine dragon screen walls are being appreciated as independent large size objects of art.

## Screen Walls of Today

Are screen walls still needed in contemporary architectures? In the vast countryside of China, along with economic development, many farmers have built their new residences which are new brick and tile

Nine-dragon screen wall, Beihai, Beijing

houses pasted with porcelain bricks from the outside; some have two or more floors. And for convenience's sake, there must be a yard in front, surrounded by a wall of the new courtyard. The gate is opened on the wall, and inside the gate, there is still a screen wall, because, just like in the past, the residence still needs peace and privacy, so the protection of the screen wall is still needed. What differs from the past is that the screen wall is decorated with new porcelain bricks. With pieces of porcelain bricks, people can patch on the wall a big character "*Fu*" in red, meaning fortune, patch pines and landscape, patch two dragons among clouds and water. The dragon walls which used to be in palaces and temples have appeared in people's houses.

The screen wall is decorative in itself; especially the nine dragon screen wall is of sacred significance. Therefore, new nine dragon screen walls are being seen in temples and gardens built today. In Putuo Mountain, Zhejiang Province, there is a new nine dragon screen wall decorated with carved bricks in a temple. In Yuanmingyuan of Beijing, nine dragons made of fresh flowers on a brick wall were in display on festival days which was really a fresh flower nine dragon screen wall.

The archway, the lion and the screen wall as well, not only have beautiful images, but also contain rich cultural connotations. Therefore, in modern society, under certain circumstances, these traditional art forms still maintain their life.

Up: flower nine-dragon screen wall in Yuanmingyuan, Beijing
Central: screen walls of new residences, countryside of Shanxi Province
Down: new nine-dragon screen wall in temples

329

# Postscript

Early last year, an editor of the China Travel and Tourism Press came to see me. She told me that in recent years, foreign visitors who are interested in Chinese traditional culture are ever increasing and the books published by the Press which only gave brief introduction to the places of historical interest can no longer meet their demands. I was asked by the Press to write a book of Chinese traditional architectural culture, the content of which should be both scientific and academic, and easy to read, not too vocational, so that the foreign tourists can have a related book to read during their travel in China and increase their knowledge of China's fine traditional culture. The book would only publish its English version, and in order to meet the needs of a sudden increase of foreign visitors, it would be the best that the book appears before the Beijing Olympic Games in 2008.

In the last few years, I have written several books introducing Chinese ancient architectural culture, among which, some are published by the Foreign Languages Press and the China Intercontinental Press in a few foreign languages, but containing mainly photos with a short text. The *Twenty Lectures on Chinese Ancient Architecture* published by the Beijing SDX Joint Publishing Company with a big circulation is also targeted at ordinary readers. If I were to write a new book, there must be repetition in content, thus, I suggested to translate the book into English. But the Press still preferred me to write a new book, the content of which could be simpler than the book, but with more photos. Taking into consideration that the book would be in English, which is also needed by our college (The College of Architecture of Tsinghua University) as English reading material, therefore, I agreed to the request. After the endeavor of days and nights of the summer months, I completed the manuscript in October of last year, which is consisted of 100,000 Chinese words and more than 600 photos. With the anticipated difficulty in translation work in mind, I avoided using the ancient Chinese language and poems when those were needed to illustrate my point, instead, modern language was used to describe the scene without referring to the ancient original.

Early this year, I was informed by the Press that in view of the content of this book, they had decided to publish its Chinese version as well at the same time. Then, whether I should put those ancient Chinese language and poems into the book as I had prepared becomes a question. But finally, I decided to use the original manuscript because it would provide convenience for foreign readers and domestic students to read the Chinese and English versions in comparison. This is a point I would wish to explain to the readers.

Lou Qingxi
March, 2007

# 部分图片来源

《中国古代建筑史》刘敦桢主编　中国建筑工业出版社　1984年　图名：第6页：陕西西安半坡村圆形住房、陕西西安半坡村方形住房、辽宁海城巨石建筑。第12页：宋、辽时期建筑屋脊正吻图。第14页：古代屋顶形式图。第15页：宋画《滕王阁图》、宋画《黄鹤楼图》。第17页：山西五台唐代佛光寺大殿斗栱。第29页：汉画像砖上的四合院住宅。第30页：北京四合院住宅。第32页：周王城图、唐代长安城图。第34页：北京紫禁城太和门、太和殿广场平面。第36页：清代北京城平面图。第37页：紫禁城平面图。第67页：北京天坛平面。第98页：四川雅安汉代高颐阙。第100页：陕西乾县唐乾陵平面。第102页：河南禹县宋代白沙墓。第103页：山西侯马金代董姓墓。第105页：北京明十三陵平面。第109页：明长陵平面。第111页：明定陵地宫平剖面。第128页：河北正定隆兴寺平面。第129页：山西五台山佛光寺大殿平面。第151页：汉代明器中望楼。第160页：嵩岳寺塔身曲线造型。第168页：山西平顺明惠大师塔、唐代单层塔图。第169页：山东历城神通寺四门塔平面。第279页：福建永定县承启楼图。

《中国古代建筑史》潘谷西主编　中国建筑工业出版社　1986年　第8页：甘肃泰安大地湾房屋遗址、陕西岐山凤雏村建筑遗址。第17页：古代房屋木结构的斗栱。

《世界建筑史·古埃及卷上册》王瑞珠著　中国建筑工业出版社　2002年　第2页：埃及大斯芬克斯金字塔。

《世界建筑史·古希腊卷上册》王瑞珠著　中国建筑工业出版社　2003年　第3页：希腊雅典帕提侬神庙。第33页：雅典卫城立面复原图。

《外国城市建设史》沈玉麟编　中国建筑工业出版社　1989年　第34页：罗马共和广场和帝国广场平面。第187页：意大利佛罗伦萨平面。

《世界建筑史图录》吴庆洲编　江西科学技术出版社　1999年　第121页：印度卡尔利支提窟。第151页：印度桑奇大窣堵波。

《中国城市建设史》中国建筑工业出版社　1982年　第187页：陕西神木城平面。

《西方园林》郦芝若、朱建宁著　河南科学技术出版社　2001年　第188页：德国海伦豪森宫苑平面。

《中国建筑艺术全集——清代陵墓建筑》 中国建筑工业出版社 2001年 第114页：清乾隆皇帝裕陵地宫石壁上雕像、裕陵地宫石门上雕像。

《西藏古迹》杨谷生著 中国建筑工业出版社 1984年 第141页：西藏拉萨大昭寺、大昭寺屋顶双鹿与法轮。第142页：布达拉宫内壁画。第143页：大昭寺屋顶。第144页：西藏拉萨布达拉宫、布达拉宫白宫、西藏寺庙用草做屋檐装饰。

《中国古代园林史》周维权著 清华大学出版社 1990年 第188页：江苏无锡寄畅园平面。第191页：西汉长安宫苑图。第192页：宋汴梁皇家园林艮岳平面想象、北京清代西苑平面。第195页：北京元大都及西北郊平面。第196页：清乾隆时期北京西北郊园林分布图。第197页：圆明园平面。第202页：河北承德避暑山庄平面。第224页：北京恭王府平面。第227页：近春园平面。第229页：江苏扬州个园平面。第233页：江苏苏州网师园平面。

《园冶注释》计成著 陈植注释 中国建筑工业出版社 1988年 第236页：《园冶》中窗图、《园冶》中门图。第237页：《园冶》中栏杆图、《园冶》中墙垣图。

《梁思成文集》（二）中国建筑工业出版社 1984年 第155页：浙江杭州闸口白塔图。

清华大学建筑学院资料室：第11页：浙江农村住宅的曲线屋脊。第13页：福建农村建筑屋脊装饰图（一）（二）。第33页：北京颐和园万寿山建筑群立面图。第81页：丞相祠堂祭祖。第83页：戏台屋顶图。第92页：浙江农村祠堂上的猪、兔、牛装饰。第125页：河南洛阳龙门石窟奉先寺。第162页：大正觉寺佛塔图。第170页：北京郊区花塔。208页：清漪园平面图、清漪园与杭州西湖的比较。第218页：清漪园被烧毁后留下的佛香阁下石基座。第268页：山西"四大八小"四合院平面图。第273页：南方四面房屋天井院住宅图。第274页：堂屋布置图。第275页：浙江武义郭洞村大型天井院住宅图。第276页：天井院住宅外街巷图。第277页：天井院住宅门头装饰图。第282页：陕西农村窑洞立面图。第283页：陕西长武县十里铺村窑洞住宅画。第302页：北京颐和园石牌楼图。第325页：山西介休张壁村住宅影壁。

《北京的世界遗产》中国旅游出版社 2002年 第38页：紫禁城鸟瞰、紫禁城后宫建筑群。第77页：北京太庙。

《中国美术全集·建筑艺术编》（坛庙建筑、陵墓建筑、宗教建筑）中国建筑工业出版社 1988–1989年 第68页：天坛鸟瞰。第95页：秦始皇陵兵马俑。第111页：定陵地宫。第123页：甘肃天水麦积山石窟。第170页：宁夏青铜峡喇嘛塔群。